Wuhu Diary

RANDOM HOUSE

NEW YORK

Wuhu Diary

ON TAKING MY
ADOPTED DAUGHTER
BACK TO HER
HOMETOWN IN CHINA

EMILY PRAGER

Throughout the book, the names of some of the parties have been changed.

Library of Congress Cataloging-in-Publication Data
Prager, Emily.
   Wuhu diary : on taking my adopted daughter back to her
   hometown in China / [Emily Prager]
     p.   cm.
   ISBN 0-375-50349-8
     1. Wuhu (China)—Description and travel. 2. Prager,
   Emily—Journeys—China—Wuhu. 3. Prager, LuLu 1994—
   Journeys—China—Wuhu. I. Title: On taking my adopted
   daughter back to her hometown in China. II. Title.
DS797.22.W85 P73   2001
951.1'225—dc21   2001019104

All photos by Emily Prager

This book is dedicated to my father,
who introduced me to China;
to my daughter, who made me love it
even more than I thought possible;
and to Robert Loomis, who has always
let me write about what I love.

Wuhu Diary

April 30, 1999
Narita Airport, Tokyo

We are close to China now and I can feel it. China, guardian of my memories, nurturer of my spirit. This time, I am taking LuLu, my Chinese daughter, there and I am so excited I can hardly breathe. Going to China always affects me this way. Even though I spent my childhood in Taiwan, China is China to me no matter who rules it. It is a matter of people, trees, birds, smells, and earth, not politics.

This is a "roots" trip for LuLu. I am taking her back to her hometown of Wuhu, in the province of Anhui in southern China. I adopted her on December 12, 1994, at the Anhui Hotel in the provincial capital city of Hefei. She was seven months old then; now she is almost five. She is my daughter now and I am her mother, but then we were just starting out.

It will be a first for me, too, for I have never seen Wuhu, though I am connected to it now by bonds almost as strong as hers.

Somewhere in that city I have never seen, my child was born and put out on the street in her first three days of life. It was near a police station. The police took her in and brought her to the local orphanage, where she was assigned to me, a single woman writer living in Greenwich Village on the other side of the earth. That's basically all we know, what is on her documents. That and what her mother wrote in her note:

This is a girl. Her Western birthday is June 8. Her lunar birthday is April 29, nighttime, at the hour of 11:30 P.M.

The birth date was computed according to both Chinese and Western calendars. Perhaps her first mother hoped she would be adopted to the West.

I consider this note in her first mother's handwriting to be almost magical. It is Lu's and my only link to the people who created her, that and the genes she carries. We know they were musical. They were expansive. They had great, strong voices, lovely long legs, and remarkable hands. They were eternally cheerful, smart, and good-looking. They had wills of iron and were awfully good-hearted.

It must have been so wrenching for them to leave her. I thought I knew this when I went to China to get her, but it wasn't until I opened the hotel room door and saw her that I truly understood.

I have to confess: I hadn't liked the tiny, two-inch-square photo of her that the adoption ministry sent me after they approved my documents and assigned her to me. She looked kind of thuggish in the picture, and I didn't take to it. But it made me understand that what I was doing was not a fantasy, that I had to be ready to love whatever person came my way, that that was the contract I was making. And I made peace with the photo and carried it proudly in my wallet.

The adoption was arranged through the Spence-Chapin adoption agency. It was like this: after a great deal of paperwork, a group of people—nine couples and two other single women besides myself—came from America together to a hotel in Hefei to embark on the most important journey of our lives. The day we arrived, I was in my room waiting. The babies were meant to come at two. It was noon.

The phone rang. Xiong Yan, the Chinese woman who had facilitated the adoptions in China, said joyously, "Would you like to meet your baby?" What a question. I was so thrilled, I could hardly move.

"Oh, yes," I gasped, and put the phone down.

I wasn't ready. I didn't have formula made. I hadn't even read the instructions on the can yet to learn how to do it. I had taken a three-hour course in infant care at Southampton Hospital in Long Island, and that was all I knew about babies. I ran around the room aimlessly, frantically, trying not to have a heart attack, laughing, jumping. Out in the hall I heard baby sounds and then there was a knock at the door.

I'm sure you will understand that opening that door was the most incredible experience. I was about to meet the person I would be responsible for for the rest of my life. I was about to have a baby. I took a deep breath and, as I am wont to do, I plunged in and quickly opened the door.

Which brings me back to the heart-wrenching deed of my in-law (as I think of her), who gave birth to LuLu. Because there before me was a truly lovely-looking baby girl, nothing like the picture, flawless, with red, red cheeks, staring at me with black, sparkling, mischievous eyes.

Her nurse, an older woman, raised the tiny creature up by her shoulders and bent her over in a little bow, whereupon LuLu—for that was the name she came with—broke into the most adorable, grand smile of hello at me. We fell instantly in love and have remained so ever since.

When I examined my child later, I felt a spasm of anguish for the woman who had had to leave her. Did it hurt her forever or did she put the baby down and never look back? I will probably never know.

And I will probably never know what made her do it. It could have been terrible poverty or conception out of wedlock that led her first mother to seal Lu's fate, or it could have been China's one-child policy.

In 1994, the governmental population decree of the People's Republic of China was still stringently enforced. Couples were allowed one child in the city, two in the country. LuLu and the girls in her group were quite probably second children, born to farming families who already had one girl and were hoping for a boy. Secondness, evidently, accounted for their physical strength as well as their destiny.

This is one of the reasons we are going to Wuhu: to see if there is anything in her orphanage file that we do not know; to see what shreds we can gather about LuLu's beginnings. It has been only four years. Perhaps someone remembers something.

When we approach the Narita lounge for the connecting flight to China, everyone waiting there is Chinese. Most are men, and suddenly they all look up, almost as one, and stare at us. I quickly bend down and advise LuLu that in China, large groups of people do have this tendency to gather and stare and it is merely curiosity, in reply to which we should smile.

I flash back to a street in Taipei in 1959. My friend Robin and I are waiting for a car to take us to the Grand Hotel swimming pool. We are both seven, daughters of U.S. Air Force and Army officers. She has flame-red hair. A large crowd of Chinese people has gathered around and stands staring at us, silent and expressionless. We hate it when this happens, because we don't know what these adults want. Robin shouts heatedly at the crowd, which embarrasses me.

In 1979, when my boyfriend and I journeyed to Beijing, a huge crowd followed us everywhere we went. We were among the youngest visitors to the newly opened republic and people were fascinated by us. We were in our early twenties.

But it's not as if the Caucasian mother and Chinese child aren't used to being stared at. On the New York subway or in the supermarket, we are oddities or celebrities, depending on the day.

LuLu has been staring back at those staring at her. She turns to me and grins. "I don't see my world, Mom," she says, and she scampers off into the midst of her countrymen and soon finds a kind Chinese man in his forties who will play with her.

Her world, as she calls it, is the white, urban, middle-class world of New York City, America. There are Asians, Arabs,

African-Americans, and Hispanics in it, to be sure, but for the most part, in her immediate world, in her family, she remains a racial minority.

It is for this reason that I sent her to an all-Chinese, Mandarin-speaking preschool in Chinatown, so that in those early years of evolving identity, at least, I would be in the minority someplace, not always she.

And I was. For the first two years, I was the only non-Chinese parent in the school, until others who had adopted or intermarried began to come. And in the beginning, until we were all used to one another, and in spite of my love for China and the Chinese, I always felt, all the time, just a little bit embarrassed, just a little bit self-conscious.

The Red Apple School taught LuLu to be proud of being Chinese and then some, which is exactly what I had hoped they would do. I don't think I could have taught her that. I could teach her to be proud of herself, of being female, of being an American, but pride in one's race is taught, I think, by seeing those of your race do things to be proud of.

LuLu had a lot of great role models at Red Apple. There was the headmistress, Joanna Fan, a dynamic young woman in her thirties who had four preschools and a son, and never stopped cheerfully working. I used to tell her she was building an empire, and she would laugh happily. The last time we saw her, she was building a new preschool in Shanghai and was pregnant with twins.

And, of course, there was LuLu's first teacher, Miss Ling, one of the greatest teachers I have ever seen at work. In Shanghai, Miss Ling had taught classes of thirty-six children under the age of three all by herself. She knew her oats. To watch her teach her class of eighteen toddlers was to see an orchestration in symphonic movements and rhythms. In her clear, singsong voice, she sang the day, and when she sensed the slightest lag of interest in her three-year-old band, she changed the tune. She always carried a little tambourine, which she shook for emphasis, rhythm, and to keep order.

Miss Ling was, in addition, totally adorable-looking, in her early twenties, with a perfectly round face that was always laughing and a ponytail that she fastened on one side of her head.

"Children this age like pretty young women," Joanna told me one day in passing, and Miss Ling certainly was one. She always did LuLu's hair after naptime, and to this day, we call the top-of-head-ponytail hairdo that we learned from her the "Ling" tail in her honor.

LuLu loved her deeply. She made LuLu feel so important. The minute we would arrive at school, LuLu would puff out her little chest and strut proudly into the classroom, and boom out in her strong, clear tones, "Good morning, *Lao Sher,*" which means, "Good morning, Teacher." And Miss Ling would boom back, "Good morning, LuLu Prager."

Undoubtedly, LuLu felt in Miss Ling some of the Chinese mother she had lost. When, after two years, Miss Ling announced that she was leaving to get married and move to Maryland, LuLu was devastated. The night I told her about it, she lay on the bed and tossed and turned. The little three-year-old told me she couldn't sleep.

"I don't want her to get married," she said angrily. And then, from the depths of her heart, "Oh, Mom, I'm going to miss her so much."

I held my little daughter close and comforted her as best I could. I was as stunned at the sophistication of her expression as I was at the depths of her pain. I went immediately into an action panic, as I would over the years whenever the anguish of her separation would suddenly surface. What should I do? How could I help? What to say? What not to say?

Fortunately, it was late spring when Miss Ling left. We went off for vacation to the beach and did not come back to school until the fall. I asked Joanna if we could be invited to the wedding, and one day there was an invitation waiting for us at school. We duly went off to a wedding palace in Chinatown, where we watched Miss Ling change into four different beautiful dresses—two cheongsams and two reminiscent of Scarlett O'Hara—and get married to a nice-looking young man she had met through a matchmaker.

It was in the wedding hall, where I was one of two Caucasians, that LuLu turned to me and said, "You're my Choco."

She was referring to a book we read in which Choco, a bird, has lost his mother and tries to find a new one whom he resembles. Eventually he hooks up with Mrs. Bear, who, though certainly different in appearance from him, is warm and loving and makes apple pie.

"You're . . . you're . . ." she continued, searching for the words.

"Not Chinese," I offered. She nodded.

She had articulated this fact only once before, the previous spring. One day she came home and said, "*You* look like this." She sucked in her cheeks as hard as she could. Then she let them out and added, smiling proudly, "But I have a Chinese face."

I laughed a lot at her depiction of the angularity of Western faces. Actually, when I was young, my face was so round that people called me "Moonface." And once, when I was an actress on a soap opera at age nineteen, the producer sent down a note to the makeup man. It read, "Do something about Emily. She looks Chinese." And that was my first personal encounter with racism.

I remember the Narita Airport transit lounge from 1994, when I went to get LuLu, although it was not so fancy then. It was here that I first saw Martha. She and her husband, Chris, had joined our adoption group on the way to China. They were film people, and wore anoraks and carried big cameras.

I instantly liked Martha and she me. We were glad to see each other across the lounge, familiar, in this place so far from home. We were being so brave and feeling so scared on this of all trips. Like little girls doing something really exciting together, we caught each other's eyes and smiled like suns.

I can see our group so clearly, sitting around this lounge, waiting nervously for the flight to Beijing: Eshel, Bernice, Martha, and to it in my mind I add Elizabeth, whom we would hook up with at the Forbidden City—the women who became my close friends, the women who accompanied me into motherhood. We sat peering in wonder at one another's tiny photographs, some a little blurry, some—like mine—dotted with ballpoint pen. Our baby daughters. Who were they, with their funny outfits and their funny names?

Joanna Fan told me once that LuLu, my daughter's Chinese name which the orphanage gave her, is a diminutive in China given to someone with the last name "Lu" who is considered very cute. Chen Lu, the Chinese Olympic figure skater, for example, is called LuLu. It translates as "Double Dewdrop," but Lu can also mean "street." For the orphanage, it had a double meaning. The girls were named, if possible, for where they were found, so, in our group, there was a Miss Bridge, a Miss Garden, a Miss Gate, and LuLu, Miss Dewdrop Street.

I kept the name LuLu because it was, besides the clothes she was wearing, the only thing my child came with that was hers, and like the birth dates in her first mother's note, it placed her nicely in both the East *and* the West, which was where we both, evidently, wanted her to be.

"Isn't it perfect?" I remember the Spence-Chapin social worker who had overseen my placement saying when she phoned and told me my child's name. "LuLu. It's the absolutely perfect name for a child for you." And she was absolutely right.

I look over at LuLu and hear her say "thank you" in Chinese to the Chinese man she is playing with. Outside of her school, she has never spoken Chinese, neither at a Chinese restaurant nor in Chinatown.

Now she turns to an American businessman and begins to play with him. I know she misses her dad, but outwardly she remains joyful. She has always been good at satisfying herself with what she actually has before her.

Her dad is Neke. I was going out with Neke when I decided to adopt from China. He already had a daughter in college. Unlike

me, he actually knew what it was to have a child. He wasn't entirely sure he could handle another one, but he was willing to try.

That was enough for me. I didn't need his surety to do it. At
forty, when I discovered I could no longer have children, I
mourned this loss. But after a while I realized what I wanted was
not a bloodline, but a family, and then I started to think seriously
about adoption. One night, I sat bolt upright out of a sound sleep.
I could adopt from China, was the message that woke me, so
strongly it was as if it had been spoken aloud, and a calm instantly
fell over my soul.

Because I have always loved China. When I was just seven, I
flew to Taiwan on a propeller plane that stopped at San Francisco,
Honolulu, Guam, Wake Island, Okinawa, and Tokyo. I went by
myself, with a tag around my neck and my Tiny Tears doll under
my arm, to join my father in this very foreign land. Although I
adored my dad, I left my mother and her new family behind, and
I was a sad, confused little girl.

But the beauty of the land and the kindness of the Chinese people saved my sanity and gave me whatever measure of joy I could
take then. And to this day, to be in the presence of Chinese people
or things always soothes me.

I wanted to have a family, and I had to admit to myself that I always wanted to be a mother more than a wife. This, I guess, was
because of my parents' divorce and because I love responsibility.
Of course, I love children, too, but I am not sure that loving other
people's children is enough of a prerequisite for the relentless caring and loving that is required to bring up a child of one's own.

And then there is what I have learned since becoming a parent:
you pretty much do with your children what you know. My father
was a great single parent, so it was not scary for me to become one,
too.

At any rate, I went right ahead with the adoption, and it was
when, as Neke tells LuLu, he saw me walking down the airport
ramp with this tiny creature who was looking all around, so alert,

smiling so beatifically, that he instantly became her father. And father her he has, with deep sweetness and dedication.

The flight is called, and Lu and I hook up again and board hand in hand. We are stopping over in Shanghai for a few days before we take the train to Wuhu. I am a bit anxious about the hotel, since we are arriving at night. It's a Chinese hotel that I found in a book called *Shanghai* (Odyssey Passport) that seemed knowledgeable. The Dong Hu Hotel, it said, was "until recently, a guest house for party cadres." That meant to me that it would be genuinely Chinese but fancy. "Building Number One," it went on to say (and this clinched the deal for me), "was owned by Yu Dusheng, old Shanghai's most famous gangster. Part of the hotel, his 10-bedroomed mansion, is very evocative of 1930s Shanghai with its dark wood paneling, its decorated fireplaces, and its stained-glass windows."

The mansion, it said, was rentable for a hundred dollars a day. The hotel was fifteen minutes from downtown and reasonably priced. I faxed and they faxed back. We have a reservation. But really, I have no idea what awaits us. It will be like many things LuLu and I have done together, a daring adventure.

Right before we board, I go over to the Japanese kiosk in the middle of the lounge and buy some gum for LuLu to chew on takeoff and landing so her ears won't hurt. The only flavor they have is green tea and it costs three dollars a pack! I had read that things in Japan are hellishly expensive, and now I believe it.

The Japanese have done so well in the last fifty years since the war. I'm reminded of this by seeing them next to the group of Chinese people who await the plane to Shanghai. The Japanese are dressed in hip designer clothes. They look healthy, well-heeled, and modern. The Chinese look dowdy and old beyond their years, and their faces are so careworn.

Since I adopted LuLu, I have read a great deal of post-1900 Chinese history. What the Chinese have suffered in this century is astounding: war, occupation, famine, floods, the Cultural Revolution. In LuLu, I have glimpsed the dogged determination that has kept the Chinese people going no matter what has come their way.

As a child in late 1950s Taiwan, I experienced the deep humanity of the people. In the afternoons, when there was no school, I roamed my neighborhood free and alone. There, by the open sewers, I saw terrible poverty side by side with incredible industriousness.

I wandered into my neighbors' dark stores and houses, curious and lonely, and no matter how busy they were, they took me in. They made room in their crowded places for me, giving me something that was very precious to them and to me—a bit of space, a place to sit, some company. I learned from them to just go on, no matter what happens, without complaint, and get the job done. Ironically, it may be this lesson that encouraged me to adopt a Chinese child alone.

It occurs to me that I am going to China again without my mother. Her death, two months ago, is fresh, and as gnawing a grief in my heart as I felt all those years ago when I lost her the first time. In some ways I never did find her again after our Chinese separation. Though I saw her often, I never lived with her again after I came back. She remained out of reach to me, like the brass ring on a merry-go-round that I was always trying to catch. I remember hugging her good-bye on the tarmac of the then Idlewild Airport and boarding the stairs to the plane. She was never mine again.

And now, this is the first trip I have ever taken in which I will not write her a postcard or phone her if I'm homesick. My mother is gone again from my active life, gone, now, for all time.

On the flight to Beijing, Lu continues to be a fabulous traveler, eternally in a good mood, friendly and pleasant to be with. When she was three and a half, I took her to the Ice Hotel in Lapland, and she was so intrepid (at 40 degrees below zero) that Sami reindeer herders not only let her into their corrals, but invited her to a special lunch at their home because they so admired her joie de vivre.

"Is she never in a bad mood?" the Sami matriarch, Maria, asked me as she watched LuLu tumble cheerily around the floor with their herding dog. Then they tried to marry me off to a cousin just so they could have her in their family.

But the answer to Maria's question is no, she's never in a bad mood when traveling. For instance, now. It's been about twenty-four hours since we left New York, and LuLu is still happy as a lark. I think she will always love traveling. After all, her first experience of traveling (to Hefei) brought her a new mother and then, once in New York, she found a new family and a new home and heritage. For LuLu, it's clear that traveling means joy and security and she is a grand connoisseur of both.

The three-and-a-half-foot dynamo with the flashing almond eyes, rosebud mouth, and deep belly laugh, whom we have always referred to as "the mayor," has already introduced herself to everyone seated around us. She loves people, and time to talk to them and experience them is precious to her.

If someone or some creature is in trouble on the street, she must rush up and see to them. She was the only two-year-old I ever heard of who rushed *toward* a dogfight. And, as I once said to a dear friend of mine, a fellow humor columnist who is her uncle Lew, it's funny that a group of shut-ins like us should have been blessed with such a lover of humanity. There is none of the reticence people usually ascribe to Asians about her.

But there is something unsettled about her, too—a frantic quality that will come upon her suddenly, a physical wildness that for both of us is impossible to control. Is this the legacy of an over-taxed infant nervous system? Or is it simply helpless, wild confusion about who and what and where she is? I know only that if I were in her position, I would have it, too.

It is lovely to have a Chinese daughter. I just love looking at her. On my twice daily trips to Chinatown, I would sometimes play a game of looking at the faces of adults and trying to imagine what LuLu will look like when she grows up.

That's an odd thing about having a daughter from another race and genetic line: you really have no idea what the child's face will evolve into. With babies of your own race or lineage, you sort of intrinsically do. Perhaps it's encoded in our cells. But I would sit on the subway or walk the streets to the Red Apple School peering into the faces of Chinese women, and one day I finally saw a face that Lulu's might one day be like.

This woman was on the subway, laughing heartily and chatting with a friend. Her energy was big and positive. I'd guess she was in her late twenties and had a straightish nose, almond eyes, an oval face, and a lovely rosebud mouth. She had dyed her hair blond, indicating a certain roguishness that was similar, too. She caught me looking at her and smiled this glorious smile, which was a rather uncharacteristic thing for a Chinese woman to do at a stranger. It was as if she knew exactly why I was staring. I was very happy with her as a future, and I never saw anyone like her again.

It's around ten that evening when we land at Hongqiao Airport in Shanghai. The airport is dead quiet. There's no one in it, no open stores, no porters. The lighting in the place is very dim, which I assume is because it is night and most of the lights are off. But actually this is my first encounter with the very odd Chinese attitude—what is it? prejudice? economy?—against bright-enough lighting.

I am looking around for the Bureau de Change or a bank, but I see nothing. We walk easily past Customs and head for the door. Just before we reach it, in the far dim corner of the lobby, I finally see a lone man in an even more dimly lit glass office. We head for him and make the change: 7.5 yuan to the dollar.

Then I take LuLu's hand and push the door open into China.

Outside, a wall of skyscrapers towers over us. Hundreds of different-colored neon signs with Chinese characters on them blink, half-lit and unsteadily, down at us. A line of red taxis stands before us, their drivers all in white shirts and navy blue pants, shouting at one another.

I summon my bravery and take out the book of hotels. I walk up to a driver and say in Chinese, "I want to go here," and point to the Dong Hu Hotel paragraph, which shows the address in characters. The man nods and puts the bags in the trunk.

As we pile in the back, I'm hoping the hotel is what I think it will be. When I read about it, I was going on a sense I have about things Chinese. I just had a feeling about it. But I could be wrong. I could be ten thousand miles from home, with a four-year-old, faced with a flophouse. My ace in the hole is the five-star Garden Hotel nearby. If the Dong Hu is a washout, we are off to the Garden until I can figure things out. We are staying only a few days and then we are on to Wuhu by train.

We drive through streets that look very much like Paris or Guatemala City. There are wide Champs Élysées–type boulevards lined with houses surrounded by stone walls, and next to them are thousands of poorly lit or dark shops. Chinese characters are everywhere in a profusion of fonts. The streets are deserted except for the occasional man in a T-shirt sitting in a chair on the sidewalk, fanning himself.

"Look," says LuLu. Out the window is a wall with wild animals—pandas, lions, tigers—gaily painted on it. Perhaps it is the Shanghai Zoo? "I want to go there," she says emphatically. I nod.

I also have no idea how far our hotel is from the famous Bund, the Shanghai waterfront, home of the term *shanghaied,* and whether getting there will be difficult.

I was in Shanghai once before, on the 1979 trip. I stayed at the Peace Hotel on the Bund in a huge room. China had just been opened to the outer world, and it was so like the Taiwan of my childhood—it looked the same, people dressed the same—that when I emerged from the airplane, came down the rolling stairs, and stood there on the tarmac, I broke down sobbing. I was so moved to be back in China. For that entire trip, emotions poured out of me that had been bottled up for years. I feel that relief again now. I feel as if I've come home.

LuLu sits quietly beside me, staring out the window at China, taking it all in. I am so glad she is getting to look at her China, the China of "you're from China, you're adopted from China, you came from China, I went to China to get you, I was in China when the phone rang and a voice said, 'Would you like to meet your baby?'" Her China. That China.

Presently the taxi pulls into a walled, landscaped courtyard before a stately, turn-of-the-century stone building flanked by stone fu dogs. Four pillars guard the entrance, which is a revolving door of dark wood and brass. Above the pillars sits an ornate stone balcony, and beyond that is a characteristically Chinese covered corridor, also in stone. The floor inside and out is marble. It's quite wonderful-looking. I breathe a sigh of relief.

I pay the driver, and Lu and I rush inside, leaving our bags to the uniformed doorman. The young woman at the reception desk speaks no English but manages to find our reservation. It seems we are eligible for the summer discount. The rate is about eighty dollars, quite reasonable, and so far the place is lovely. Our room turns out to be huge and rather soviet, in that it is comfortable and serviceable but not especially gay.

As we fall into our big bed, I ask LuLu how she likes China so far. She thinks about it, then replies slowly, "Everyone is Chinese. I'm Chinese."

"How does that feel?" I ask, really wanting to know.

She grins at me. "It feels like good."

May 1
Shanghai, Sunny

I don't know what to call myself, really. Am I a Westerner or a Caucasian or an American or what? I hate this race thing, but I have to deal with it so I try. In Chinatown, I'm an American or white, and a Chinese person seems to always be Chinese even if he or she has immigrated and become a U.S. citizen. To me, LuLu is a Chinese-American; but to the Chinese, I think, a Chinese-American is someone who was born and raised in the United States and perhaps doesn't even speak Chinese.

In China, I'm definitely a Westerner or foreigner first, then an American. I don't like to define myself as "white" and my child as "non-white," although I know a number of Chinese people who do quite freely and refer to their skin as yellow. The whole thing of typing by skin color makes me uncomfortable. I was brought up during the civil rights era and cannot entirely expunge evil "Whites Only" signs from my mind.

When they told us at the adoption agency that we would have to deal with questions of race, I was perplexed. I never thought of the Chinese in those terms, but I have learned that others do.

The summer LuLu turned three, she went to precamp in our summer community. As she walked up the path to the building where the precamp crowd had gathered, every child and adult turned to stare at her, then me. She was the only non-Caucasian child in the camp and the only child with a mother of a different race.

It was a terrifying moment for me, and God knows what it was like for her. But that morning, clearly knowing more than I, she insisted on wearing this pair of "golden shoes" that I had bought her for dress-up along with a "pretty dress." I argued, of course, but finally gave in. Within two weeks, every child knew her name, and gone were all shorts and sneakers. Every little girl in her camp group was wearing a dress and golden shoes.

I remember that morning as we descend to the all-Chinese street in the all-Chinese country. It pleases me that while we are here, she will have an entire country behind her for support. I wonder how that will change her.

There is a bit of garden in front of the lobby with a tiny fish-pond in it to ward away ghosts. In the center of it stands a rather Greek-looking white marble statue of a water-pouring maiden. Two other buildings on the grounds also have rooms, one with a lovely wooden staircase up to a casement-windowed conference room. Around the grounds are planted flowers and weeping pine trees. There are several of these "Garden Hotels," as they are called, in China, and I think they are the nicest. They remind me of the China I used to know, with lots of houses with pagoda roofs and gardens all around.

Above the wall around the hotel tower half-built skyscrapers, and near them their pals, the cranes, dangle girders in their spindly jaws. The hewing sounds of construction are constantly in the background, even though the immediate neighborhood dates from the French Concession period of Shanghai's history and—for the moment, at least—seems safe from the wrecking ball.

We walk down the street toward the hotel coffee shop, which, curiously, is outside the wall and looks rather like a French patisserie. LuLu is making Chinese sounds to herself. I don't know how much Chinese she actually speaks. For two years at Red Apple, she was taught entirely in Mandarin, but we never spoke it at home. The idea was for her to have the linguistic map in her head so she could learn later. Sometimes I think she thought it was a special way of talking reserved only for school.

A little way down the block, a man has set up a wooden table and people are eating noodles. I would like to eat there, but I am as yet too shy. A middle-aged woman, nicely dressed in a linen blouse and long skirt, passes us and points to LuLu.

"Pretty," she says in Chinese, and smiles.

I make a note of that. These little shards of information I collect like an archaeologist: she is considered pretty in her native country as well as mine. Her name is cute. Second children are stronger.

I have consulted my travel book and planned our day. It's Sunday, so we are going to the Fuxing Park, which is nearby.

I have learned from the *Lonely Planet, China* travel guide, which my stepfather Stephen pressed into my hands as I was leaving, bless him, that there are only two taxi fares in the country—ten yuan and twenty yuan, depending on the opulence of the cab. The larger cab is more like a town car, with white curtains and doilies on the seats. The smaller cabs do not have partitions like ours in New York City. Here, only the driver is surrounded by plastic, walling him off from us.

After breakfast, the taxi drives us past Huaihuai Zhong Lu, the shopping street near our hotel. The stores are in clusters, as they are in France. Fifteen huge skirt and blouse stores in a row, enough skirts and blouses for an army. Then hundreds of men's suit stores. All of them are quite empty at this hour of the morning.

We pass what looks like a children's department store. I take note of the streets. Tomorrow I will buy a stroller if I can. A stroller is a necessity for sight-seeing with children in a foreign land. On the street, taxis, town cars, bicycles, foot-driven and motorized pedicabs, and motorbikes whiz around.

The driver comes to a halt at the edge of a park. Before us is a large concrete area on which about twenty middle-aged couples are ballroom dancing to Chinese pop music emanating from the old Maoist PA speakers.

It's lovely to see the couples glide around. This I remember from my last trip to China. I went to the province of Sinkiang, which is home to some of China's minority people and is below Inner Mongolia.

Near the city of Urumchi, we visited a mountainous park. Suddenly we came upon a group of Uighurs, a Chinese minority that retains Chinese coloring—black hair, black eyes—but whose eyes do not have the epicanthic fold and look Caucasian. They were ballroom dancing on the grass to a little record player. Everyone turned, still in dance poses, and smiled at us. That scene, as this one in Fuxing Park, had an air of such gentleness about it.

Beyond the dance platform at the entrance to the park proper sits a row of people selling massage, cupping, and various medical cures. They sit in white coats in front of small wooden tables with glass jars on them that contain snakes, toads, and lizards. There are also strange acupuncture charts on the tables, showing the sensitive points of hands, feet, and brains. The medical men and women are in earnest conversation with people who sit at the tables, seeking their advice.

Behind the purveyors of medicines, the park divides into two populations. On the left, the elderly are together, doing tai chi exercises and playing mah-jongg or cards. Occasionally, someone stands on a platform and speaks to the crowd. Off to the right is the children's area of the park.

To her delight, LuLu finds that there is a huge outdoor table covered with pots of brightly colored sand for making pictures. I figure out that in order for her to play, I must buy a picture from the man, who has all kinds of Disneyesque drawings displayed on a board. LuLu chooses a drawing of Sailor Moon, the adolescent Japanese superheroine whom she likes a lot. When the man gives us the picture, we find that it is sticky so the sand will adhere to it. Lu makes her picture happily alongside about twenty other children.

I am feeling pretty relaxed, although I am the only Westerner in the park. It will take a week or two for me to change myself so I can walk around China. My awareness of myself has to vanish completely. Right now, I am still too self-conscious. After all, this is a culture where the whole is greater than the individual, and I have just come out of a culture where the individual is more important than God. But becoming one with China is something I have done before. I should be able to do it again.

When LuLu finishes her picture, we take a rest on a bench with a youngish couple and their daughter. "*Chungkuo?*" the man asks me, indicating LuLu. Is Chinese?

"Yes," I reply. "She is *Chungkuoren* [born in China and Chinese]. *Wode nuer* [She is my daughter]."

"*Baba Chungkuo?*" he asks then. Is the father Chinese?

I mull this over. I have been asked this in America, too. Sometimes it's just easier to answer yes, but I don't. I'm interested to see what he decides when I say no. I want to see whether the city man knows about foreign adoptions.

"No," I reply. The man looks confused. Funnily enough, I don't know the word for "adopted," so I leave it at that.

It was after Miss Ling's wedding that LuLu and I had our first real conversation about adoption. It was in November, when she was three and a half. I know exactly, because it happened at a "multicultural" Thanksgiving dinner Joanna held at Red Apple. We were the "multicultural" part. Everyone else in the class was so Chinese that not one parent spoke a word of English.

The other mothers tried to be nonchalant. But even as little as three years ago, Westerners didn't go down to Chinatown and march into fully Chinese institutions. And there was not much consciousness of Chinese adoption then, among Americans or Chinese.

It didn't help that I was a lot older than everyone else. "You're like a grandma," LuLu said to me one day, and she was quite right. I was forty-five when she said that to me, about the age of the grandparents who often picked up her classmates at the end of the day. Most of the mothers were in their twenties.

But it wasn't until the Thanksgiving dinner that LuLu seemed to fully grasp the oddness of our situation. Faced with a classroom full of young Chinese mothers and me, a lightbulb seemed to go off over her head.

She began to run aimlessly but frantically around the room. Then she started to bring me food from the table, as if trying to find a way to include me. She refused to sit at the table where all her classmates were sitting. She sat apart from them or just ran to and fro. She was clearly profoundly uncomfortable.

When we left and were out in the street, I bent down to her in the stroller. "Are you embarrassed that I am not Chinese?" I asked.

his happens to grown-ups. There's so much
art that it spills out my eyes."

hugged her and prayed that she could feel the
saying. I held her close and said softly, "I love

close. "I love you, Mama," she whispered back.
ter, on a Sunday morning, she was sitting with
did not live with us but came and stayed on
oked suddenly very sad. I asked her what was
id, "My parents left me. They went away and
grandparents." I looked over at Neke. We were
h, Mom," she suddenly said, "I don't want to be

around her. I was so torn up with emotion, I
k. "You won't have to be adopted again, my dar-
er leave you. Don't worry. Please don't worry."
six-month period in which she seemed to be
at she had learned. She became noticeably calmer
the time she had learned to walk, she'd had long
he couldn't stop running or moving. In my igno-
ught her high activity the result of having been
e first six months of her life—she, who was so ath-
e, in part, it was. But as she worked on the prob-
tity, it became clear that part of her drive to move
ety, confusion about herself and her whereabouts
in her a desire to run. Because the more she under-
er origins, the more tranquil she became.
ly added the "first parents," as I called them, to the
y she wanted to hear each night. But I could not as
elf to tell her that they had left her on the street near
n. I couldn't figure out how to soften that. Perhaps
art because of something my friend Eshel, Sasha's
brought to my attention.
d one day and said that her husband had brought

"Yes," she replied.

I felt a terror in my heart that I tried to cover. "It's all right," I told her. "That's okay." Still, I went home scared. It was time to have the talk.

I guess every adoptive parent fears the moment they will have to discuss adoption for the first time. I know I was terrified of telling my child. I was terrified I would say something irrevocably wrong, something that she would never get out of her thoughts. And I feared that when I told her I was not her birth mother, she would no longer love me with the strength she had. Actually, I would probably never have even gotten the word *adoption* out of my mouth were it not for Barney.

Yes, let no man speak against the big purple dinosaur, for it is to him that I owe this debt.

One day when Lu was about two, she was watching Barney (and, hence, so was I) when suddenly adoption was mentioned. It appeared that one of the little girls on the show was supposed to be adopted.

I seized the moment, and in a falsely cheerful voice, strangled with avoidance, I managed, "Oh, LuLu. She's adopted. You're adopted, too." LuLu nodded disinterestedly.

But the dreaded word was out of my mouth, and for a while I used it if people questioned us on the street. "Yes," I would say offhandedly, "Lu is adopted from China." And I repeated it until I felt that we were both accustomed to hearing it.

Once I had said it aloud, I no longer strangled on it, and it lost its bite. But saying "adopted" and explaining its meaning to a small child are two vastly different things.

I had read several books on the subject. One was a hellish text of grim accounts of sadness and suicidal feelings from adoptees. But another, called *Talking with Young Children About Adoption,* by Mary Watkins and Susan Fisher, was really helpful, and from it I got three pieces of important advice: 1) keep it simple—don't overexplain; 2) children can't really understand adoption if they don't understand birth; and 3) even very young children know more about their situation than you think they do.

The night of the Thanksgiving dinner, when we were lying in bed, I said to her, "LuLu, I want to explain something to you. I want to explain why I am not Chinese." She focused on me intently.

"I am not Chinese," I went on, "because I did not give birth to you. But I am as much your mother as any mother in your class, and you are my daughter. We just don't look alike, that's all."

She seemed relieved to hear this.

"Do you want to hear the story of how I adopted you?" I asked. She nodded yes fervently.

So for the first time I went into it, telling it much as I have told it here. The parts she liked best and asked for over and over were the part about the adoption ministry deciding she was the perfect baby for me and sending me her picture, and the part about how Xion Yan had called and asked, "Would you like to meet your baby?" and how she had bowed and smiled when we met. The birth part of our story, if you will.

It gave her instant relief to have talked with me, and the next day when she came home from school, she sat down and asked me this exact question: "Excuse me, Mother," she said with odd formality, "I wonder if you could tell me—why don't I speak Chinese?"

It had never occurred to me that she might wonder about that. It was a darn good question from her end. She looked Chinese. Why didn't she speak Chinese? Perhaps all this time she had been thinking that she was dumb in some way.

I replied that she did not speak Chinese because neither Neke nor I speak Chinese and so we did not speak Chinese at home, but since we live in an English-speaking country, she is very lucky that she speaks such good English. This seemed to comfort her.

It brought her a lot of comfort, too, to hear about how her dear friends Sasha and LiLi and Emily and Gianna were there at her adoption, along with our friends, their parents.

In the next
night over and
ing—and every
bring myself to

Finally, one nig
story, and before I
the story." Her ea

"The story reall
And they gave birt
you want to. I call
you, but they could

"Why?" Her little
toddler gone. This
find out about but
they?"

I swallowed. I was
stuck to the truth.

"We don't know," I t
government wouldn't I
We don't know. But I'n
you to the Wuhu Child
best mother for you, and
ture"—I pointed to it w
when I saw it I thought, T

I held my breath and lo
thinking, how this inform;

"LuLu," I whispered, be
son, a humorist who's sca
down deep inside myself to
felt. "The best day of my lif
happy to be your mother."

And tears exploded down
was terrified that she would th
three, after all. "I'm crying 'c;

mered. "Honest, th
happiness in my he
I grabbed her and
truth in what I was
you so much."
She hugged me
About a week la
me and Neke. H
weekends. She lo
wrong, and she s
left me with my
both stunned. "O
adopted again."
I put my arm:
could hardly spe
ling. We will ne
Now began
working out wh
right away. Fror
periods when s
rance, I had th
swaddled for th
letic. And may
lem of her ide
was pure anxi
that produced
stood about h
I immediat
adoption stor
yet bring mys
a police stati
this was in
mother, onc
Eshel call

home a book of photographs of China in the twentieth century. She'd been flipping through it and had seen a shot of a bunch of people standing on line, and on the pavement near them, wrapped in rags, lay an abandoned baby girl.

"It is incredible to see it," she said, the sadness in her gentle voice, "but there it is. Just incredible."

For a long time I searched for that book, and then one day at a friend's, by accident, I found it. And it was incredible. A young woman in line is looking down at the little ragged wrapped bundle curiously, as if to say, What's that thing?

My daughter's first days were that stark, that real, a little ragged, wrapped-up bundle placed on a street near the Qing Yi Jiang Canal Police Substation. And having seen that photo of the reality, I could not pretend well enough that that was perfectly okay, so I couldn't tell her.

Although watching LuLu struggle to understand was almost unbearably moving to me, at the same time I was relieved to see that she was trying to make sense of it. In *Talking with Young Children About Adoption,* Mary Watkins warned that children must mourn their losses and that among the signs of mourning is a profound grief at not having been in the adoptive mother's stomach. This surprised me, that little children would think about that. But it happened exactly as the book said it would.

"Okay," LuLu would say to me, "pretend you are getting your new adopted baby." And we would reenact the "birth" scene of the adoption.

That led to "Pretend someone's in your tummy," then to "Pretend I'm in your tummy." Then she wanted me to give birth to her, and I would pretend to, and she would lie on her back between my legs with her head on my stomach and wiggle out and cry. Then I would pretend to suckle her at my breast for a bit.

"I feel like I gave birth to you," I would tell her as we played.

"I wish I was borned from you," she would murmur from time to time.

Then we entered a period where she was the one who gave birth. I bought her a baby doll so she could have a new adopted baby of her own, and although LuLu was ordinarily completely uninterested in dolls, she played with it instantly, giving birth to it and employing it in our reenactments.

Once she put the doll to bed and propped its little milk bottle on the pillow near its mouth, exactly as they did in Chinese orphanages. Another time she gave birth to the doll and said to me, "You're the sister. Tell me to throw it away." And I did reluctantly, and she threw it in the bathroom and slammed the door. Then there was the rhino game she and I acted over and over after seeing Babar and the Rhinos war on a Babar video. "Rhinos are taking your baby. Cry!" she demanded of me.

She began to have nightmares. She dreamed she was having a birthday at school and she went to the bathroom to pee, and her mother left the school and went away.

She dreamed she was in a museum, and a baby with an outstretched arm and bloody nose grabbed her. "She liked me," she said.

And in between, moments of grief surfaced. "I'll never see my Chinese parents," she said sadly one afternoon. I took my reply from something my friend Sara had so wisely said to her Chinese daughter when she had voiced the same sadness.

"Look in the mirror and you'll see them. They are in you." I took LuLu to the mirror.

"In my legs?" she asked.

"In your legs," I replied.

Once on the subway, LuLu sat next to a Chinese woman and asked her, "Are you my mother?"

"Why did you ask that?" I questioned her later.

"I want a Chinese mother," she said angrily.

"You have one," I told her. "We don't know her, but you do have one." And she smiled.

Then there was the final game, which she orchestrated with

three stuffed pandas. One panda was the baby, one was the mother, and one was the adopting mother.

When she started this game, she made me the birth mother and she was the baby. She tried to give me money so that I could keep her. I tried to explain that poverty was not cured with one payment. Then, as the birth mother, I took the opportunity to try to explain in simple terms the reasons behind the Chinese government's one-child policy: China's population problems and its relative lack of arable land for food, and how because of this the government deemed that I was not allowed to keep her.

This was not exactly simple stuff, but I felt I owed it to the woman who might have been forced to give her up—I wanted to lay the groundwork in the hope that, someday, LuLu would understand.

For months we played with the pandas. Sometimes I was the birth mother, sometimes she was. Mostly she was the baby. We both gave her away and readopted her many times over.

Then one day she announced to me with finality, "Okay. I'm going to call you Mama instead of Emily."

And that was that. Her work was, for the moment, over. She came out of it more self-assured. It seemed that she had resolved something to her satisfaction. We took up hands again as mother and daughter and went on with life. We continued sporadically to play birth and suckling, but we never played the panda game again.

We journey on through Fuxing Park and discover a small merry-go-round and a small but beautiful Ferris wheel. Lu insists on getting into one of the oxidized green metal oval cars that hang off the central spokes like seedpods on a stem. A man shuts the door and she revolves slowly through the treetops, beaming down through the grating.

We stroll on through the park, past a man who is selling only goldfish. Bowls and aquariums sit on the pavement. An aquarium in the house wards off evil spirits. You need a pond at your entrance or a bowl of fish so ghosts can't come in.

We walk out the way we came in, and right nearby we find a rather nice-looking restaurant. I take LuLu up some stairs and into a spare but pleasant room, with lots of round tables covered in crisp white tablecloths.

When the waiter comes, I ask for *jiaodzes,* dumplings—the only food (besides duck) I can as yet order in Mandarin. Families are filling the tables. Everything has a nice formality to it, partly because most of the women are wearing skirts and the men are in suits. It is like the 1950s in that way. We wore rayon then, too, and skirts and suits.

The waiter brings the *jiaodzes,* and they are delicious—fresh and delicate, their broth fragrant and light. LuLu and I both eat heartily. After we have finished, I pay the check and we leave the restaurant. People have cast sidelong glances at us the entire time, and now they openly watch us leave. But really, it is very different than it used to be. I'm thankful for LuLu's sake. Had we been constantly surrounded by people staring, it might have really spooked her.

We notice, as we walk along, that there seems to be a hairdressing salon every two feet. Somewhere I read that Shanghai is renowned for its hairdressers, so I decide to have my hair washed and cut. I steer Lu into a salon, and everyone inside bustles over, pleased as punch to see us.

They dress me in a robe and wash my hair, and then the attendant proceeds to give me a fifteen-minute head and neck massage that leaves me limp with pleasure. For a while, she hits me on the head with a mallet with a soft ball on the end. When she's done, everyone plies me with questions about us—*Chungkuo? Baba Chungkuo?* I answer as I have before: *Ta shi Chungkuoren, Wuhuren.* She is Chinese, I tell them, from Wuhu. They are thrilled to hear she is Chinese. It interests me that, as Chinese as my daughter looks, the Chinese make no assumptions. I guess that's one thing they've learned this century. They talk among themselves, trying to figure us out.

The hairdressers, men and women both, are playing with LuLu. They chat to her and let her touch whatever she wants. She asks if they can do her hair, and I say yes. LuLu wants the massage with the mallet, but they won't do it for her. Evidently it's not good for children.

We return to the main street to get a taxi, and LuLu wants badly to go back in one of the motorized pedicabs. These are like Vespas with cabs in the back and are obviously the least expensive of the taxi family. I make a deal with the man, and he takes us back to the hotel.

It is a ridiculously bumpy ride, and scary, as we are quite close to the other, larger vehicles on the road. When we arrive, we are both vibrating. It turns out that by mistake, I promised the man thirty yuan, ten more than for the most luxurious taxi. He is angry and shouting at me. Basically, I don't approve of screwing tourists, so I stand my ground.

The hotel doorman emerges, and I can see from his face that he is rather shocked that we took that sort of cab at all. I decide to pay the thirty yuan, and as we enter the hotel, the doorman mimes to me not to go near that type of cab again.

May 2
Shanghai, Sunny

In the morning, we get ready for our trip to the Yu Garden, a big tourist attraction. According to my book, it is a giant, fully restored, classical Chinese garden, the layout for which was designed in 1537. There is also a five-sided teahouse there, the Huxinting Teahouse, which is supposed to be the actual teahouse pictured on European "willow pattern" plates. The Bridge of Nine Turnings (bent because evil spirits cannot turn corners) leads to a five-sided teahouse, the book says.

Fine. I realize this will be the playground and garden tour of China. Were I alone, I would visit Sun Yat-sen's former residence and the tomb of Lu Xun, the great poet. But we are here this time for LuLu to absorb the present rather than the past. Anyway, she's too young to grasp the concept of fifty years or five thousand. And maybe she doesn't need to, maybe all that history is encoded in her DNA.

We breakfast in the coffee shop again. The door is open to the sounds of Shanghai waking up, the distant pounding of construction like its heartbeat.

I pass by the reception desk on our way out and manage to explain that we need "soft seats" (first class) train tickets to Wuhu. "Perhaps four days," the lady replies.

"But I don't want to stay four days more," I stammer. In the *Lonely Planet, China* guide they did mentioned getting train tickets could take a few days, but I forgot. "I want to go day after tomorrow," I tell her.

She gestures helplessly. "Holiday," she says. I urge her to try, and slink out.

I'm upset because Leo may be waiting by now in Wuhu. Leo and I first met when he and another professor came to my apartment in New York. They were doing a study on what happens to Chinese adopted girls when they come to America. Leo was taken with the idea that LuLu was going to a Chinese preschool, and when I told him I would be bringing her to China one day soon, he offered to help get us settled when I did. So, we are to meet up in Wuhu two days from now, which means I must get tickets as soon as possible.

In the meantime, however, the Yu Garden. First we will stop by the children's department store to see if we can get a stroller. I read the guidebook again as LuLu plays with the waiter and manages to wangle her way into the patisserie kitchen. She loves to go backstage, as it were. The way things work is an obsession with her.

She and her friend Sasha played together from the time they returned from China as babies. One day we went over to Sasha's, and Lu and Sasha had their first conversation in words. Lu picked up Sasha's kiddie tape player and held it out to Sasha. "How does it work?" was the first sentence she ever said to her friend.

We hop in a taxi and I direct him to go up Huaihuai Zhong Lu. We come to a large building with a group of children singing, a full band playing, and a blowup rainbow over all. This is it.

We get out and walk into a wonderfully festive store. The dress department alone is an explosion of yellow and turquoise sundresses, with little purses and sunhats to match, all tacked up on the walls. The styles are simple but very different from ours. The skirts are round and full, the bodices cut in all kinds of shapes, and all have long sashes. They remind me of young women's dresses from French movies of the early 1960s, very feminine but not frilly. They don't look especially childish, although they are obviously for children. I love them and resolve to buy some later.

The stroller department is not vast, but I find a strong umbrella stroller with a cute bear-patterned seat for a whopping two hundred yuan (twenty dollars). It must be the most expensive thing in this clearly upscale store.

The stroller folds and unfolds easily and lo and behold has a little metal handle that makes carrying it much easier than American umbrella strollers. I buy it and bundle Lu into it, and off we go back into a taxi.

We stop in front of a wall, and the taxi driver gestures that we should walk left to the entrance. I put LuLu in the stroller and push her. Suddenly she says, "That's a funny head." I look to my right, and there is a child around three and a half whose head has been so terribly burned that all the hair is gone and the facial features have melted. The burned child was just leaving his little begging mat when we approached.

I immediately start crying, although the child seems very lively and not at all in pain. Ever since I became a mother, there are things I simply cannot hear about or read anymore, let alone see. LuLu is looking to me to explain about the child, and I bend down and tell her why the child has a head like that. Even though I assure her the child seems all right now, she is very abashed.

Well, welcome to Asia. I had been dreading something like this. Actually, Shanghai seems to have relatively few homeless or beggars. I can remember seeing all manner of poor souls with misshapen or missing limbs when I was a child in Taiwan. It always made me both sad and curious.

We find the rather undistinguished entrance, and I push Lu through it into a tunnel lined with packed stores selling hair ornaments, fake antiques, the useless Austrian crystal figurines of China, and all manner of merchandise. Lots of Chinese people are milling about.

We emerge into a central area and weave our way through the throngs, and suddenly I realize that we are by a little lake. There at the end of a zigzagging bridge is the Huxinting Teahouse.

It is absolutely beautiful, like an old drawing from the eighteenth century. The building supports both square and hexagonal rooms on two levels, with four separate roofs of very long, very coiled pagoda curls. It is our first genuine Chinese pagoda-roofed building.

The roof color is gray. The teahouse beneath is made of that lovely reddish wood—is it a kind of teak? Across the lower half of the teahouse walls is an ornate wooden grating backed with white so that you can see its intricate pattern. Cut into the upper part of the wall is a series of square casement windows that open onto the lake. The building stands on stilts in the water and is small enough in circumference to walk around in about five minutes.

I would love to have tea there, but the bridge and the teahouse both are overflowing with people (although no foreigners that I can see). I push Lu down another corridor, and we run into a man selling watercolors of the Chinese astrological signs. He's a wonderful painter, so I buy a Rooster for Sasha and a Tiger for LiLi.

There are a lot of people around us and we are both still too jet-lagged to cope with too much. I can't seem to find the actual garden part of Yu Garden and I have forgotten my language book, so I can't ask where to go. Now I just want to get us out.

Finally, I find another corridor that leads outside. It seems to be full of map stores and I would like a giant map of China—but in English, which of course is unobtainable here.

The Huxinting Teahouse has got to be one of the most extraordinary whimsies I've ever seen. How beautiful teakwood is, and those pagoda roofs make a building seem so magical. When I was a child, the beauty of Chinese design gave me immense pleasure. I lived in a Chinese house made of teak. I awoke every morning in a room that smelled of camphor and seven kinds of tea. The shapes of dumplings and brooms and hats and sandals and the colors of paper fans and kites helped so much to keep my sadness at bay.

Lu and I take a taxi back to the hotel and lunch in the patisserie because it is there and therefore restful. LuLu strikes up a conversation with Mr. Fridman, an American businessman sitting at the next table. He is a big man with a thick Yiddish accent and a kindly face.

After a time, I begin to chat with him, too, and find that he's a salesman who just moved back to the States after living in Hong Kong for thirty years. He tells me he stays at the Dong Hu because it's so quiet compared to the hotels on the Bund. Then he says he likes everything about the Dong Hu except the lighting, which is too dim to enable him to sell his fabrics. He's having a word with the manager about that tomorrow, he says.

He also tells me that the hotel has very elaborate rooms in Building Two, one of Japanese design that offers a "Presidential Suite" complete with whirlpool bath. Mao is rumored to have slept there.

While LuLu is rushing around, playing waitress, he and I talk about our experiences living in China. He mentions how wonderful it was for his two small children to be brought up in China, how much the Chinese love children. It is nice to hear this from someone else. At home, I'm always the one trying to convince people of this, and they often look at me like I'm nuts. It is so hard for Americans to understand when all they hear about is grim Chinese orphanages and the one-child policy.

After lunch, I drag Lu away from her waitress duties and we stop at the reception desk. There we find that our train tickets have been reserved, but they are not for three days. All right. Tomorrow the Shanghai Zoo, the next day the Bund, and the third day to Wuhu. We have the tickets, the "soft seats." I feel better.

I ask if I can see the mansion that once belonged to Yu Dusheng. A magazine editor has asked me to look into it. When the manager appears with the keys, he explains that they do rent the mansion, but only to corporations for months at a time, and not at one hundred dollars a day, but more like five thousand a month. Ah, inflation has hit since my Shanghai guide was written.

We accompany him down the block and across the street to the corner, where there's an entrance to some grassy acreage dotted with four condo houses that they also rent. Not far from the last of those stands the mansion, a large French colonial–style building with a circular driveway, fronted by a huge lawn.

The manager lets us right into the history of Shanghai. Giant wood-paneled rooms with stained-glass windows sit silent, their furniture covered in sheets. I imagine Chinese women from the 1930s in bias-cut gowns, smoking opium pipes over by the French windows, then stumbling laughing onto the great lawn. According to The Soong Dynasty, by Sterling Seagrave, Chiang Kai-shek was an enforcer for Yu Dusheng's "Green Gang" before he married one of the Soong sisters and rose to lead the Kuomintang.

In the afternoon, I push LuLu in the stroller over to the Garden Hotel. This five-star Japanese extravaganza has computers available for public use, so I can e-mail Neke that we are safe and sound.

The Garden is two blocks away and composed partly of the old Cercle Sportif Français, which later became the Jin Jiang Club. The old pre-1949, semicircular pillared building now balances on its shoulders yet another skyscraper. But for now, at least, the old French Concession area has a number of elderly buildings that give one the feeling of being somewhere in Europe . . . and yet not.

The hotel is opulent inside. No dimness here, it is lit up like a Christmas tree and bustling with foreigners in designer gym clothes. We ask for the computer room, and a young woman in a tailored navy blue suit and Dorothy Collins tie tells me that Internet use costs fifteen dollars for three minutes! Sitting at the console, I have to quickly learn a new method of getting onto the Net and end up spending thirty dollars to send an e-mail to Neke. I could have called.

We walk outside and cross the circular driveway to the garden for which the hotel is named. One grassy area unfolds into another and finally into a third, where two young Chinese mothers sit on blankets while some little girls a bit older than LuLu run around.

The mothers glance over at us, then look away discreetly. LuLu engages with the girls, who are immediately friendly and invite her into their game. The mothers now take a good look at LuLu and offer her their food. I feel a little left out, like the odd duck in the nest. And I wish I spoke more Chinese. Never mind, I tell myself, hang on, this feeling will pass.

The few gardens and parks we have visited so far seem very quiet inside, shut off from the outside world. But looming above them and around their edges are those ever-present cranes and skyscrapers, waiting to encroach. It makes me nervous, seeing them, as if the days of tranquillity are numbered.

After an hour or so of merriment, I gather LuLu and we walk

back to the Dong Hu. At the edge of the garden are a number of businessmen's cars, all with their drivers waiting outside, smoking and leaning against them.

As I stare at them, I am right back in Taipei. This was always part of any outing—the drivers leaning against the cars, smoking and laughing. I watch their faces now, as I did when I was little, taking note of the nice ones and those who look a little mean. I choose a nice one and give him my camera, and he takes our picture.

The sound of men laughing and joking follows us into the lobby. I nose around and discover the hotel restaurant hidden around the back of the reception area. An odd contraption by the door turns out to be a receptacle for umbrellas. Many are locked up in it, each in its own little hole. Clever, I think; if you forget your umbrella, it will be there when you get back.

We sit down and are given menus. Grilled bullfrog is one of the delicacies, and when I ask LuLu if that is what she will be having this evening, she shrieks with delight and insists on being shown the words on the page. I don't even mention the "dogmeat stew" because of her love of dogs. But it does remind me that since we arrived, we have not seen an animal on the streets except for the goldfish and some birds.

We eat well again, dumplings and pieces of roasted duck this time, and then we go upstairs to our room. As we pass the reception desk, I learn that Leo has called and left a number. Later I return his call.

I am embarrassed to learn that he is already in Wuhu. I feel we are putting him out so much, and I thank him profusely. He speaks English fluently but sounds a bit rusty, and I find it impossible to explain why we have to wait three days here since I don't really understand it myself. He doesn't seem to know that train tickets take a while to get, which is upsetting because I don't want him to think we are delaying in order to sightsee while he waits there. But such are the problems of communicating in a foreign language: you often look like a boor.

He will meet us, he says, at the station in Wuhu when we arrive. He adds that although we do not as yet have permission to visit the orphanage, it looks good. At this point, I can hardly wait to get to Wuhu.

I am armed with the adoption papers of three other Wuhu girls. One of them, Francesca—or Lao Li, as she was once known—is the daughter of my friend Janine, who is herself adopted. "Anything you can find out is good," Janine had said, and I take my cues from her. It is Janine who suggested that I visit the places where the girls were found and take photographs of them. The places are listed on our documents. On LuLu's it says, "Found nearby the Qing Yi Jiang Police Substation of Wuhu City."

Then, of course, we want to visit the Wuhu orphanage. LuLu wants badly to see it and perhaps meet her special care nurse. It is the one place she knows she came from, where she spent the first months of her life.

Thanks to a video made at the time, LuLu has seen the special care nurse who handed her to me. The adoption agency told us that many of the girls were assigned such nurses for a month or so before we got them, so they would get extra attention and wake up a bit before we got there.

I remember the nurse saying, "I don't worry about LuLu," which seemed to suggest that she knew my baby, had cared for her long enough to be aware of her positive nature. Perhaps we can find the woman and reintroduce her to my child. It would mean a lot to Lu to meet someone from that time, a person from her past.

Since I got LuLu, the present has assumed paramount importance. But in the two months since my mother died, I have been reminded of the intoxication and even the necessity of the past. My sister and I have talked and talked about where our mother came from and her parents and grandparents, the massive infusion of Irish talent and angst, the crazed progeny of the Rickards and the O'Keefes.

My mother's mother and her father were both actors on Broadway in the twenties and thirties. When she was eight, her father, Charles Romano, died at the dinner table between the matinee and the evening show of a play he was doing at Radio City Music Hall. He had angina. From that time on, my mother supported her mother as a child actress until she married my father at the age of seventeen. It wasn't until my mother was in her twenties that she learned that Romano was her father's stage name. His real name was O'Keefe, maybe.

It was in the middle of hashing and rehashing my mother's life, and seeing how important this was to our grieving, that I realized LuLu would never be able to do this in the same way. Of course, she has me and Neke and is now part of our heritages, in the kinship charts. Yet the mysteries of her genetic code, how old it is, how far back it extends, what characteristics it wrought in those now dead, are lost to her, probably forever. So anything we can find, any tiny nugget that might lead us back, we will take and store. If paleontologists can build a race from just a jawbone, surely we can glimpse a mother and father from an entire town.

The orphanages are closed to foreigners now, so Joanna at Red Apple has written a letter for us, stating that we are of good character, to aid in our petition to be allowed to visit the one at Wuhu. And I wrote a letter pleading our case, which Lu's teacher, Miss Ch'ien, translated into pinyin. These I will give to Leo to give to the people in charge. But he'd said on the phone it looks good. It looks very good.

We take a long taxi ride out to the Shanghai Zoo, which is near the airport. On the way, we pass an amazing-looking new building, which I dub "the flying saucer apartments." For that's what it looks like—a flying saucer. One thing about the Chinese architect: he is not afraid of rounded shapes in building, the legacy, perhaps, of the pagoda.

The air is so full of rubble dust that when we come home at night, we are covered in a thin film of dirt.

We get out of the taxi at the entrance and a child of about five greets us, hand outstretched. I give him ten yuan, which is a lot here, and his father, a few yards down, nods in thanks.

"Is he begging?" LuLu asks. I explain that he is and that his family is very poor.

LuLu knows a lot about poor and homeless people because she is a New Yorker. One day, walking in the city near our bank, we saw a man living in a big cardboard box. LuLu was at the age when living in a box seemed very like Nirvana, and she wanted to know all about it. She thought it looked like fun.

"Not so fun when it rains," I said. She thought about this and ever since has made sure that we give a little money to those in need. I didn't know how she would take to begging children, whether, as she says, it would hurt her heart too much. But her interest in their lives seems, for the moment, to be her main preoccupation.

I buy tickets at a kiosk and we walk onto the zoo grounds, past vendors selling sunglasses, plastic fans, and stuffed pandas. Immediately the strong, sweet fragrance of jasmine hits me. And there are flower beds everywhere, planted in intricate patterns of red and white carnations and roses. All kinds of trees are arranged together, their differently shaped leaves and shades of green creating a tableau of greenery. Through them wind paths to each group of cages.

The zoo land used to be Shanghai's golf course and comprises 173 acres. The zoo buildings date from 1954 and, though shabby, often have pretty little round or hexagonal stained-glass windows and wooden pagoda roofs.

I push LuLu in her stroller down the fragrant paths, and she is very happy and chirping. Immediately, we come upon a strange sight. It is a real lion that has been very badly stuffed. A hilariously awful piece of taxidermy, it is the life-size equivalent of those tiny, real-fur lions and tigers you can buy in Chinatown. But this one was once a real lion, and it's standing on a piece of wooden board, its mouth propped open in a mock roar.

I pose LuLu by it and take a picture, and then I notice at a small table nearby a man with a camera. He's looking irritated, and I realize that the lion is his or the zoo's and I'm supposed to pay him to take a Polaroid or pay him for use of the lion backdrop. So I do.

We walk on and it's evident that we are passing the lion house. The stuffed lion was a kind of signpost of things to come.

Up ahead is something called Pets World. As we approach the entrance, the air suddenly swells with the sound of a scratched recording of Paul Robeson singing "Old Man River." Before us is a cute live dog sitting on a desk, behind which stands a man with a camera. The dog is white and fluffy and friendly, and LuLu rushes up to pet him. This is the first dog we've seen in China.

To the cracked but amazing velvet baritone of Robeson, the great black legend—revered here, I guess, because he was himself a Communist—we enter what I can only call a most Dadaist area of the park. Here, I discover to my amazement, are dogs and cats in cages. Poodles, shihtzus, labs, Siamese, and Persians, you name them—in the dingiest and dankest of barred areas.

Uh-oh, I think to myself, but as yet LuLu is still pretty excited by the idea of dogs and cats in a zoo. Actually, it isn't that bad an idea, because children do love to see dogs and cats. But as with all good ideas, the proof is in the execution, as it were. And the snake-pit appearance of things is pretty grim. The scratched, skipping voice of Robeson adds to the insane quality of the experience.

And as I'm trying to whip out of there as fast as possible, LuLu suddenly says, "Mom, why is that dog alone? That's not right."

She is referring to a truly pathetic-looking poodle that is in a cage by itself, filthy and incredibly sad-looking.

"No, no," I mutter. "That's not a good thing at all. But you know, he's got other dogs around. . . ." And we are out of there quick, and I'm winging it down the path, Robeson's barrel chest now a visual in my mind.

The condition of the animals is standard. China is no place as yet for an animal rights person; it would just drive them mad. But Pets World has me a bit stumped. As we trot down the path, I wonder what exactly they were thinking of.

Next we come to a children's ride that is really cute, although by Chinese Communist standards, it could not be considered politically correct. The ride consists of a group of three colorful pedicabs—red, ocher, and mint green, with red-fringed pagoda roofs—that go around in a circle, each manned by an ape doll in old-style Chinese pajamas. LuLu and a little boy hop on and ride around.

We then continue on, and the next thing we come upon is—oh, no!—a life-size stuffed giraffe in a glass box, signaling, I now know, that the live giraffes are around the bend. The badly stuffed giraffe is really bizarre, and I speed around a corner to find a little girl about LuLu's age hand-feeding a live giraffe. The child is holding a thorn branch and the giraffe has bent down over the fence to munch it until its face is level with the child's. Its long fat black pointy tongue scoops up the leaves greedily. It seems hungry. The keeper is urging the giraffe closer with more good leaves, and the parents take a picture of the giraffe's face almost up against the little girl's.

LuLu is thrilled with this, and wants to pet the giraffe and snuggle it, too. The keeper is about to oblige her in return for some yuan, but I tell him no because all I can think of is a rabid giraffe bite on my daughter's cheek. Obviously the keepers earn extra money this way. The Chinese parents are clearly not afraid of a giraffe bite, and LuLu is quite disappointed. Before she can ask if she can kiss the tigers, I roll her away.

By now I am really laughing, because this zoo is so unlike an American zoo that it's almost a satire. And as we come to a group of men moving a camel, I've decided that the place is a child's dream and a Western parent's nightmare.

The camel is in a big wooden crate with no top, and by means of pulleys in some trees, the men are hoisting it up into the air. This is a mesmerizing sight that reminds me a lot of *Jurassic Park*. Come to think of it, the whole place has kind of a *Jurassic Park* feel to it—it's a little anarchic.

For a while, we watch the men maneuvering the camel. They shout to one another and almost drop the creature as they pull and strain. The camel snorts and spits, and finally a flatbed truck arrives, and they ease the crate down and drive off.

LuLu is loving it here. She is up out of the stroller, gamboling down the pathways, leaping and twirling. We turn a corner and there is a pony ride, her absolute favorite.

"Look, LuLu, a pony ride," I blurt out before I can stop myself. Then, as we both watch, a small child is put on the pony by the attendant, who then spanks the pony's rear and sends the kid off around the ring by himself. The child's mother does a double take. She is worried but calms as the child keeps his seat.

When LuLu sees that no one will walk her around, she hesitates, her usual fearlessness gone. We opt instead for the pony cart ride, which we take together. We get in and a man drives us around the ring so fast, it's like being in a chariot with Ben-Hur.

LuLu and I are giggling maniacally as we stagger off and straggle toward the main gate. There we run into the hamster, parakeet, and guinea pig saleslady. She has an open stall and sells the little pets in pink and blue cages. They look pretty good, and it makes sense somehow that you should buy your little pets at the zoo, which makes me think of Pets World again and Paul Robeson singing in his thunderous, skipping voice.

We get a cab and, once in, LuLu gasps, "Can we go again tomorrow? Please, Mom. Please!"

I begin to explain why we can't go again when LuLu falls instantly asleep. What a day! It is my first taste of the non-insurance-driven society, where anything can happen because no one can sue. It's a bit dangerous, but a lot of fun.

I'm still chuckling when we stop in at the hotel restaurant for dinner, where we do not order the bullfrog or the jellyfish.

That night, LuLu gets a fever. I have brought children's antibiotics from home, so I administer them to her and she falls into a deep but restless sleep.

May 3
Shanghai, Cloudy

When we awaken, LuLu tells me she dreamed that "they shot my mother. Now you're my sister." The feeling of the dream, she says, was not scary, just matter-of-fact. Outwardly, she is in a fine mood. Inwardly, she is beginning to work.

I think about this as I take her temperature, which is normal again. It seems to make sense that she is examining our relationship in her mind. "Shot" does not upset me. She learned the word *shot* from Babar and Disney, but I don't think she knows exactly what it means other than removal from the scene. She doesn't know it can mean death.

I take the dream to mean that her surety of me in the role of "mother" has gotten rocky now that we are in China, surrounded by Chinese women and all manner of questions about her origins. But her surety of me as family member, even caretaker, is still okay (hence I am still there but changed into sister). I am, it seems, moving from above her in the kinship chart to by her side.

We have one more day to fill before we leave for Wuhu. Lu is feeling all right, so we set off to see the Shanghai waterfront, or Bund, as they call it. We decide to eat breakfast at the Peace Hotel, where I stayed in 1979, and take a taxi there. I bring with me my hotel book, which contains a map.

The first thing we see upon alighting at the hotel entrance is the promenade along the river. Of course, it's under construction, so we can't go up there. Beyond the promenade, across the river, we can see the Oriental Pearl Tower, which sits in the new Pudong business area and is a feature of the reconstructed landscape. The Oriental Pearl Tower is a strange-looking thing, like an Eiffel Tower bisected by two balls. It's a wacky World's Fair–type creation, especially when contrasted with the old Deco sturdiness of the buildings on the Bund. It represents modernity, prosperity, and the future. Shanghai is clearly booming. There are tons of stores, all overflowing with goods.

When I was here in 1979, there was one store, the Friendship Store, where foreigners could shop in Shanghai. I remember walking in and seeing a tiger-skin coat on a mannequin—an actual tiger-skin coat, which would then have been worth quite a bit of money. Of course, the design was soviet, boxy and bulky, but I considered buying it for the paltry six hundred dollars they were charging and having it remade, since the tiger was dead anyway and this was pre-PETA. But it was against Customs law, as the tiger was an endangered species, so I restrained myself.

I still have the beautiful embroidered pillowcases I bought then. The simplicity of China in 1979 compared to now is astounding, but even then you could see what she would become. You always have to remember that when they reopened after twenty-five years, the Chinese sent out one pair of cloth Mary Janes and changed the Western world's concept of dressing. In my opinion, the Chinese understand mass appeal better than any people on earth.

The Peace Hotel is a Deco skyscraper, like the Empire State Building in shape, leading up to a pointy top with a short spire. We ride up in the elevator to an elaborate buffet breakfast in a dining room that is very Chinese. The walls are bright blue, with ornately carved red moldings and wall plaques and carved screens. We take a table looking out on the waterfront.

LuLu eats her cornflakes and watches the river excitedly. She loves the water. Once, when she was three, I took her out on an excursion boat from our summer town, and the peace and happiness that emanated from her little face as she stared at the horizon came from very deep inside her.

Water and planting are part of her soul. Once, earlier, when she was two, we were passing a community garden near our house and she saw a woman planting there. She let go of my hand and rushed through the gate to the gardener's side. She squatted right down and planted with her intently for a solid hour. For a child who was always moving, and often frantic, this quiet concentration was unusual and profound. I took it as another shard of information. Boating or planting seeds was as relaxing to my daughter as deep massage.

But when we come back down from breakfast, we remember that we can't reach the waterfront because of the scaffolding. Disappointed, we turn onto Nanking Road, or, as it was once known, Horse Road #2.

Our destination is Renmin Park, which was once the racecourse in the 1930s. Nanking Road is supposedly the major shopping road, but within minutes, there is nothing on either side of us except white concrete blocks, enormous pits, and stacked girders. Up ahead are uninhabited, unfinished buildings, white and empty. It is dusty and deserted and decidedly futuristic. Can they be tearing down every old building in Shanghai? White plaster dust puffs out under my feet.

We press on and finally come to an elaborate set of entwined elevated pathways reachable by stairs. LuLu gets out and we climb up it to find the department stores I had read about, one after another in a row. These are open for business but, like the ones on Huaihuai Zhong Lu, are without patrons. The amount of goods for sale is staggering. I buy a blouse with a Mandarin collar in a jazzy lightning-bolt print. It is cut quite well.

After a long trek past store after store, we reach the place where

Renmin Park should be, according to the map in the guidebook. But across the street there is only a construction wall. I push LuLu into the Park Hotel, so named because it is supposedly across from the park, and ask the clerk at the reception desk, "Where is Renmin Park?" He points to the construction wall. "There?" I ask mournfully, surveying the barrier, which doesn't seem to be enclosing a very large area.

"Renmin Park much smaller now," the man explains.

As we pile into a taxi, exhausted again, I wonder if one day the Chinese will regret building skyscrapers over all their parks and gardens. But then I know that if they do, they will simply tear down some of the skyscrapers and put back the parks and gardens. In China, there are no obstacles.

It is lunchtime as we reach Huaihuai Zhong Lu. Out the taxi window, I see that the deserted stores in which we browsed in the last few days are now so packed with people that no one can move inside. Each of the ten thousand shirt stores is stuffed like the New York subways at rush hour—no, worse. People are sort of falling out of the doors. Surely it is hard to breathe? The sight is incredible, like stuffed buses I saw once in Cairo. How can they shop like this? Suddenly I get a sense of what the one-child policy is all about. I point out this sardine phenomenon to LuLu and she nods and watches.

I can hardly get the vision of that crush out of my head as I stop at the desk and order a wake-up call for five-thirty the next morning. The train leaves at seven and the station is far away, near the zoo. As I leave reception, I hope the desk clerk has understood my broken Chinese and gotten the time right, and I resign myself to unremitting anxiety until we have reached Wuhu.

Up in our room, I pack up and LuLu chooses the dress she will wear for her arrival in her hometown. She picks an outfit that I bought in Chinatown, a pink sundress with a ruffled skirt and a little white jacket. It is the dress she feels is her most beautiful—a princess outfit, the perfect outfit for a triumphant return.

May 4
Shanghai, Sunny

At dawn, the phone does ring, thank God, and we sleep-walk out of bed and into the elevator. Lu says she is feeling good, and I am relieved. The patisserie is open, barely, and I get them to give us ham sandwiches for the trip. I don't know if there will be food on the train.

Once, in 1990, when I was traveling from Berlin to Warsaw just after the Wall came down, the train clerk in Berlin told me there would be food; but after we entered the Communist bloc, all food vanished and we were stuck on the train for the next ten hours. That's when I learned that communism doesn't mean taking care of the people. Warsaw in 1990 was, in fact, the only city I've ever visited where I never saw any food on the street, not a bun or a piece of fruit or a candy bar. The town had a desolate, cold, famished feeling to it. So I'm bringing food just in case.

The taxi takes us back past the spaceship apartments, past the zoo. Surrounding the station are several half-finished skyscrapers, and one that is evidently all finished and just open. I know this because two strings of "grand opening" flags, just as we drape them across new storefronts in the United States, have been stretched from the top to the bottom of the skyscraper and reaches the entire length of twenty-six floors! The building looks wonderful this way, decorated like a huge birthday package.

The driver drops us outside the station and I am reminded, as he does, that there are no porters in Communist countries. You carry your own bags. In Poland, women would come up and take a handle of my bag to help me.

But I knew in advance that I would be doing the carrying, so I have a backpack with wheels, a suitcase with wheels, a shoulder bag, and the stroller with its blessed handle, and LuLu has a back-pack with wheels. Mule Mommy, I struggle into the station, and after a time of muttering, "Wuhu? Wuhu?" and showing the tick-ets, a clerk directs me to leave the bags in a heap and sit down in the main waiting room until Wuhu is called.

The room contains a number of old couches and chairs and, in the center, a grand piano. Evidently, at more crowded times of the day, a pianist comes and plays for the waiting passengers. We wish it were now.

LuLu studies piano in New York. She is, the music teachers tell me, a gifted musician. I found this out down at Red Apple when they started giving piano lessons to those who wanted them. She was three and a half then.

The first day, when I appeared to pick her up, the music teacher was ecstatic. Before she even had lessons, LuLu had taught herself to play chords and two-handed songs. After the school year ended, I took her to one of the city's quality music schools and the director assigned her a special teacher.

As we wait, LuLu approaches the piano and tinkers with the keys a bit. Sometimes when she is playing, I imagine this musical family she must have come from. I see them on a summer night, outside near the rice fields, under the clear, bright stars, playing traditional Chinese instruments—the *pipa* and the *erhu*—and singing Chinese classical songs. They are always laughing.

Twenty-five years ago, each county had a theatrical troupe and a musical troupe. I often wonder if LuLu's birth family was the-atrical, like mine. Was it the mother who was musical or the fa-ther? Or was it the grandparents? "Her hands are so beautiful," her Russian teacher murmured after her first time teaching her. And they are. Like little doves. Her long, slender fingers make them look like the tiniest of adult hands. One of my delights is giving her manicures and painting her nails with what she calls "pol nailish."

The train is called, and we collect our bags. I hand the man the tickets and struggle down the ramp. Next to me, a man and his wife offer help. They look around and spy a man in shirtsleeves, who, it transpires, is a sort of freelance porter who for ten yuan will get us into the right car. I thank the couple profusely. The freelancer takes the bags and I rush along behind. LuLu keeps up with him, proudly pulling her little suitcase behind her.

He leads us into the train car and leaves our big bags with a pile of other luggage at one end of it. Here, at last, are the soft seats. The car is light mint green with royal-blue velvet seats, the tops of which are sheathed in crisp, easily changeable, white cotton covers, against which you lean your head. Four velvet seats surround a small table by the window, hung with lacy white curtains. The whole car has an old-fashioned look to it, which I like a lot. As if we are traveling in the late forties.

A group of two men and two women at one of the tables gesture that there are no assigned seats, first come, first served. So Lu picks our seats and we settle down. Suddenly, as the train leaves the station, Chinese Muzak lilts from speakers in the corners of the ceiling. These strains of Chinese classical music are played orchestrally and are not high-pitched or loud: another touch of grace added to the ambience.

Presently, a woman in a uniform and cap appears with a cart, selling tea and, surprisingly, coffee. I buy a glass of coffee. She has two giant teapots made of tin that sit in quilted wicker baskets. She takes one and pours out coffee the color of tea into the glass. To this she adds sugar. It tastes almost like tea, but with a little bite. I'm glad to have it.

LuLu is very quiet and falls asleep lulled by the purring sound of a large machine engine. After about four hours, we are finally in one of the areas where my daughter might have come from. We are about two hours from Wuhu, and from here on in I look carefully at the farmland out the window. It is rice farmland, rice paddies with an occasional water buffalo plowing or farmer bending over, picking or maybe weeding rice plants.

The farmhouses are two stories high, shaped like old saltboxes, with pitched roofs that have long, skinny extensions at the corners that curl up into pagoda ends. Sometimes, at the top of the roof, two wings jut off toward heaven so that the house looks as if it has little horns. Sometimes there's a large group of buildings, a communal farm often with some sort of factory attached to it. Once or twice, a new farm building appears, four stories this time, with royal-blue glass antiglare windows. I wonder what that must be like from the inside and whether a certain amount of darkness is preferable—perhaps because of summer heat.

Around two farmhouses, rice paddies extend in either direction for several miles. Then come another two farmhouses built on the edge of a pond, with a water buffalo grazing nearby. The settings are quite sylvan and beautiful. I imagine my farm-loving, animal-loving, plant-loving, water-loving daughter opening her infant eyes to this perfect view, and I see her with the same expression she had when at one and a half she woke in her safety seat in the midst of an apple orchard, where we were parked for fall picking: bliss, as if she'd seen heaven itself.

Eshel saw it first, for she and Mark and Sasha were there. "Look," she said. "Look at her face. Have you ever seen such happiness?"

We know what these girls have gained: respite from poverty, families, love, in many cases life itself. But what I'm here to see, as much as anything, is what they've lost. For few speak of that. And right away I see that they've lost this—the beauty of this land, which helped my heart so long ago; the special luster of the water plants; the seedlings in the lake. I remember years and years of driving past the rice paddies, walking on the muddy rims between the paddies, the long, slow *moo* of the water buffalo, his huge nostrils flared, the long black eyelashes that framed his giant eyes, the yoke eternally around his dutiful neck.

A woman comes down the aisle with a tin cart, selling maps, old coins, and old paper money. Funny timing, because now some hard, dusty poverty is going by outside the window. Backyard middens. There's an old pool table, odd, unfinished blocks of flats on deserted streets that never came to life.

Was it on one of those dusty alleys that my little girl took her first breath, coughed out the mucus from her tiny lungs, and cried out in her strong, clear voice? LuLu is not the only one who thinks about her birth.

Like an overly possessive lover, I want to know all about my daughter, every moment that she wasn't with me. But I am not jealous of her former life or of what it means to her, only curious to know. But how will I feel if I actually find something—a family, a person, a relative of some kind? I have no idea.

Two big pine trees come into view, planted side by side in a nice-looking, countrified station. Ma'anshan, the conductor calls out, and I see the sign in English letters. I've met little girls from there in my playground in New York. So, here it is: Ma'anshan. The next stop, the people at the table say, is Wuhu.

I wake LuLu and she doesn't look so well. She's also subdued, which usually means she is ill. She's very excited, though, and stares in rapt attention as we pull into what is a large station. The men at the table kindly help us off the train car, and then others pick up the bags and steer us through a doorway to the street outside.

The first thing we see is a miniature Eiffel Tower. How odd. After all, we are six hours inland from Shanghai, 250 miles north of Hanoi in a small south China town on the Yangtze River. The temperature is about 75 degrees. It is May 4, 1999. We have arrived in Wuhu.

LuLu is ecstatic now. With what energy she has, she runs up and down the street, searching for Leo. But he's nowhere to be found. I do have the name of the hotel we are going to, Tie Shan Hotel, so I hail a red taxi and bundle in the bags and LuLu, and off we go.

It's a snappy little town we are driving through, no question about it. Another town designed on the French model, with roundabouts and streets branching off them like spokes and wide boulevards like the Champs Élysées, with fenced-off lanes on both sides of the street for bicycles only.

As in Shanghai, there are many new skyscrapers, many half-finished and empty. Sometimes, an old wall containing a circular moon-gate doorway will be left standing, as if they have some plan for it. That royal-blue antiglare glass is on every new building, and often it is used as a colorful design element, like blue buttons on a white shirtfront. The architecture is kind of a cross between Disney World and Miami Beach and is decidedly whimsical.

I can't get over the rounded elements in every new building I see, ball shapes or tube shapes, which perhaps make up for the lack of doorways shaped like vases and hexagons and such. And everywhere we see the same sign that says something like "Building for the year 2000." Evidently, that's when it will all be done. That's when the construction is slated to be over.

But in the meantime, it seems they are tearing down every old building, not just in Shanghai, as I thought, but in China, an entirely monumental task.

The driver asks about LuLu right away. *"Chungkuo?"*

"Wuhuren," I reply. He's astonished, of course.

"Wuhuren?" he repeats, and a huge smile breaks across his face.

After about ten minutes, we turn off a main avenue up a long, hilly, dead-end street, at the top of which is a guarded entrance. On one side is a large sign in English and Chinese brass lettering that reads "Tie Shan Hotel." We drive into a big plaza that surrounds an enormous, ancient pine tree. To the right of us is a long, two-story building, which I will learn is Building One: the lobby, stores, doctor, hairdresser, and reception. Before us, dotting the mountainside, are the five four-story buildings that make up the hotel and will be our home.

We drive in under two glass pillars holding up a silvery roof and come to a stop before the ornate lobby building. We are helped out of the cab by a very young Chinese doorman dressed in a light-blue-and-white uniform straight out of the 1930s, complete with pillbox hat that attaches under the chin and band jacket with brass buttons. As we emerge, I spy Leo come bounding out of another taxi. I am awfully glad to see him.

Ever since I first opened the door to Leo in New York, I was drawn to him. His craggy, kindly face, so evocative of wisdom, sensitivity, and suffering, perches on his tall, rail-thin, almost concave body. He laughs a lot as he darts around, driven by a kind of spirited energy. A highly respected professor of social studies at Anhui University in Hefei, he was instrumental in convincing the adoption ministry to allow Chinese families to adopt girls in China, an incredible boon for these children.

He is relieved to see us. It turns out that he was at the station, but we missed each other. Apparently we came out of a VIP door. Immediately he rushes into Building One and up to the reception desk, to see about getting us accommodations.

I assume we are just going to check in, but instead we leave our luggage at reception, and walk with Leo and the general manager to see a room in Building Four, which is situated at the very top of the property.

We trek up the road to the left of Building Two, which sits across from the reception building on the main plaza. There is also a road to the right of Building Two that leads up to Buildings Five and Six. Leo carries LuLu, who clings to him like a feverish koala. He chats to her as he bounds forward.

I am aware of how exhausted I am and struggle to keep up.

The road this side is lovely, long and winding, with overhanging trees giving us shade all the way up. The birdsong is almost deafening. A wall along the side divides the hotel property from the Anhui University housing compound. A series of large but discreet framed advertisements for beer are pinned up at intervals on the wall, as if it were a gallery display.

We climb up and up, passing a number of intriguing buildings that I later learn are the conference room; the Canting (canteen);

the restaurant, which is perched on a little peak above a steep stone stairway; and Building Three.

Finally we reach Building Four, which, according to the Garden Hotel system, is a world unto itself, with its own manager and lobby. Four's lobby is pleasant but tiny, with a polished wooden reception desk and a few armchairs to sit on nearby. We tread softly down a carpeted hall to a room that overlooks the mountainside. The room is minimal but fine and has a little refrigerator.

I ask how much it costs and find that it is too expensive, about fifty dollars a day, primarily because of the kitchenette. We are staying for several months, so it will add up. Also, it's too quiet. We need some fun. Finally, envisioning having to carry LuLu up all the way up here when she's too tired, I decide to look at something closer to the main reception building, something around twenty-five dollars a day. I tell Leo, and he tells the manager.

We stroll down to the plaza again and go into the building right in front of the giant pine tree, Building Two. I choose a much bigger, sunlit room on the second-floor front. It faces the main plaza but is hidden from sight by some hedges. We will be much closer to the action here, which will be better for both Lu and me.

We return to reception and Leo asks us to sit down at a table in what seems to be a tiny bar area. I thought we were just going to check in, but it seems we must have a discussion first.

While we wait, Leo goes to the desk and calls a friend who works at the Tie Shan. She in turn calls another friend, who teaches the general manager's child as a pupil in school. The teacher acts as a reference for us, and thus I am introduced to *guanxi,* or the Chinese system of favors and influence I have read about. Leo's friend, the hotel employee, a smiling lady with red-apple cheeks, appears now; alongside the general manager, she sits at our table to join in the negotiations with Leo and me.

Leo begins by explaining why we have come: that LuLu is from Wuhu, that I want her to see her hometown, that we have traveled all this way to introduce her to China. The general manager nods thoughtfully.

Wuhu, and it seems there is one on our street that is affiliated with the university. So we are off to enroll her.

Exhausted, LuLu begs to be carried again, and Leo picks her up. She drapes herself around his neck and I pet her back. I hope those antibiotics are working.

We hurry down to Geng Xing Road and I get a closer look at it. It stretches about two city blocks, dead-ending at our hotel and making a T down at a main avenue called Laodong Road.

The left side of the road is very colorful. A beautiful wall, about twelve feet high, separates the sidewalk from the Anhui University housing compound and extends from the hotel about a block down. The top edge of this wall is trimmed with rounded and elaborately molded dark-green tiles. The middle section is white and bisected with a series of little curvy windows that run its entire length. Beneath the windows, the white plaster melts away into a mosaic of green and blue river stones. Gorgeous. This wall encloses the pink and light-green apartment buildings where the professors and their families live.

The wall ends by an open gate that leads into the housing compound, and vendors hang out there, selling sweet pancakes and whatever fruit they have brought in wooden handcarts from the country.

Next to the housing compound gate stands the three-story white primary school building, with its wide-open wooden casement windows. From the pavement one can see the covered balcony, with the portraits of Karl Marx and Lenin that hang there. There's a permanent wind song in this part of the street, a tiny chorus of children's high-pitched voices. And right past the primary school, at the corner of Laodong Road, is a French-looking bakery.

On the left-hand side of Geng Xing Road, as we leave the hotel grounds, is an ancient pagoda with an ornately carved wooden peak and pagoda curls over a doorway in the shape of a vase. Leo tells me this is an approach to Tie Shan Park.

Then Leo suggests a price for the room. The general mana[g] nods again.

Leo gets up and motions to me to get up, and we walk arou[nd] the lobby. "They have agreed to one hundred and eighty yua[n a] day," he says, about twenty-five dollars. "What else do you [de]mand?"

Somewhat taken aback, I think quickly. "Umm . . . quiet[,] good air-conditioning. Television, I guess."

We go back and sit down, and Leo and the manager discu[ss] again. Finally, after about ten minutes of talk, we all shake h[ands] and then Leo tells me I must pay the whole stay up front. [They] don't take credit cards.

"But what if I want to leave early?" I ask.

"They give you your money back," he replies.

If we stay two and a half months, that's about two tho[usand] dollars I must pay now. I feel rather anxious about giving ov[er] much money in advance. As an American and, further, a [New] Yorker, I find it hard to believe that anyone who already h[as] much of my money would ever easily give it back. But w[here] we don't trust in the long run, the Chinese don't trust in th[e short] run, and I am theirs and must give in. I pay them in cash.

The doorman, an adorable young man in his late teen[s,] name, we learn, is Tao Liang, has been playing with LuL[u.] about six feet two inches tall and weighs about one hun[dred] eighteen pounds. His hair is buzz cut and sticks straight [up;] his mustache is very fine and downy. He looks as if he [has] grew six inches this year.

His expression is one of amusement as LuLu peers u[p] and then runs off, embarrassed, flirting shamelessly. He [is] in his uniform, but so thin that his pants are folded [in a] bunch under his tight belt.

"Mom, he's so cute," Lu whispers to me as we push [the] glass door. We are following Leo, who turns left to leav[e the] grounds and go back down our street, which I learn is c[alled] Xing Road. I had told Leo I would like to send Lu to p[lay]

Right next to it is a preschool (not ours) that can be entered via a round, bright-green moon-gate doorway set in a white wall painted with squirrels and ducks. There are wooden and metal animals to ride in a courtyard in front.

A short wall, about five feet in height, continues down the right side of the street, running the length of the park, opening once for an alley of houses, then closing again for another block until we reach the preschool that Lu is to attend.

At the end of the short wall (conveniently opposite the open gate of the university housing compound) stands the portal of the university preschool. A little farther down from that, we can see a back entrance to the university itself. A man selling roast ducks from a glass-enclosed cart works the sidewalk.

A sign in English and Chinese brass lettering welcomes us: "*Fu Shu You Er Yuan*" (University Preschool). Its sky-blue iron door is painted with a red-and-green diamond pattern and rests rustily between two plaster pillars. We climb through a little side opening and find ourselves in front of a turreted gatehouse guarded by a smiling man in his mid-seventies. In front is a small, circular fish-pond to ward off demons.

We gain entrance and are led to the headmistress's office, which is in a building that must date from the eighteenth century. It is two stories high, with hexagonal rooms at either end, and is extremely narrow, only about twelve feet wide. Since she has not arrived yet, we take a walk around the school.

There is a fenced-in playground across from the guardhouse. The equipment is metal and pretty rusty, but very imaginative and quite pretty. There is, for example, a yellow fish skeleton with an open mouth that you can crawl into and play in. There is also a merry-go-round with a red-and-turquoise umbrella top.

The actual school building is across from the headmistress's office: brand-new white concrete, two stories high, with a pointy roof and decorated with strategically placed red half-moons (rising suns?). When we walk through the main doors, glass in wood casings, we come face-to-face with a bedroom dressing mirror, the kind that pivots on a stand. At first I think this is for kids to check their attire, then I realize it is antidemon feng shui.

Once we are through the doors of the new building, I see that the architect has incorporated some old school buildings into the new one in the most beguiling way. The old buildings are very sweet—one-story red brick with wooden doorways and slanted red tile roofs. One of them even has a small tree growing in its middle court, which is open to the sky and surrounded by red pillars.

Connecting them with concrete paths and overhead ramps, and surrounding them with walls ending in stairways, the new building embraces the old ones, winding around and between them, giving the impression that it is holding the old buildings in its pristine lap. The new building is not completely finished, and one end is still rubble.

The part that is finished is adorable. The second story has an open balcony all around that is decorated with red, turquoise, and yellow suns, earths, moons, and other planets. The first floor is built around a central concrete assembly area open to the sky, where the students play at recess. The classrooms are on both floors, and all the doors are pink. Four separate stairways at the ends of the central court lead to the upper floor.

The prettiness of the place reminds me of Red Apple. The Chinese take great care to make places frequented by children aesthetically pleasing. It is something we in the West, for some reason, don't think is important. The Western preschool in New York City that LuLu attended for a while was a great school, but visually it was unprepossessing, all garish primary colors.

While we are waiting for the headmistress, we walk back outside, past a class of small children in the yard doing exercises that are clearly tai chi–ish. Finally we go back to the headmistress's office, a small, dark room with a wooden desk and a picture of President Jiang Zemin on the stark wall. LuLu still clings to Leo.

In a minute or so, the headmistress, Yu Jie, trots smartly into the room. She is a young, energetic woman, no more than thirty, wearing a miniskirt and extremely high platform ankle boots that remind me of the Chinese opera. It suddenly occurs to me that platform shoes may be particularly useful with all the rubble around. Yu Jie looks friendly and amazingly hip, and I take to her right away.

Leo explains who we are, who LuLu is (*"Wuhuren"*), and that I want her to go to school and experience China. Yu Jie nods and smiles. She and Leo talk, and they agree on a price for two months of six hundred yuan (about fifty dollars a month), "because," Yu Jie tells Leo, referring to me, "she has a kind heart." The hours are nine to eleven-thirty, then home for lunch, then back from two to four.

After school, Yu Jie explains as she takes us back into the new building to see the classroom, all the children come to the central area and roller-skate. At this, LuLu perks up considerably. Actually, she can't believe this news. Yu Jie assures LuLu that they will lend her roller skates.

LuLu's classroom is on the second floor in the corner. It is really nice inside: Little turquoise chairs and tables. A blackboard on one wall. A piano with a red covering over it. A few toys on little blue shelves in a far corner. Tons of light.

Out the window is a serene view: a single old Chinese-style house within a garden near a tree. A bent old man is tending the plants near a tethered donkey. Perhaps much of Wuhu once looked like this, although in a book called *No Dogs & Not Many Chinese: Treaty Port Life in China, 1843–1943,* historian Frances Wood describes turn-of-the-century Wuhu dwellings as "thatched, mushroom shaped," which sounds intriguing.

The classroom has its own bathroom near the door. It is the "two footprints and a hole" kind, but much modernized, with gleaming white tiles and flushing capability. It is quite pristine.

"What's that?" Lu asks, and I explain to her how it works and suggest that she will learn quickly how to use it. She looks a little dubious.

I wonder if she's feeling any better. As we go downstairs, Yu Jie introduces us to the school doctor, who is a hearty, friendly woman in her late forties, wearing a checked flannel shirt and jeans with butterflies embroidered down the leg. I ask her to look at Lu, and she takes us to her office, which is part of the guard-house.

The doctor takes LuLu's temperature, confirms that she has a fever, and gives me a packet of powdered antibiotic for her to take. She advises that if Lu is not better tomorrow, we should go to the hospital.

That unnerves me, but I decide to trust that the antibiotics will work. I have often found it to be true that one country's medicine will not cure another country's bugs. And our antibiotics are clearly doing nothing for Lu.

As we walk out the gate, the headmistress and the doctor both assure me they will take good care of my baby.

We walk back to the hotel and up the red-carpeted stairs into Building Two, our new domicile. I notice that our lobby is furnished with a leather sectional sofa, one of those lumpy, craggy scholar's rocks, but this one's in wood about eight feet high, and a smoked glass mirror for feng shui against the back wall.

By the door is a desk womaned by a pretty young miss in her early twenties, who smiles warmly at us in greeting. Yet another beauty in her thirties appears and introduces herself. She is Mrs. Chang, the manager of our building. She speaks a little English.

We walk up the stairs to the second floor, where for the first time I notice another desk, this one for the floor attendant. A pixi-eish waif of a girl rises and introduces herself as JingJing. She wears the Tie Shan uniform for women, a navy skirt with a long-sleeved white shirt, Dorothy Collins tie, and black velvet Mary Janes with one-inch rubber high heels. JingJing's hair is a gamin cap on her head. Her keys are pinned to her waist.

JingJing hurries down the hall and opens the door of our room. Leo places LuLu on one of the two double beds, and she instantly falls asleep.

I stay up talking to Leo for a while. He says it does look good for visiting the Wuhu orphanage, that the man in charge of permission is well-disposed to us, but I must mail my letters of petition to him tomorrow. Leo invites us to dinner, but I decide not to wake LuLu. So, I thank him for everything and he leaves for the university, where he is staying.

As I get ready for bed, I feel good and very much at home. Wuhu is different than I thought it would be, much more modern, much more cosmopolitan in a way. I had envisioned a very small, very poor town, which it definitely isn't. The Tie Shan Hotel seems great, too. I wonder what I can ever do for Leo to thank him for helping us.

May 5
Sunny

In the morning when we wake, LuLu is very sick. I take her temperature and it's 104. None of the antibiotics have worked. I bundle her into her clothes and go down to the lobby, where Leo and I had arranged to meet around nine A.M. When he comes, I tell him we must go to the hospital. He helps LuLu into the stroller, and he and I immediately set off walking down to the Laodong Road.

I assume that the hospital is close by, since we are going on foot, but we walk and walk and it seems incredibly far. Actually, it's always like this in Communist countries I've visited. The people are very hardy, used to walking miles at a time, and I feel like a pampered weakling.

We take a left onto Laodong Road and eventually reach an enormously wide street, which Leo tells me is Sun Yat-sen Boulevard, a main thoroughfare of the city. When I was here in the past, main streets were named only for heroes of Mao's revolution. Dr. Sun's presence could signify a major identity shift for China. Dr. Sun Yat-sen was a scholarly revolutionary who helped overthrow the Ch'ing Dynasty and in 1911 became the first president of the new Chinese republic. He was also one of the founders of the Kuomintang, or Nationalist Party, which, led by Chiang Kai-shek, fled to Taiwan after World War II. Dr. Sun was sympathetic to Communistic ideology, but he was definitely not a heroic Communist. As an icon for the new China, Dr. Sun's is a far more modern, educated, intellectual, and less warlike image. Interesting.

Sun Yat-sen is so wide that it's more like an oval assembly area than an avenue. From its appearance, it might almost have been planned for massive demonstrations. Or perhaps the Wuhu government was thinking ahead to gridlock of the future. Traffic is as yet scant, with red taxis going 20 mph, bicycles, and occasional cars.

Many streets branch off Sun Yat-sen, like spokes off an oval wheel. Rather majestic-looking, pillared buildings (which turn out to be uninteresting utilities) reign around the edges. We, however, parade straight across, skirting taxis that don't actually come to a stop but somehow don't hit us, onto what looks like a completely bombed-out street.

The rubble sometimes reaches heights of nine feet on either side of us. Dust clogs the air. It is hard going pushing the stroller over the stones and rocks, but I slog forward and soon Leo says, "Here it is." I look where he's pointing and then down at my little daughter, flagged out in the stroller. I wish to God we didn't have to do this. Then we struggle by the debris to get in.

Fu Yuan Workers' Hospital, when we reach it, is minimal and shabby. The lobby is covered with rubble dust and smells like urine. A spittoon sits against a pillar in the middle of the front hall.

I am aware of one important fact as Leo walks up to a cashier's window and pays 2.5 yuan (30 cents) for our visit: this is the kind of hospital in which my daughter was born—if she was born in a hospital.

There are several women around us carrying babies tied to their backs, the first we've seen of that. Modern Chinese women don't do that anymore. I remember being taught by my amah how to take the long cloths and tie the baby, one-handed, to yourself. I was so proud when I learned to do it. I can still do it to this day.

To take my mind off what's going on, I look closely at the women and their children, trying to see a resemblance to anyone we know.

We are ushered into the doctor's room, which is very spare but clean. There is a double desk, with a nurse sitting at one end and the doctor at the other. There is no examining table as we know it, but under the window behind the doctor is a long bench, which he does not use for us.

The doctor is a jovial man with a flattop haircut. Leo tells him the symptoms while the nurse takes Lu's temperature by placing the thermometer under her armpit. She is limp with fever but manages to be intrigued by this. It comes out 104 degrees Fahrenheit.

"Very high," the doctor says, and indicates to me that this is not good. He tells Leo that LuLu must have a shot immediately to bring down her fever.

Now I begin to panic. I don't want her to have a shot here. I'm scared. I ask if they use disposable needles, and Leo asks and reassures me: "Oh, yes." Still, I ask the doctor about using pills instead, but he says he doesn't want to wait. In children, Leo translates, it is best to bring the fever down quickly.

Now LuLu suddenly goes berserk, which she has never done before. She is screaming and crying, "I don't want a shot! I don't want a shot!" I burst into tears because she is so upset and sick and I don't know what to do, and I'm sobbing and clutching her.

Leo and the doctor mistake my terror at the possibility of dirty needles for worry about LuLu's illness. (And mind you, I *am* worried about that, but not as much as I am about hepatitis, AIDS, etc., etc.)

They try to reassure me, explaining she has bronchitis, which is common in China among children and not serious. Then Leo rushes out to the cashier's window to pay for the shot while I turn my attention to two lady pharmacists who are setting about mixing up the solution for it. Both in white coats, the two are bent over wooden desks before little wooden shelves stacked with pharmaceutical bottles, from which they measure and combine ingredients.

My grandmother and grandfather on my father's side were both pharmacists, and when they had their first drugstore in the thirties, they prepared medicines just like these ladies. My grandmother stopped practicing, she told me, when drug companies started concocting the pills and shot solutions themselves. I am praying now that these ladies are good at their jobs.

Shots are given in a different room across the front hall. Lu is still screaming and crying as I carry her over there. A woman in a surgical mask waits for us and indicates that she will give Lu the shot in her rear. Leo holds LuLu still while I pray that I am not doing the wrong thing. The shot is given. Lu is still sobbing, but barely a minute later, she begins to sweat and instantly calms down. She says she feels better. I almost faint with relief and decide not to think anymore about anything negative.

We return across the hall to the doctor's room. Now the doctor says he wants her to have penicillin shots every day for a week, that it's best. Lu goes nuts at this thought, and needless to say I am horrified. No way is this going to happen. But he adds that first she must be tested to see if she can take penicillin. So we walk back across the hall to the shot room, where LuLu is tested. A twelve-year-old-girl is there as well, going just as berserk as LuLu, only she's a lot bigger and is running out of the room and around the lobby like someone out of a cartoon. This sight cheers LuLu, and we watch as the girl is subdued and returned to the room for her shot. The nurses and doctors laugh kindly, and once the shot is given, the girl and LuLu are laughing, too.

LuLu is now sweating profusely and clearly feeling much better. The shot nurse appears and informs Leo that LuLu can't have penicillin because the test showed she is allergic to the drug. I make a note to tell this to her pediatrician at home. I'm also feeling sheepish now, because clearly the medical personnel are much more careful here than, in my Western prejudice, I've given them credit for.

In fifteen minutes LuLu is back to normal, no exaggeration. I recall that in the 1950s when I was little, I had shots every time I got sick, not just the standard vaccinations. And I wonder why they so rarely give antibiotic shots to children now in the United States, since they clearly work so fast. I decide that it must have something to do with insurance.

We go back to the doctor's room and he writes out a prescription for some sort of antibiotic pills. I thank him very much, and Lu and I go wait in the hall while Leo, at his insistence, pays for the pills. He then takes the scrip to the two ladies, who make them up.

No longer a raving nut case, I look around more closely at the faces of the babies waiting near us. They are all boys.

"He looks like me," LuLu suddenly says about one little boy baby. Is she wondering, as I am, whether someone here might be a relative?

On the walk back to the hotel, I ask Leo, who has been doing new research on abandoned baby girls, what he can tell me about LuLu. He says the fact that she was found near a police station indicates that she is probably from the outskirts of the city. Girls found at a railroad station are generally from the country. It is very hard, he explains, to find out any real information about their families.

I tell him that there is conflicting data on her documents. The official document says her date of birth was estimated by the doctor at the hospital where she was taken after being found on the street. Her mother's note gives an actual date and hour. People have told me that some of the mother's notes are mere fabrications by orphanage directors trying to please foreigners, whom they have heard want "notes." Which should I trust? "Trust the mother's note," Leo says, quashing that rumor. He says of the orphanage directors, rather eloquently and succinctly, "I have seen many, and most are kind."

While Leo waits with LuLu in the hotel plaza by the big pine tree, I run upstairs and get the letters requesting permission to enter Wuhu orphanage. I come back and give them to Leo for perusal. He writes out the address of the official in Hefei in Chinese characters, and I copy it onto the envelope. Then I hand the letters to the young man at reception to send to the post office.

"I think it should be fine," Leo says again. "I don't think there will be a problem."

We arrange to meet again around six to dine. After he leaves, I flop into one of the big leather armchairs in the main lobby and watch LuLu, who seems completely recovered, playing with the young doorman.

It is not the same boy we met earlier. This one is in his early twenties, with a perfectly oval face, a very narrow, straight nose, and hair parted on one side. He is about five feet ten inches tall and muscular, a young man, not a boy. He is laughing as LuLu hangs and swings from his wrist. I ask him his name and he tells me it is TohToh. He, too, wears the 1930s bellboy outfit. That pillbox hat that fastens under his chin is so jaunty.

Nobody seems to mind them playing together. The manager who sits at a wooden desk by the bar is taking no notice. The two young men behind the reception desk are oblivious. A wiry man in his early thirties—Mr. Liu, as I will come to know him, another manager—laughs to himself about them as he hurries past. Everyone is remarkably relaxed around here. So I relax, too.

And I start to think. Why did I bring her now, as opposed to later—say, when she was around ten and could understand more? Because I'm afraid any information that might exist about her, any files at the orphanage, will vanish with time, that people's memories will dim, that the woman who took care of her might not be there anymore.

But there's another thing: at four, LuLu judges things purely. A place is warm or not warm, fearful or not fearful. She doesn't see shabbiness, or if she does, she doesn't care about it. What if the orphanage is draconian and terrible? Well, she is young enough that I trust I can steer her away from it without her realizing what I am doing.

And I wanted her to be a child in China, small enough to breathe it in without prejudice or consciousness. I would have brought her to China now if she were Caucasian and my birth child.

I take her little hand and drag her away from TohToh, and we push the stroller back to our building. As we climb the red-carpeted stairs to Building Two, I look back at the main lobby building and notice that in front of each opulent silver pillar is a wastebasket in the shape of a little white sea lion balancing a green-and-red ball on its nose. This is the kind of juxtaposition that makes me love China so much.

In the early evening, Leo invites us to the new dumpling restaurant that has opened on Laodong Road. We passed it when we walked to the hospital. A full ten-piece band is playing outside to announce its opening. A huge, inflated red rainbow surrounds the entrance. Red lanterns dangle from the window, and huge bouquets of flowers festoon the doorway.

Inside, the place is simple and white, with wooden tables and chairs. We take a seat with Leo and everyone glances at us, then away, in that "not meaning to stare" fashion. We order dumplings and duck, and when the meal comes, along with duck meat, the ducks' heads are nicely arranged in a fan shape on the plate, eyes staring at us rather accusingly. LuLu is rather aghast.

When I take her up the stairs to the restaurant bathroom, I notice that the wall-to-wall, AstroTurf carpet on the second floor has not been tacked down and is bunching dangerously. What China really needs, I decide, are contractors who know how to finish a building job.

We walk home in darkness. There are no streetlights, and many of the taxis have their headlights off. Fortunately, traffic is light and moving very slowly.

May 6
Sunny

The next morning, we meet Leo early. He is going to help me set up my Internet account before he goes. It seems there is an Internet office in town, where, for a fee, I can send e-mails to Neke and friends.

While LuLu plays out in the plaza, we sit in the lobby with Mr. Chen, the young man in charge of computers at the hotel, to discuss the question of Internet use.

One can hook up a computer to use in the room, but unfortunately, both Chen and the hotel are baffled by Macs. The next possibility is the town office, but after some talk, Leo and Chen come to the conclusion that it would be more convenient for me to use the hotel computer in the Xerox room, which is next door to the reception area. Why Chen didn't think of this right off is interesting: they don't use the computer at the hotel for much besides word processing, so it didn't occur to him. Clearly, computer use is not run-of-the-mill in Wuhu. We haggle over price and decide on eight yuan per hookup. When we finish, Mr. Liu and Leo escort LuLu and me to the bank so I can cash traveler's checks.

Liu takes us all in a taxi, and I try to memorize the route so I can come by myself. From Sun Yat-sen, the cab takes one of the left spokes, which leads into the street behind the little Tie Shan (the miniature mountain) that the hotel and the park are on. We hop out at the bank and go in to the teller, who turns on a small timer as she begins to serve us, to make sure, I guess, that she does her job promptly. Neither Liu nor Leo can fill me in on the optimum time for bank service.

I take out my traveler's checks and realize that I never signed them at time of purchase. I try to convince the teller that they issue them in America now without making you sign them first, but she does not believe me. We are turned away and I can't get money.

Liu takes a taxi back to the hotel and we accompany Leo to a special duck restaurant for lunch. To do this, we taxi back to Sun Yat-sen and take another spoke, which leads us to the Jing Hu (Mirror) Lake. I think it's fair to say that the lake is considered the centerpiece of Wuhu. Around it is the shopping area, the department stores, the market, and the main entrance to the university.

The duck restaurant is at the university end and looks remarkably upscale. The manager comes over and chats to Leo, who introduces us to him. We are invited to come any time and he says he will look after us.

The meal is hot pot, evidently a local specialty: duck and vegetables are cooked in a swirling, oddly spiced, almost nutmeggy broth. "Pungent" is the word for it. LuLu eats more roast duckmeat, provided on little side plates, with gusto.

We walk back to Laodong Road down a street just below the main entrance to the university. As we pass by, I examine the very elaborate, heavy steel accordion gate that closes the school up at night. At present, it is unfolded and definitely seems the most aggressive mechanism in the town. Are they keeping people out or in? The back gate near the preschool is infinitely more flimsy.

We stroll past the university bookshop, past some clothing

stores, and past a group of electronic, video, and CD stores that open half onto the pavement. One has a man-size robot outside. I name that store Radio Shack.

The whole area reminds me of Washington Square by New York University in Manhattan, where I live, with Jing Hu Lake substituting for the square: lots of students and student clothing and CD stores. The only difference is that things are simpler here, not so many gadgets to choose from, not such a mountain of stuff to wade through.

We walk on farther and, at the corner of Laodong Road, come upon a sporting goods store. I can buy roller skates there and make a note of it. We pass by a photo store just before we get to Geng Xing Road and I make a note of that, too.

Back up at the hotel, I take leave of Leo and thank him for everything. We plan to meet again when I bring LuLu to Hefei, to see the famous Anhui Hotel, where there was the knock at the door and I first met my baby.

After Leo goes, I feel a tremendous sense of excitement. We are on our own in the middle of China, in LuLu's hometown. We actually got here! LuLu seems thrilled, too. I can see she likes the Tie Shan. There is plenty of space to run around, the grounds are beautiful, and young Chinese people are everywhere and ready to play.

We go back to our room for LuLu's nap and I watch her unpack from her little case the special items she brought with her to Wuhu. Her sudden illness kept her from organizing her things, and she does so now. Her little fingers deftly remove her stuffed elephant, Ellie, her special blanket, two diaries, a ballpoint pen, some markers and alphabet cards, two books, her toothbrush, and a Mennen skin bracer deodorant stick. This last came in an airline dop kit that Neke gave her, and she often uses it at night before bed, telling me that it makes her feel "fresh" when she wakes up. She places these items neatly on the carpet by the bag, all except for the toothbrush and deodorant stick, which she takes carefully into the bathroom.

She has always had ramrod-straight posture, just like my mother. And I love watching her sit and move, just as I did my mother, both so ladylike.

I bed her down for her nap and use the phone on the night table to ring up a young woman named Anne, an American who teaches spoken English at the university. Leo has given me her name as a contact, in case I need one. Perhaps she can find me an interpreter; I need one to accomplish several things.

First, I want to go to the Children's Palace, the institution that offers art and music lessons for children in China, and set up lyre lessons (*gu zun*) for LuLu. She has taken them for two years at Red Apple with a Miss Lee, whom she despises. Miss Lee was so mean that I once went to Joanna and said, "You know, you can't have this woman teach kids, Joanna. She's too horrible."

"My son hates her, too," Joanna replied, surprisingly. "But she's very good," she added. "She gets results."

"She's got to tone it down," I said. "She's making everyone cry."

Miss Lee did tone down, and LuLu, though she still hated her, learned to play the lyre in sync with five other little girls. It was really charming to watch and lovely to listen to. And LuLu agreed to continue lessons before she loses the knack.

I also want to take a taxi ride and visit the places where LuLu and Francesca (or Lao Li) were found. I have in my luggage the documents of two other Wuhu girls, Mary, Alice's daughter, and Maya, who is from our original group. But only Janine has given me the address of the place where her daughter was found.

The others don't care to know or forgot to give me the information, and I can't say I blame them. Because if you show your daughter where she was found, you are telling her that she was left someplace, and that is very hard for an adoptive mother to do.

I couldn't do it. In the story I told LuLu, her first parents took her straight to the Wuhu Children's Institute, where she was assigned to me. But that isn't true. They left her near a police station, and because I want her to have all the information when she is older and perhaps better able to understand it, I'm going to find the police station and take a picture, for later.

I ask Anne whether there is a student who would interpret for us for a fee. She says she will ask her class and call me back. She sounds very nice.

I lay back on the bed and reflect on what I have learned so far. My daughter's birthday is probably real, as is her mother's note. She most likely comes from the outskirts of Wuhu. She is allergic to penicillin. She comes from a town where people seem very kind. It's a lot for just a few days. A lot.

And I know a few things more. I know from her first dental exam in New York that her teeth are good, which indicates that she had good nutrition in the womb. Either her mother was not so terribly poor or she meant to keep her until she found out she was a girl, or perhaps even that she meant for her to be adopted to the West.

I look over to the bed, where my little daughter is sleeping soundly. She is such a healthy baby. She eats well. She sleeps well. She is so loving. She lives with her whole being. I focus on her pink mouth, and her straight black hair, and her funny straight nose with its little flared nostrils and tiny hook. I am so attuned now to her coloring and features that Caucasian children look pale to me. Ghosts . . . isn't that what the Chinese call us?

Once, when I was walking down to LuLu's school in China-town and passing by Sun Yat-sen Junior High School, I ran into a gaggle of Chinese teenage girls. I was examining their faces and bodies, musing on what LuLu would grow into, when I suddenly wondered what they envy among their peers.

Among Caucasian teenage girls (when I was a teen), the dark-haired girls envied the blondes, and the brown-eyed girls wanted blue eyes. The curly-haired ones wanted straight hair. What do Chinese girls envy among themselves? Maybe body types, although what could there be to envy when the entire female population has no cellulite? And obviously there are standards of beauty. Still, so many of them are adorable.

Maybe they don't envy each other at all. At Red Apple, the Chinese mothers would say to me, "You are lucky you have a daughter. She will never leave you." Girls don't seem to hate their mothers at puberty in China, I think because they see that their mothers' lives are so difficult.

Wuhu, the orphanage director told us when we got our babies in Hefei in 1994, is known for its beautiful women. From the women I've met here so far, it does seem true.

After LuLu wakes up, we walk down Geng Xing to the French bakery. We buy little sponge cakes and long-life milk to keep in the room. They also have real milk in refrigerated glass cases, a big change for China. When I was little, there was no pasteurized milk in China. Since I couldn't stand the powdered variety, I never drank milk at all. I remember once taking a pedicab all by myself to a missionary's house to get home-baked chocolate-chip cookies. But they were made with powdered milk, and I was so disappointed that they tasted funny.

We walk back up Geng Xing past grandmothers who have brought babies and toddlers to hang out in front of the three schools that line our street. I sense that this is part of the training to get children to respect education. It is also on this street that the babies are learning to walk. LuLu takes the hand of a toddler and helps her stagger forward. The grandparent looks on without worry and, of course, inquires if LuLu's father is Chinese.

A line of taxis is parked in front of the ancient pagoda entrance to Tie Shan Park, awaiting passengers from the hotel. The drivers are playing cards while they wait for business. We stroll past them into the main plaza and decide to explore the road on the right side of Building Two. We walk on past the reception building.

Adjacent to reception is another two-story structure: the ground floor houses an antiques store full of vases and teapots, while the entire second floor is a games room. We make a note for later. On a plot of grass in front of it is a big sign advertising "bowling" and "Ping-Pong" and a gym and giving their locations.

Past the games-and-antiques building is a concrete parking area and basketball court, where cars are being washed by a group of young men. Across from that, on a little rise, we suddenly come upon a lovely little man-made lake, circular, with a stone, moss-covered walkway all around it, and overhung with weeping willows and swaying pines. Sitting on the surface, like tablecloths, are perfectly round, bright-green lily pads topped with cup-shaped lotus flowers. A viewing pavilion with a pagoda roof juts out over the water. There are some benches to sit on and a scholar's rock on a marble pedestal. The road to Building Six, the luxury building, and to the fancy guesthouse where the Chinese dignitaries stay, winds around the lake.

The vista is quite dramatic. On the far side of the lake, stone steps lead down to the water; and behind those, a red-pillared walkway with a tiled pagoda roof—to shield guests from the rain as they contemplate the lake—extends the full width of the lakeside. Behind that, a grove of bamboo bends and shivers in the breeze. A deep green film of moss covers everything, and I recall reading somewhere that where there is moss, there is no pollution in the ground or air and the plants and trees are thriving.

It is astonishingly scenic, and I sit with LuLu on one of the benches and we breathe in the ancient Chinese beauty before us. It smells green and earthy, and the air rings with birdsong. At this edge of the lake, there are steps, too, which LuLu uses to go down to the water's edge. She almost falls in, to her vast delight.

For a long time, LuLu plays around the lake's edge, looking at bugs and examining leaves. Then we return down the road to reception and the Xerox room, where one of the young women managers, a Miss Smith, turns on the computer for me and connects me to the Internet. While I e-mail home and check my messages, LuLu fools around with Tao Liang, who is back on duty at the lobby door.

I feel composed but exhausted as I write Neke. We made it. We are here. We are doing it. We are connected to home by e-mail. LuLu was sick, but she's okay now. Everything is going well.

After ten minutes or so, I log off and go get LuLu. I stop at the little store near reception. They don't have postcards, so we buy maps of Wuhu to send to the Wuhu girls we know. This is also the place to buy Oreo cookies, soda pop, and spirit mirrors.

"I'm going to marry him," LuLu gushes about Tao Liang as we leave. "He's my boyfriend."

Tao Liang, who has overheard and understands the spirit, if not the words, blushes amusedly.

Back in the room, we eat our snack from the bakery. LuLu has her milk and I put her to bed. After our duck lunch, neither of us is very hungry, and she is still recovering from her illness.

She falls right to sleep, and I turn on the TV and discover, to my joy, that there is news in English at eight on Communist Chinese TV.

NATO is still bombing Kosovo. The news on CCTV has a pro-Serbian slant and focuses on how the bombing is playing havoc with Serbian civilians there. There is no mention of ethnic cleansing atrocities against the Bosnians at all.

The phone rings and it is Anne, reporting that several girls in her English class are coming tomorrow to "help their foreign friends." No payment is necessary. A girl called Caroline is the best English speaker among them.

After thanking Anne and inviting her over to see the hotel, I hang up and turn off the TV. In seconds I am blissfully asleep.

May 7

I am sick. I stagger into the bathroom and hunt out the adult antibiotics I brought from the United States. As I'm downing them, there's a knock at the door and I open it to three giggling, very shy Chinese girls in their late teens. One of them is Caroline.

I ask her if she wouldn't mind coming back after lunch and taking us around then. This seems to please them all and they rush off.

While I rest, LuLu watches a kids' show on television, and just before we leave for lunch—lo and behold!—the English-language news comes on again. We are rushing out, but I linger to catch the highlights. The commentator, a matter-of-fact woman in her mid-thirties whom I dub Barbara Walters Wong, announces that the Chinese embassy in Belgrade has been bombed and that investigations are under way to see who is responsible. There is a possibility, she says somberly, that the United States may have done it.

That's impossible, I think. Clinton would never do that. I shut off the TV as Wong begins to talk about preparations in Beijing for celebrations of the May 4th Movement.

The May 4th Movement was the first mass demonstration in Chinese history. In 1919, after World War I, five thousand Chinese university students protested the Versailles Conference mandate assigning Kiaochow in Shantung Province to Japan. Their outrage led to a nationwide boycott of Japanese goods and a whirlwind of intellectual discussion, which led to attacks on Confucianism. Marxist and democratic principles were taken up, and modern ideas (like women participating in politics) were espoused. Out of this foment came the founding of both the Chinese Communist party and the Kuomintang.

LuLu and I trot up the leafy roadway on the other side of Building Two to the restaurant, or Canting, as I see it is misspelled. We pass by Building Three and then turn right to climb a very steep set of elderly stone stairs. These stairs remind me of the ones I have seen in the Forbidden City and are separated in the middle by a smooth stretch of stone so heavy that carts can be pushed up them. It is evidently a very ancient construction design.

We go through glass doors into the restaurant and a hostess greets us as we enter. She looks like a model and stands about six feet tall, wearing a floor-length cheongsam slit quite high on the sides.

The Chinese girls we have seen so far are of a pretty good height, many of them very tall. The days of short Chinese are clearly over. LuLu has always been tall for her age. Right now she's in the eightieth percentile for American boys, although the pediatrician told me that Asian kids sometimes shoot up early, and without seeing her genetics, he couldn't tell how tall she would actually be.

Funnily enough, that is something that really irks me. While I don't mind having my authenticity as a parent constantly questioned, I do mind not knowing how tall my daughter is going to be. I have a health record at home that says LuLu was 7.7 pounds, twenty-three inches, at birth. I think they got it wrong. She was only eleven pounds when I got her at seven months, and twenty-three inches at birth would probably mean she'd end up six feet five inches tall.

Right inside the doors of the restaurant are two banks of fish tanks full of live lobsters, eels, and fish. LuLu loves these, of course, and spends time checking on the inhabitants while I take one of the vast number of empty, white-tableclothed tables. I try not to feel self-conscious.

The dining room itself is about four thousand square feet. At the far end, away from the entrance, is a stage decorated with hanging red lanterns and flanked by golden pillars. Some of the tables are big and round, some are small and square, but all the chairs are dark wood and Chinese style, such as we see in antiques stores in America.

The room was once opulent but is a bit worn now around the edges, although clearly it is an expensive restaurant by Chinese standards. About fifteen waitresses—all pretty, with their jet-black straight hair pulled back in buns and clipped with velvet bows, all in their early twenties, all wearing bright-blue skirts, white long-sleeved shirts with black velvet ties, and black velvet high-heeled

Mary Janes—stand around, ready to assist. But at present, we and another Chinese couple are their only clients.

I order fried chicken, rice, and green vegetables. While we wait, the man at the next table comes over and gives LuLu a book, a Chinese paperback, which, when I examine it, turns out to be humorous. LuLu is thrilled, and the man and the woman smile at us.

The food, which comes quickly, is freshly prepared and utterly spectacular. The taste of the rice makes me understand for the first time why the Chinese love it. It is almost sweet but not, almost fragrant with jasmine but not. It tastes light pink.

The green vegetable is local, fresh, and sweet and very plainly sautéed in an oil that is more like butter in taste. It is also not greasy. The chicken is lightly fried in bits and is juicy.

They do not automatically bring tea, which I think is funny. You have to order it. I do, and they give me a glass with what looks like an aquarium plant growing in it. This is Wuhu's local tea. Everyone carries around jars of it. It tastes very green.

After a wonderful lunch, I feel better. We go down to the huge pine tree in the main plaza to meet Caroline. In my purse I have the addresses of the places where LuLu and Francesca were found. Since I don't feel so well, I figure we will take a taxi ride to locate these places and photograph them. As far as LuLu and Caroline are concerned, we will simply be sight-seeing.

Caroline is twenty years old and about five feet seven. She comes from Ma'anshan and is studying to be a teacher. She wears the characteristic fashion of the Wuhu college girl, a cotton ankle-length jumper dress, very simply and geometrically cut, which gathers with a pull string at the neck. Underneath is a white cotton long-sleeved blouse. Over all, she carries a cloth backpack. The whole outfit, which in America would look trendy, in China resembles a modern version of ancient Chinese women's dress as seen in scroll painting. Her shoes are black and platformed. She has a plain, sensible, affectless face.

We walk out to the taxi queue and I choose the one woman

driver, an energetic, no-nonsense gal with a ponytail who looks like a dancer in a Broadway musical about China. Her name is Miss Swallow. I bundle LuLu and Caroline into the backseat of her cab.

I show Caroline the address of the place LuLu was found and tell her I want to go there. She and Miss Swallow confer.

LuLu leans back and stares out the window at her town. The taxi goes down Geng Xing to Laodong Road, turns left, goes up to Sun Yat-sen, takes a left spoke, and swings around Jing Hu Lake. As we do this, I notice swan and duck boats in the water for rent, the kind you paddle with your feet, just as they have in Boston. In fact, Wuhu in some indescribable way reminds me of Boston. I'm not sure what it is—the size, the formality, the lake, or what.

The lake is divided by a picturesque round-backed little bridge that looks so like the bridge that's a clue in *Big Bird in China* that LuLu gets all excited when she sees it. The taxi weaves around the rubble and half-built skyscrapers at this end of the lake, and comes to a halt before a modern bridge over a small canal that feeds into the Yangtze River. You can just see a little sliver of it in the distance.

On our side of the bridge is the department store Xin Bei, fronted by rubble. On the other side of the bridge lies the rest of Wuhu, which has not been so rebuilt and, I can see, looks kind of gray and grim.

"Here," Miss Swallow tells Caroline, who tells me, and she stops the car. "Here is the Qing Yi Jiang Canal."

"Here?" I echo hollowly.

LuLu stays in the car and plays with Caroline while I jump out, taking my camera.

Here? My daughter, the child I adore so much, was abandoned here? Here.

Fortunately, there is not much traffic on the bridge, which allows me to run up on it and just stand there and stare. I drop my eyes down from the heights of the bridge to the little canal, where a number of wooden houseboats are parked. Was she born on one of those houseboats? Did they sail up the canal to the bridge to leave her here?

I look up. In the distance, a little pagoda rises like a lighthouse, facing the river. It stands like a tiny beacon at the end of the canal. There are pictures of it in Building Two. It is the one tourist attraction in Wuhu.

The bridge I am standing on is industrial and modern. The people of the city are crossing on bicycles and in trucks, and it's a busy place.

But I find it totally surreal. I hadn't expected the place to look so . . . what? So urban, so twentieth-century. I don't know what I thought: that it would be more ancient-looking somehow? Just as I thought that Wuhu would be more like a village, with a dusty main street.

But no, Wuhu is a city and LuLu's bridge is modern. Was it this way four years ago? I ask Miss Swallow. The bridge was the same.

I walk to the other end of the bridge and look down at some of the older houses. Yes, it was definitely slummier at one time. Was it by this ramshackle, redbrick house at the bridge's corner that she was left? I imagine my baby as she was, lying there, wrapped up and crying—her familiar cry that I've known so well for these last four years, that I could pick out of a crowd of crying babies.

I remember when she first came home, there was a dog that barked in the courtyard in back of our brownstone. It was the only thing that made her cry loudly and fearfully, and I always thought, when she was out there on the street, had a dog bark scared her?

But there are no dogs in Wuhu, and when she cried out, she wasn't on a dusty village street with dogs running about, as I once fantasized. She was lying right here, in the middle of her city, near this bridge that half of Wuhu crosses every day.

I stare down at the canal. Did her people bring her on a houseboat? Lu, with her love of boats and water? They could have. Did they bring her up out of the houseboat and place her right here?

And how long was she in the street here? They found her at three days old. Was it one day, two days, or all three?

I suddenly realize the importance of this journey we are taking. It is absolutely true that very soon all trace of what we can know of her past will be bulldozed away. Trying to sound very casual, I tell Caroline that we would like to visit the Wuhu Children's Institute. Could we drive there right now? I call it, as she does, "the Welfare," so LuLu will not understand.

"Oh, sure," replies Caroline. "That's easy." And she talks to Miss Swallow, who nods and drives across the bridge into the older part of Wuhu. Miss Swallow weaves the car through what are clearly slums, and now and then stops to ask people directions.

"Not many people know the address of Welfare," says Caroline, to explain Miss Swallow's difficulty.

"Do you?" I ask.

"Oh, yes. I went on a school trip there," she replies.

"What was it like?" I persist.

She bows her head and looks away, knowing LuLu is from there and not wanting to offend. "It was miserable," she says softly.

I slough off this comment as prejudice, since I know that there is a sort of 1950s horror here about orphans, the disabled, and the mentally disabled, all of whom are more or less lumped together. To a Chinese, having no family is the metaphorical equivalent to having no limbs.

I have made the snap decision to drop by the institute just in case we are denied entry through channels. I was always nervous about asking permission, because once you ask, they know you are here and can refuse you. It is my friendship with Leo that has made me go through channels. He is the citizen here, not me.

The officials in Hefei probably aren't in daily contact with the orphanage director in Wuhu; and if they are and there is a problem, I will simply say that, knowing Lu's story, the taxi driver drove us there on her tour before I realized.

Miss Swallow is driving around, turning here and there and asking people. She talks with Caroline as she does so. It seems that the institute has moved recently and the building that it was in was torn down.

So . . . it is not the place LuLu was in as an infant. I digest this slowly. It is nearer to the main part of the city and in better shape, evidently. Okay. I take in this disappointment. She will never see the actual place. Okay.

LuLu does know we are trying to visit "the institute" while in Wuhu, but she doesn't seem to realize that we are on our way there now. I want to see the place first, make sure it is palatable.

Pretty soon, Miss Swallow comes to a halt in a congested area by a railroad track. She points across the street, and we all get out. Lu and I follow Caroline as she crosses the dusty thoroughfare and enters a narrow alley, past a market set up there.

We walk by a live-eel salesman and a live-chicken salesman, and then we come to the live-frog salesman. The man is skinning the bodies of live frogs from the neck down. Lovely. But, strangely, the frogs seem not to mind this and are hopping about quite well, skinless, looking as if they are wearing frog heads. Four-year-old LuLu is fascinated by this and insists on watching the process intently. I can't take it.

I drag her away by the hand and Caroline leads us down the alley, which becomes a street of the very *hutongs* that they are tearing down all over Wuhu: small, dark, one-room shacklike structures built across from one another on a cobblestone street as narrow as two human arm spans.

Along this rather fetid but ancient and picturesque cobblestoned way, there are open stalls selling magazines, candy, some clothing, and food. Presently, we come to a run-down gated compound. Between dirty stone pillars, a metal gate allows me to look in and see a drab courtyard. One grim-looking leafless tree grows in the center of it, mired in a bed of mud. A long, low wooden building hunches down behind it, all shut up tight. There is no evidence of little children anywhere and nothing green.

I crane my neck and see an archway that leads to another, interior court. In there, a disheveled and rather grimy adolescent girl is sitting silently, lost in reverie.

A gnarled old man at the gate, the security guard, tells Caroline that since it is Saturday, there are no officials about and we cannot come in. As he is saying this, suddenly, LuLu drops my hand, squeezes by him, and runs as fast as she can through the courtyard and beyond into the interior court. Once there, she stands motionless, looking all around her, finally fixing on the adolescent girl. I can almost see the energy popping out of her tense little body.

It happens so fast that for a minute I'm stunned. Then, before I can stop him, the old man runs after LuLu, shouting harshly. I rush in the gate after him to get her, but LuLu doesn't stop or come out; she runs farther into the interior courtyard. Again, she stands her ground and looks all around her.

The adolescent girl, who I now realize is retarded in some way, becomes scared and cringes as the old man harshly shoos her away to somewhere inside. Lu watches this for a moment and then speeds back toward me.

Tears course down my cheeks. Someplace less congenial than this is where my daughter spent the first seven months of her infant life. And it is not that it's so awful or even that I didn't expect it to be minimal, or even harsh. It's that I am really looking at it. It's not a fantasy. And I can't help it: I'm devastated.

"Pick me up, Mama," says LuLu, which I do as fast as I can. I hold her close, explaining that the old man is afraid and not to worry. She rests on my neck and hugs me back. I try to stop my tears, but they are streaming down my face.

Caroline and the old man assume that I am crying because we are not allowed to go in. The old man apologizes profusely now but says I must go to the police station to get a permit with a stamp, and then I'll be allowed in. Clearly he is shaken up. He asks us to leave.

I walk out through the gate silently, carrying LuLu.

As soon as we are beyond it, LuLu asks to get down. She has seen some children her age, with whom she now goes off to play. The kids accept her instantly and they invent a game, jumping off some little stairs and poring over the cobblestones, looking for spiders.

I stand there composing myself, thinking frantically how to make this all right for LuLu. I am in shock. This was definitely not the return I had envisioned. I have no idea how much LuLu has really understood of what has gone on. But somehow, without my saying so, she certainly seemed to understand that this was a place she should take a good look at, and no one was going to stop her. Perhaps she even intuited that this was the institute.

Suddenly, she appears back at my side and tugs on my shirt. I look down at her and she stretches her little hand up to me. Clenched in her little fingers is a bouquet of the tiniest red flowers I've ever seen. She hands them to me and her little almond-shaped eyes look into mine so lovingly. Then she quickly scampers away to play with the children.

I am so moved by her gesture that I can barely stand it. I go over to where she is playing and take my little girl's hand and kiss it. I look around on the dusty, squalid street. There are certainly no flowers anywhere around, anywhere at all. I can't imagine where she found them.

"Thank you, LuLu," I manage. "Thank you so much." She gets up from playing and walks back by my side, down the cobble-stoned street.

"I'm sorry, LuLu," I say, leaning down to her. "Did the man upset you? He was afraid."

"Where are the children?" she asks. So she knew.

"I think they were inside," I reply. "Maybe napping."

"I want to see inside," she says.

"All right," I say. "Okay. We will try. We will go back next week and take some toys to the children. Would you like that?"

"Yes," she replies matter-of-factly. "Yes. I would."

Next to me, Caroline is still horrified that her countryman has made the foreign woman cry. To console me, she buys me a piece of special Wuhu candy from a stall.

We get back to the taxi and I hand Caroline the address of the police station where Janine's daughter, Francesca, was found. As we drive off, LuLu falls to sleep, lulled by the sound of the car motor.

We drive over the railroad tracks and down a rather busy avenue crammed with pedicabs (bicycle rickshaws), red taxis, people on bicycles, and the occasional truck. We pass a Catholic church with a big stone angel in front. I make Miss Swallow stop, and I get out and take pictures of the environs and the big angel for Janine.

After some maneuvering through crowds of bicycles, our taxi stops at a rather dreary-looking police station building. Near here is where Francesca was found. The avenue turns out to be another end of Laodong Road. To make the place look a bit more festive, I take a picture of a man selling red cloth from a little glass stall, leaving the police station in the background.

But once again, I am staggered. This is a busy avenue. I try to imagine a little bundle containing Lu's friend Francesca lying here near the chaos. I then switch to LuLu and Francesca riding together in Francesca's Barbie jeep out on her lawn last summer. It's unbelievable. And what I realize is that their lives now are so vastly different from what they would have been that it is not that these girls are "lucky," as people are wont to say; no, their collective fate is some sort of miracle.

I get back in the car and let Miss Swallow take us on her tour. She drives us far out of town to "the new urban area," as Caroline calls it, a stretch of green farmland where enormous industrial factories, many of them German, have been built. Caroline and Miss Swallow are both very proud of this complex.

There is nothing else here but the buildings, unkempt grass, and rice paddies. It has the empty look of Mayan temple complexes overgrown by the jungles of Guatemala. There's no city out here, no people visible. I guess this is where the foreign businessmen who stay at the hotel go all day. This is the area that will save Anhui from the terrible poverty that has always gripped it.

On the drive back to the hotel, I ask Miss Swallow whether she minds all the old buildings being torn down in Wuhu.

"I can't wait to see them all go," she replies, laughing. Caroline explains that everyone wants light in their apartments and air, and, of course, the rooms are bigger.

Caroline and I make a date to meet the next morning. She will take us to a children's park called the Water Palace. I love that name.

As we disembark at the main plaza, Lu spots TohToh, the doorman on duty, and runs to play with him. She shrieks with joy as he teases her and throws her up in the air. I collapse on the red-carpeted stairs in front of our building and think over what occurred.

I was surprised that Wuhu Children's Institute is such a small facility. Very small. And it was interesting that there were no children outside. I had thought they would be out. Some babies in our group were very tanned from being outside in the sun so much. I had always pictured the babies sitting outside.

I think back to when LuLu handed me the bouquet of tiny flowers. They were as small as pinheads. What was she saying with them? I know only that the expression in her eyes was so wise, it melted my heart.

Deep in my daughter lies a knowledge that I will never have. I have always been aware of this. She has shown it to me through her hyperawareness of who and what is around her and her lightning ability to grasp the relationships between people. She is a little child, yet she trusts herself before me, her own ability to survive before my advice. In this she differs from all birth children I have met. And she is right to. It is she who survived her circumstances, not me. How could she view it any other way?

But I didn't really know the extent of what she knew until the day we visited my mother in the hospital.

It was the week my mother went in for tests. As yet, they had not found her cancer, but she was in terrible shape. I took LuLu with me because I knew it would be one of the last times she could see her grandmother, who was fading quickly.

I had started to prepare LuLu that Grandma would not always be with us, that soon she would die. LuLu asked me what death was, and I explained what different religions believe death to be. I told her about heaven and hell; merging with the cosmos; rebirth and reincarnation; and just disintegrating. She instantly embraced rebirth and reincarnation (as befits a descendant of Buddhists), and decided to believe that. She derived clear comfort from the idea that my mother might be reborn as a baby.

Anyway, I took LuLu to the hospital, and when we arrived, my mother was asleep. She looked pretty ghastly, emaciated and worn out.

I took my mother's hand and held it, and Lu held her other hand. After a few minutes, we left.

When we got home, my stepfather called and I told him that he should prepare himself because I didn't think it would be long for Mom. Ever the optimist, he started to demur. LuLu, then just four, took the phone out of my hand and said in a deep, serious tone I had never heard her use before, "Grandma is going to die, Grandpa. Very soon. I know it. She's going to die soon."

I was startled. I took back the receiver, and my stepfather was silent for several moments. Finally he said, "That was very definite." And for the first time since my mother had become critically ill, he began to deal with it.

Later that evening, I asked LuLu, "Why are you so sure Grandma is going to die? Have you ever seen someone die?"

"Yes," she said without hesitation. "In the orphanage. The mother went to feed the baby, but the baby was dead."

Chills ran down my arms. LuLu had never mentioned the orphanage before, ever. I don't think she had ever uttered the word. And she was not the kind of child who made up fantasies. In fact, she rarely fantasized, which worried me, as if she was, as yet,

afraid to leave her present, safe reality. So when she said this, even though I had fed her the idea, I was pretty sure she was not just making up a story.

I knew from what Spence-Chapin told us that in the orphanage, the infants often slept together, five or six to a crib, for company and warmth. This was why, Spence said, some of the babies considered it a punishment to sleep alone. LuLu always refused to. She would cry pitifully in protest, and it was the only thing she cried about. Later, when she started to talk, she told me that she could see no point to sleeping alone at all. Why would anyone want to sleep by themselves, she would ask, when they could snuggle?

So she had probably slept with other babies. I knew from a friend who had visited a large orphanage in 1992 and was among the first to adopt from China, that the sick babies were not, at that time, necessarily separated from the well ones, especially in the poorer facilities. It was entirely possible that one of the babies in Lu's bed had died in the night and that the nurse—in an infant's mind a mother—had come to feed them in the morning and discovered the child.

Had my daughter lain all night next to another infant who was dying or dead? I don't know. I know only that LuLu was correct in her assessment of my mother. The hospice nurse gave my mother three to six months to live, but she died as Lu prophesied, "very soon," several days later.

I watch LuLu as she plays with TohToh. She seems full of happiness now, running around and hiding from him, chortling with gaiety. Her long black hair streams behind her round baby body as she flees. I dash into the computer room and e-mail Neke and Martha about what happened at the orphanage. I write down Neke's e-mail to LuLu to read to her later. I am very glad to have this means of near instant communication. Martha always reassures me, bless her.

I gather up LuLu and we go to the Canting, where we eat a din-

ner of dumplings in soup. Again, about fifteen young waitresses are standing around, with only a few people to serve. When we are finished, LuLu goes outside to look for bugs at the edge of the stairs while I pay the check. Twenty yuan is a lot to pay; a typical bill is about ten ($1.25).

When I get out to her, LuLu is chatting with three friendly-looking men whom I will come to know as Mr. Tong, Mr. Wu, and Mr. Tchang, managers, respectively, of the Canting and the hotel. They are all dressed in navy pleated trousers and white shirts, and when they talk among themselves, they are exactly like men of their age in America discussing business, only more relaxed somehow. They laugh a lot.

Mr. Tong is a robust man in his late thirties with black wavy hair and a dimply, round-faced smile. He is the Canting manager. Mr. Wu is in his mid-thirties and very handsome in a tall, Harrison Ford–type way. Mr. Tchang, also in his mid-thirties, is slender, wiry, and intelligent-looking. He is the head manager.

LuLu is laughing and showing them her finds. They are teasing her about her spiders and bugs.

I nod to them and take her down the hill to our building. There is a new attendant on our floor, a strong-looking girl whose name is LingLing. She opens the door for us, and I go in and turn on the TV.

The English-language news is pro-Belgrade, but there is no mention of anything new. Nelson Mandela is visiting Beijing. There are big celebrations going on to commemorate the May 4th Movement. And a ban on learning Mandarin has been lifted in Indonesia. Hearing the news in a Communist country is always like peering out at the world from the other side of the mirror.

As I put LuLu to bed, I see the housemaids have noticed that Lu and I sleep together, and have turned down only one bed. I read to LuLu from *Stuart Little* and she drops effortlessly to sleep, with me following suit soon after.

May 8

It's a warm morning, but overcast. On our walk up to the Canting we pass the basket salesman, a man on a bike festooned with baskets. The bike looks as if it's covered with wicker flowers.

At breakfast, LuLu spies a friendly black man who speaks English, and she sits right down and engages him in a chat.

"Are you Chinese?" she asks him.

He laughs and tells her he is from Zimbabwe. He is a cellular phone salesman. Near our table is a little girl about seven or eight, breakfasting with her dad.

Caroline appears for our trip to the Water Palace. We choose Miss Swallow again to drive us, and after circling a number of roundabouts, we reach the train station where we arrived. I recognize it for its Eiffel Tower, which, according to Caroline, has no particular meaning. It is there just because it is fun.

Miss Swallow parks in a small lot adjacent to the park entrance and a ticket booth. I go up and the ticket taker asks me for twenty yuan, which Caroline talks down to ten. It is clear that there is a price for foreigners and a price for natives in Wuhu, and they can differ by a fair amount. We walk through the iron gate into a small amusement park that, though a bit tarnished, is lovely.

A kite festival is in progress, and hanging everywhere are the most elaborately made kites, primarily in red, yellow, pink, and green. One is a five-foot-long peacock with an exquisitely beautiful fantail, thousands of little pieces of colored paper, laboriously glued together. There are box kites and tail kites. A continuous soft breeze in the park causes the gentle sighs of rippling paper and the tinkle of little bells on the kite tails.

The effect of all these lovely kites hanging everywhere is joyous. It makes you feel you are inside a fairy village. LuLu and I both gasp when we enter. She instantly begins pirouetting with pleasure down the walkways. We are greeted at the gate by one of those white plaster nude Greek ladies with a fawn. (I call them Greek because that's what they look like to a Westerner; an Easterner most likely sees them as Chinese goddesses.) The wastebaskets in the park are in the shape of little mushrooms and decorate the main walk.

The Water Palace itself is an odd amalgam of buildings and events. There are the usual amusement park rides—the spinning teacup, the Ferris wheels, the roller coaster, and something the Chinese love a lot, the Dragon Boat, which swings from side to side on a giant pendulum.

Then there is a ride that makes me laugh out loud because it's so un-Western and un-PC. This is the Big Game Hunt. You get in a jeep car painted with camouflage colors. On the dashboard are two realistic-looking rifles. As the car shunts around through real bushes, different metal African animals come into view, such as a rhino, monkey, or lion, and you have to shoot them. If you fire the gun, though, nothing comes out of it; you hear just a *ping*ing noise.

LuLu gets in and has a great time riding around and shooting everything. Farther on we discover the indoor playground, which has crawling tunnels, pits full of balls and bars to swing on, and a trampoline. Down a wide, breezy walkway and over a bridge, we find a wonderfully kept lawn dotted with little log huts and fenced in by a glass enclosure. On the glass is the silhouette of a generic infantry soldier. Evidently, this is a place to play soldier for children who don't have lawns. What a great idea. The grass is perfect in there, and I can picture little boys crawling around.

Right next to it is a small, circular roadbed edged with rubber tires. A kid-size tank is parked there for playing army on the move. Where I live, kids don't play army anymore. I wonder if that's because Western military strategy now favors short skirmishes between computerized missiles in complex aircraft. I don't know for sure, but it's definitely odd to see this army stuff for kids. It's been a long time.

In the afternoon, we meet up with Caroline again and go to the Jing Hu Lake, where we rent a swan boat. It's very hot out, but there's a good breeze on the water and some boys are windsurfing in a small boat.

Caroline and I are pedaling while LuLu sits in the middle. We are all staring through the big eyeholes of the swan. The bright sunlight glints off the lake, making it look as though it's covered with diamonds. The little pagoda island looks dreamy.

It is superior exercise maneuvering the swan boat around, and for mothers trapped with young children, it seems the perfect thing to do to keep fit. LuLu could ride the boat all day, but even young Caroline is panting when we finally glide into port.

We get off near the round-backed bridge at the midpoint of the lake. We move along the edge, through milling crowds of old people and various men vending their paintings and drawings. One young man has some watercolors with science-fiction overtones, modern horror stuff in dark purples and greens that seems unusual for China and Wuhu. Then a really obviously gay man walks by us, the first and only patently gay man I have seen in China. I wonder if we are in the nonconformist section of the lake, where the avant-garde types hang out.

Presently we reach the southern end of the lake, which resembles the south of France or a piece of Coral Gables, Florida. Here, there are lots of low, cream-colored two-story buildings with red-tile roofs and Moorish-arched arcades on the street level. A line of trees has been planted before them. Open shops selling fans, visors, beach balls, and children's clothing front the sidewalk.

It's very pleasant at this end, and we discover a market through one of the arcades. It is the pet market, Caroline tells us. Here are kittens in cages, parakeets, and fish, as well as toys, teapots, and crockery. I buy LuLu a little green plastic dog pendant because she was born in the Year of the Dog.

I browse while LuLu plays with each kitten. Then she finds a mechanical game that she wants to play. It is called Beat the Rat: you put in a quarter and rat heads pop up through holes, and you hit them on the head with a mallet. Fortunately, I can't figure out the correct change, so she forgoes the pleasure.

We've got the stroller with us, and by now I've begun to see that nobody in China uses one; children walk or are carried. That, I guess, is why it was so expensive—and why, when LuLu is in the stroller asleep, people often ask me if she is ill or perhaps paralyzed.

Caroline points out the Children's Palace, where I want to see about lessons in *gu zun,* a lyrelike instrument that is played with pluckers worn on the forefinger and thumb. Every town and city in China has a "Children's Palace," as it's called, the center of art and music lessons for kids. In Wuhu it is housed in a nondescript concrete high-rise built around a central court.

We wait on a short line to talk to a guard in a glass booth at the entrance. Behind me, I sense something and turn to see a grungy-looking type who is surely a pickpocket. He looks homeless and has that weird energy. He starts as I turn, then grins, and the guard, seeing him, shoos him away.

As we climb the stairs to the administrator's office, we hear a group of children singing German classical songs. The glorious clear sound of their voices echoes off the walls. I have rarely heard children singing with such perfection.

The administrator, a stern woman in her forties who is wearing a navy print dress with big, padded shoulders, doesn't seem to like us much. Generally, she says tersely, they don't teach children younger than seven at the Children's Palaces, but they might make an exception for LuLu. I suggest three lessons a week, and she agrees (at twenty yuan per lesson) but insists we talk to the teacher.

The teacher in question—a pretty woman around forty in an artsy, 1950s dress with a full skirt and a wide, tight belt—is really furious. LuLu takes one look at her mean face and starts to bail out. She refuses to play for the teacher, which makes the woman angrier. In front of my eyes, LuLu is becoming frantic. These people are a far cry from Yu Jie at the university preschool.

The teacher is conducting a *gu zun* class of ten-year-olds. She commands them to play for us, and they do so wonderfully. Miss Lee's group of five-year-olds played lyrically and delicately, making harplike trills. These girls play strongly and deeply, with a huge, tragic sound.

But I can see LuLu is not going for it. She is acting crazily now, running off and refusing to behave. The two women are seething with disapproval. Maybe all *gu zun* teachers are like this.

We return to the administrator's office, and she changes the price to sixty yuan per lesson. "She can pay," Caroline translates what she's saying about me. "She's a foreigner." Caroline whispers to me that they are not being very nice about us at all.

I stand up, thank the administrator for her time, and leave with Caroline. LuLu has already run down the stairs and waits by the glass booth. "I'm not going here," she states.

And I tell her she doesn't have to. We hail a taxi and ride home quickly, after letting the taxi driver know that LuLu is *Wuhuren*.

It is interesting to me that they don't start teaching children seriously until seven here, quite different from Chinatown, where they begin everything very early. LuLu had her first piano lesson there at three and a half.

I arrange with Caroline to come in a few days, and LuLu and I emerge from the car to find a wedding under way at the hotel. We sit on the steps of our building and join the photo shoot of a bride in Western white dress and groom in tux. No one minds us. There is a general unspoken rule in Wuhu that if you are present when it's happening, you can be part of it and welcome. For LuLu, who loves people and their doings, this relaxed attitude is

Nirvana. I'm beginning to see that she really is *Wuhuren* to a greater extent than I imagined.

As Miss Ling did in Chinatown, this bride changes her outfit. She goes off and returns in a very red Scarlett O'Hara number with a parasol to match. LuLu applauds.

We go straight up to the Canting to eat. The wedding party has filled the dining hall, so we are escorted past "the bug area," as I now call it, where LuLu plays, to the building next door. It has private dining rooms and we are seated in one of them with a man in his late fifties, who is wearing a Mao suit and is clearly some sort of cadre. He is drinking beer and looks red-eyed and tipsy. He smiles at us, and LuLu begins to chat with him and orders herself a Coke.

"What's your motherland?" he asks her.

Not understanding fully, she replies, "America."

"You are Chinese," he thunders, and I look at him, astonished.

But LuLu ignores his tone completely and chats right on. "My Chinese parents are gone. We don't know where they are. This is my new mommy." She gestures toward me. "Well . . . my old mommy—my real mommy."

He doesn't get this at all and looks puzzled.

"My mom's mom died a few months ago," she adds, which confuses him further.

It's a really wonderful speech, and I am cheering inwardly for her because she put this guy right in his place.

In the uncomfortable silence that follows, I remember a similar incident in Urumchi in 1979. The unpleasantness that took place concerned my buying a pack of cigarettes at the kiosk in the lobby of our hotel. The lobby's only decoration was a spectacular wool rug, eleven by fourteen inches, with a huge portrait of Chairman Mao's face on it. I bought some cigarettes, and when I turned around to go back to my room, I found myself encircled by ten older women in Mao suits. They all were staring at me menacingly.

Led by a mean-looking woman in her sixties with chopped-off gray hair, they began ranting at me in Chinese, and it was pretty clear they were denouncing me for being an immoral Western woman. After a few minutes of their chanting, I denounced them back for being inhospitable to a foreign tourist. Then I flounced off. It was just a taste of the tag end of the Cultural Revolution, but it was quite unsettling.

After finishing our meal quickly, LuLu and I return to find a message from Anne, the American teacher from the university, which cheers me up. I'm about to call her when the phone rings and she calls me.

She is ringing, she says, to tell me that NATO *has* bombed the Chinese embassy in Belgrade, killing three Chinese journalists. The Chinese government is furious and blaming the Americans specifically; and her foreign adviser has told all Americans at the university to stay indoors until they tell them otherwise.

Great.

Instantly I'm back in Taiwan, lying on my father's bed, burning with fever. My father's secretary, Letty Wu, is walking in and announcing that an army enlisted man has shot a Chinese and they expect rioting and looting in the city. As my father is away in Hong Kong, the office is evacuating all military dependents who do not live in American compounds. She bundles me quickly into the car, and our driver ferries me up the mountain to an American army colonel's house. I spend the weekend lying on his couch. I recall being mortified that I was in my nightgown around his teenage sons.

"Don't worry," I find myself soothing Anne, "it will blow over. Just wait it out."

Anne, who has never been through an anti-American event in China, seems perplexed but not unduly frightened. She finds it hard to believe that any of her students would harm her, and I do, too. But she has been trapped inside all day and has no sense of the outside world right now.

Ignorant of political events, of course, I have been out with my daughter all day in the thick of Wuhu. I recount the meanness at the Children's Palace and the anger of the party cadre at dinner, both of which make more sense to me now, but add that Wuhu seems otherwise friendly and unchanged. Anne is relieved to hear this. I arrange to come by in the morning to visit her after I take LuLu to school.

I hardly have a minute to think about this latest nightmare when Leo calls from Hefei. Though he does not sound overly concerned, he does let me know that the Chinese government has, as he puts it delicately, invited students to demonstrate. They are having marches in the cities tonight, and he suggests we stay inside. When I ask him about our chances of visiting the orphanage, he is not optimistic. It is definitely a bad break. I do not tell him we have already dropped by the place, lest knowledge of it cause him any trouble.

After we hang up, I turn on the TV. Unfortunately, the English-language news is already over. But there is President Jiang Zemin speaking to the camera, looking grim. I turn off the TV.

Outside our windows, which are curtained with gauzy material, I hear commotion and see lights flickering in the plaza by the pine tree. It's the torchlight parade of students from the university, which I once thought was so conveniently nearby. As there were no other Westerners at breakfast this morning, I assume the parade is for me and LuLu. I'd like to take a good look, but LuLu is still up. There is no need for her to know any of this.

After she is asleep, I lie awake in a rising fury. How could this happen? We bombed the Chinese embassy? Can this be true? I can't believe such stupidity! I don't exactly know what to do. I trust the hostility will blow over, but a lot depends on the Chinese government's reaction.

My paramount mission is to keep LuLu safe and sound. When I see Anne tomorrow, I will ask how we can get out of Wuhu quickly and go back to Shanghai if we have to.

Such is the fate of a Tiger, like myself, traveling in the Year of the Cat.

May 9
Sunny

In the morning, I awaken mortified and furious. All my self-consciousness is back and I am in a state. Also, I am dreadfully confused. Why would we do a thing like bomb the Chinese embassy? Can it be true?

How to face the hotel workers, the school officials? I decide to behave as if it never happened. After all, I didn't do it, and it is the polar opposite of my mission here. I will simply have to hope that the people of Wuhu realize that.

When I first became a mother, I was unused to having attention brought to me in public. I was used to fading into the background and observing. So whenever LuLu did something unwonderful that might cause people to look at us, I would pretend I was Eleanor Roosevelt and that whatever she was doing was absolutely up to snuff. This I am going to do now. I am going to walk tall, with all the strength and pride of Eleanor, my grandmother's favorite person.

I decide that LuLu will be safer away from me, a Western-looking person, at this moment, so I go right ahead with our original plan and determine to take her to her first day of school.

I go to dress and find that most of the T-shirts that I have packed were chosen for their American symbolism, because I thought the Chinese kids would enjoy them. The Gulf War shirt, the one with lots of little American flags, the New York City one, all in one way or another shout "aggressive American: stone me!" I can't believe this. I pull on a shirt I bought in Shanghai.

First, we have to come out of the room and face JingJing. I smile sheepishly and say hello, and proceed on. LuLu beams at her. She smiles back broadly, a sweetheart.

We walk up the hill to the Canting. The fifteen waitresses are there, and I smile at them. And they smile back, sweet girls. I pretend I am Eleanor Roosevelt and try to be as well-bred and gracious as possible.

LuLu, who knows nothing of the situation, eats like a horse. Every morning, there is a free buffet of Chinese breakfast foods: dumplings, pickles, rice *congees,* and such. LuLu has turned away from American breakfasts on a dime and fills her plate with Chinese delicacies. We talk about her first day of school. She is nervous but eager.

We walk down the hill hand in hand to the school gate, and LuLu greets the security guard effusively. Around us, university parents are dropping off their children in the manner of working parents in the United States. No one pays undue attention to us. The doctor is in front of her office and I give LuLu into her hands. She smiles and her eyes show such deep understanding. She nods her head reassuringly. I kiss my daughter and zip to the university to find out how we can escape if we have to.

There are few people on the campus walkway, which is lined with pine trees. I follow Anne's directions to the foreign visitors guest house and walk briskly along, vigilant. I hurry up a steep little bridge, then up a hill, and there it is: a small four-story building fronted with balconies enclosed with that blue antiglare glass.

This is where Leo initially suggested we stay, but I had said no. I wanted to be in a Chinese place surrounded by Chinese people. And I love the Tie Shan Hotel. The people are gracious and the grounds are truly spectacular. I hope it turns out all right.

A smiling Chinese receptionist at a big desk directs me to the second floor. I knock on the door and it is opened by a kind-looking American woman in her early twenties. We take to each other on sight.

Anne is with a Christian teachers association. She has been in China for three years, teaching English as a second language. She has lived in Wuhu for a year and thrives on it. Her home here is a small two-bedroom apartment that she shares with another teacher. I walk out on the balcony to see what the blue glass looks like from the inside. The light it filters is navy blue and very dark.

The crisis consumes us. Anne says if it were up to her, she'd be going right on with life as usual. But she must do what the association tells her, so she will stay inside until further notice. Evidently, in Beijing and in other cities that are home to American consulates, there's a lot more organized hostility and more reason to keep off the street. At any rate, she says, she is close with her students and trusts them.

Just in case, I ask, is there a quick way out? We are, after all, in the middle of south China, six hours by train from Shanghai in a town that during the Opium Wars had its share of attacks on foreigners. Anne knows of a Chinese military air base somewhere on the outskirts of Wuhu. One of the teachers has gone to Beijing on one of their planes. We could fly out if we had to. Okay, good, I say, and change the subject.

We discuss our mutual affection for China, and Anne says that from the moment she arrived, "I felt that my heart was home." It's so interesting how some people have this visceral reaction to this country. What is it about China that makes some people, myself among them, fall in love so fully?

There's a knock on the door and Kay comes in. She's the wife of another teacher, Max, who has taught in China for eight years. Kay is in her thirties and is not a China addict. She'd just as soon go home.

Anne and I talk politics a bit. The Chinese see the Belgrade situation much as they do that of Taiwan, she explains. The Albanians want their own nation and are trying to secede. I find this fascinating, since I've never heard this at all, that the Albanians want their own nation. What about ethnic cleansing? I ask, and

Anne knows nothing about it. So I explain what's been happening. We both end up perplexed by the whole thing.

I mine Anne for information about the countryside. Some towns suffer from 80 percent unemployment, she tells me. What about the empty buildings everywhere? They are 60 percent empty, but government officials want new buildings, so they keep erecting them. Well, I think, I guess they will have them for the future.

We talk about my bringing LuLu to Wuhu, and they say they know of another adoptee living in Hefei with her American teacher parents. Apparently this little girl refuses to speak Chinese, perhaps in an attempt to show solidarity with her English-speaking parents. Interesting.

I tell Anne that I will ring her tonight after I have seen the news on CCTV. I bid Kay good-bye and I'm off.

I get back to Geng Xing without incident and then decide to go down to Laodong Road to visit a stuffed-animal store I saw right across from the bakery on the corner. I stand waiting to cross, head held high, the only Western person in sight. No one looks at me at all. They won't, Anne has said. That's their way of dealing with it. But I'm not so sure. Perhaps they are just all going about their business and paying no attention to politics.

I buy twenty stuffed bears, lions, tigers, and mice for the Wuhu orphanage. The store owner is delighted with me, foreign devil or not. I lug my package back across the road and up Geng Xing to the hotel. Then I head for the computer room. I have to let everyone know we are okay.

While I log on, people gather round to watch. This is a feature of my daily e-mailing. I think it's funny that they stand there and peer at everything I'm writing. I wonder if any of them can read English. Maybe they can. In any event, I have nothing to hide.

I e-mail Neke, and then suddenly I feel sick again. Stomach trouble, on top of everything.

It's starting to rain, too. I don't think we will go into the town itself today, but not because I'm afraid. I might have tried to take a walk. After all, we were out all day yesterday during the height of President Jiang's televised fury, and people left us alone. I feel more shame than fear, really. We can't have bombed them on purpose. It must have been incompetence.

I trot down the street again to pick up Lu for lunch. When I get there, Yu Jie has gathered a group of women to welcome me, and she introduces me to Lu's teacher. Under the circumstances, it is so thoughtful of her to do this that I'm overwhelmed. It is her way of saying that governments and people are two different things, which I believe is also some kind of Chinese proverb.

Another mother, a professor at the university who speaks English, says hello, too, and reminds me that what we do now is go home, take a nap, and bring the kids back at two-thirty. She smiles and rushes off. At this moment, I am very grateful for these little kindnesses. But I know from living with a *Wuhuren* that if they like someone, they support them wholeheartedly and nothing can change their minds.

Today in the Canting, LuLu helps the waitresses set the tables. Then she sits down at the table and declares, "You know, Mom, I don't speak Chinese, so I need a mother who doesn't speak Chinese." And she is quite pleased with this explanation for why it is a good thing in the end to have me, a non-Chinese woman, as a mother. I think it's a pretty ingenious reason myself.

"That's true," I affirm. "That's very true."

After nap, I return Lu to school, and we run into one of the teachers. She's on roller skates and having so much fun that I vow to try it.

All afternoon I remain in our room, and read and rest. At four, it is raining torrentially. I pick up Lu, who is ecstatic. She loved her first day at school. Silently, I bless Yu Jie. She's a miniskirted, platform-booted saint. The school with its open court is very wet, and I wonder if it is cold in winter. There don't seem to be heating elements, but maybe I don't recognize them. LuLu and I huddle together under the umbrella, and when we arrive at Building Two we discover one of those locked umbrella stands like the one we saw in Shanghai.

We run into Mrs. Chang and her adorable daughter, Yue Yue, LuLu's schoolmate. They demonstrate the umbrella stand, which works a bit differently than I had imagined. You can rent an umbrella from it for about a quarter when you go out. The attendant unlocks one and hands it to you. When you come back, you replace it in the stand and relock it. You don't store your own umbrella in it after all.

Mrs. Chang invites us for a playdate in a conference lounge on the second floor. There's a sectional sofa all around the wall. The girls jump on it and shriek while Mrs. Chang and I talk. She is completely unperturbed by the kids' raucous playing.

Mrs. Chang has a Loretta Young kind of beauty and bearing. She looks to be in her mid-thirties, and her face is composed in a gentle expression. Her hair is tied back in a tail at the base of her neck. She is a gracious woman.

She begins our conversation by asking if LuLu isn't cold without a sweater. She has noticed that LuLu doesn't wear many clothes. This is true. All the children at school are wearing heavy sweaters and woolen tights despite the fact that it has been warm enough for LuLu to wear only a T-shirt.

The Chinese believe in dressing children warmly no matter what the temperature. When we got our babies in 1994, they came dressed in multiple pairs of knitted pants and sweaters. If we removed but one, people on the street would chastise us.

I tell Mrs. Chang that I could not get Lu to wear a sweater when it is so warm out. How do Chinese mothers manage it?

"Sweaters are easy," replies Mrs. Chang. "But Chinese children refuse to wear rain boots."

We laugh pretty hard at this strange cultural difference. Then she confides that she is worried that Yue Yue, who is very slender with tiny bones, is too thin. How, she probes, did I get LuLu so strong?

"Milk," I reply, and she nods and tells this to Yue Yue.

"She won't drink milk," she says with a sigh. Many of the adopted Chinese girls I know do not like milk, either, perhaps because the diet here is not dairy-based. It is much less fatty, mostly vegetarian, and very healthy. And they don't eat dessert. In all of Wuhu, I have seen only one plump child, and by American standards that child was average weight.

That evening, while we are eating in the Canting, a flute player appears on the stage and plays Chinese classical flute music. What a wonderful thing! His playing is haunting, and for a time I cease worrying and simply listen to his artistry. LuLu rushes across the dining hall to the stage and stares up at him, rapt. When he finishes, she applauds loudly, as do I.

Later in our room, though, we thud back to reality when I turn on the English-language news. The news anchor reports there is growing anger toward NATO and the Americans, and they show demonstrations in Beijing. But at least they do not go overboard. Tomorrow, the reporters promise, everyone will be going back to work. Please God, let it be so.

I call Anne and report in. We are both aware that this news is directed at the American business community and is a sort of missive from the Chinese government. Tonight's installment was continuing anger, but on the way to calm. Anne tells me that the secretary of state has advised foreigners to stay near the hotels.

It's not over yet.

After the news, there is another program in English called *Around China,* a travel magazine program. Tonight it's about the goldfish breeders of Beijing. They have been breeding goldfish for the emperor since the seventeenth century, but what with all the building, their facility now lies in a modern-looking suburb of Beijing. I'm beginning to like the idea of having goldfish and aquariums. Maybe we will get some when we get home.

In the humidity from the rain, my hair has frizzed up into a big bush. One odd by-product of my hyper-self-consciousness brought on by the bombing and its anti-American fallout: I have come to think that my bushy hair is drawing attention to me. I hate it. I am conscious of it all the time. And I feel it makes me really noticeable on the street. Of course, if my hair were straight, people would still know that I am Caucasian and notice me. So all this is simply some terrified paranoia compounded by the fact that I am living in a town of bone-straight hair. Is this what victims of racism feel like?

May 10
Rain

At breakfast in the Canting, while LuLu is eating dumplings and pickles, I spy a young Western man. He is Australian, touring around China. Have you been out? I ask. Do you think it's safe? He doesn't know. It occurs to me that I could pose as Australian on the street if there's a bad scene, there is that.

After dropping Lu at school, I run back to the computer room. Miss Smith, the manager who boots me up and logs me onto the Net, can't get a connection today. She tries and tries, but no go. It is very disturbing. She calls in Mr. Chen, who also tries. No luck. For all intents and purposes, we are cut off from the outside world.

I decide to walk off my nervousness by going around the block. I venture down to Laodong Road, turn left, and nose along past a photo store and then a milliner who sells handmade ladies' sunhats with lace trim and wide, flowered brims.

I round the corner at Sun Yat-sen and take one of the spokes that lead to the lake, the one with Radio Shack on it. I enter the sporting goods store and look around to see what they have: soccer balls, basketballs, Ping-Pong paddles, and some sports outfits, much of the same equipment we have, but less of a selection. They do not have Rollerblades, and there is no evidence of safety pads and helmets. To cheer myself up and soothe my capitalist nature, I buy two pairs of roller skates, one for Lu and one for me.

By four, the rain has stopped and I bring the skates with me to the school. I collect Lu from her classroom and we go downstairs, where the little kids are massing. I tie on her skates, adjust them with the skate key, as I did so many times when I was a little girl, and off she goes into what can only be described as a jolly melee.

The entire school of children is there, on the concrete court, skating and shrieking with euphoria. They fall down frequently, laughing hysterically at themselves and each other. LuLu pushes off into the fray, determined to learn quickly. I sit on the edge with the other mothers, basking quite happily in this explosive communal baby joy. What a brilliant idea this is! By the time half an hour has passed, the kids have had a lot of exercise, and have honed their balance and coordination to boot. Every single child is in a delirium of pleasure.

It occurs to me that prohibitive insurance premiums would prevent such goings-on at an American preschool, but I have rarely seen little children having so much fun together. Their cheeks are all apple red from effort, and the screams of excitement reverberate off the walls. They hold on to each other and skate together in terrific camaraderie.

One girl is particularly good, and I indicate to her mother that I am impressed that her daughter is doing so well. "How old is she?" I ask in Chinese.

"Seven," she replies.

I'm surprised there are seven-year-olds here, but another mother explains that, in China, children go to preschool until they are seven, then advance to primary school. So basically, the Chinese begin children's formal training in music, art, and educational studies when the kids are almost fully cognizant.

After an hour, I can barely drag LuLu away, and she insists that I skate with her before dinner. Needless to say, she can hardly wait for her next day at school.

I strap on my skates on the steps of Building Two, and we are off up the road around the lake. I almost fall several times. LuLu loves this, and we laugh hysterically together. The car wash guys wave and laugh, too, and everyone we meet thinks it's really wild and funny that I am skating with her.

She thumps to the ground often, but she perseveres, as I have seen her do before with physical feats she wishes to perform. Last summer, she was determined to swing from ring to ring in the playground. Although she was sobbing from the pain of the blisters on her hands, she didn't stop until she had mastered the skill.

At one point, she falls backward and hits her head hard. For the first time since we arrived in China, she cries loudly and long. I cradle her in my arms and look up to find that both TohToh, the doorman, and JingJing, the room attendant, have appeared at the doorways of their respective buildings. Both look worried.

"She hit her head," I call to them, and I can see they are a bit disapproving that I let her do this. Later, one of the women managers at reception tells me that generally, children would not be allowed to skate outside of school. I guess they feel that skating on the school court is less dangerous, more controllable.

In the evening, LuLu plays with the waitresses, one of whom is her favorite and is also named JingJing. Wei Wei is another of the girls who particularly like LuLu. They take her with them into the kitchen.

While I'm sitting alone, the man from the father/daughter breakfast the other morning comes by and says hi. I smile at him gratefully. (We are all of us trying to deal with the wretched incident.) Then the flutist comes on stage and plays again, enchantingly. LuLu runs back from the kitchen and stands at his feet, again transfixed. There has been some luck on the trip: this man is a great musician.

Later, on the news, Clinton, thank God, apologizes to China. NATO apologizes to China. And Madeline Albright is promising to get to the bottom of it. Anne calls, and I tell her the good news. But her teachers association has not sprung her yet, so she still has to stay in her quarters.

In the morning, when Lu awakes, she tells me she had a dream.

"Captain Hook takes me to my park. Then I get in a car with you and later we meet Daddy. I went to Captain Hook's house. He was sort of mean. I had to sleep in his bed, and I didn't want to, but I had to. He pushed me in the bed. The next morning, I told Captain Hook to take me to my park. Then I came home by myself to our New York house, where I belong, and where you picked me up in a car, a big black van. Then I went into the van with you, then we picked up Dad. The whole time it was snowing. I got angry at Captain Hook. I did not want to sleep in his smelly bed."

It seems to me that LuLu is finally processing the events of our visit to the orphanage and interpreting them. When she has finished recounting the dream, she tells me she wants badly to take the stuffed animals to the children there, so I call and leave a message for Caroline to come over. LuLu does not have school today. She and I have decided she will go only two or three days a week.

In an hour or so, Caroline appears at the door. She is a rather docile person, affectless. Her face never shows what she feels. So when I ask her if she thinks it is safe to go out in the city, I don't expect her eyes to light up with a bit of passion and fire.

"Yes, it is safe," she tells me, but her voice rises. "The president has told people not to hurt foreign tourists. The reason, you see, that we think you are terrible is that you bomb innocent people and are aggressive and—"

It takes me a minute to realize that she is denouncing America and, by association, us. There is a memorized quality to what she is saying. Perhaps student leaders urged her to attack me. I interrupt her icily.

"We would never bomb your embassy on purpose. Why would

we? Why, when we have all this business with you? Clinton has always been a friend to China. Ask yourself, why? Why would we do it?"

She glares at me in return. "You have killed two young people, you see." She puts emphasis on the youth of the couple killed.

"That is awful," I reply. "It is awful when anyone is killed. It's a terrible thing, a dreadful mistake."

I don't add but want to that the couple was working in a war zone, which is pretty dangerous place to be in.

We clam up now, both of us. I shouldn't be talking politics, but it popped out because of her certainty that we did it on purpose. That we are evil, Machiavellian. I realize I'm quite angry at everybody involved.

LuLu, who has been playing in the hall with JingJing, runs in, and I thankfully grab the toy bag and we set off in silence for the orphanage.

Unfortunately, Miss Swallow is not around. We take one taxi and have to abandon it when it becomes clear that the driver has no idea where we are going. Caroline can't remember the street name, either.

We drive around and get another good look at Wuhu, which has a neighborhood with high-rises that are older and look kind of middle-class. Finally, we get back to the railroad track and the old *hutong* alley.

The market is in full swing today. For sale are roosters, raw meats, eggs, eels, vegetables, clothes, and housewares, all packed together on the narrow street. Bicycles and pedicabs are miraculously squeezing by us, too. We thread our way along, and through *hutong* doors, which now are wide open on either side, we glimpse live ducks waddling about within.

At the orphanage gate, the old caretaker immediately tries to shoo us away. I'm ready for him this time, though, and insist on seeing the director, whom we catch sight of, scurrying along the side of the building.

He doesn't look familiar to me. He wasn't one of the men who signed the papers when I adopted LuLu. I remember them well, and they had some humor to them. This man looks like a scared rabbit.

We introduce LuLu to him. Caroline tells him LuLu is adopted from here, but he hardly glances at her. He couldn't be less interested. Fear is his one reaction. He tells Caroline what the security guard said last time, that we must go to the police station and get a permit to enter.

I inform him that we have applied and are waiting for permission. As soon as we get it, he says, visibly relieved that we are going through channels, we may come back. There is no problem.

Caroline now tells him we have brought gifts for the children. LuLu hands him our bag of toys. I tell him I bought twenty animals. Is that, I ask, enough for each child to get one? But he won't tell me. The number of children is, evidently, privileged information. He becomes terribly nervous again and flees back into the compound as soon as he has gotten us out the gate.

LuLu has run out before us and is in the alley, pretending to beg and be poor. She seems to be trying out the life she might have had. She has always done this, try out other lives. She used to try out other children's strollers, for example, when she was a toddler.

I am disappointed that we are here and can't do more for our orphanage. I would play with the babies. I would buy medicine or whatever I could see they needed. My original plan had been to do volunteer work here. What a pipe dream that was.

On an already bad day, I leave in a huff, but a hidden one so LuLu won't see. It has pleased her to give the toys to the Wuhu children. She stops begging and seems pleased.

When we return to the hotel, I make a halfhearted date to see Caroline the next day, but I don't really want or expect to see her again—and, in fact, she never comes back.

Lu and I eat a wonderful lunch of *xiao cingsai* (water spinach), soft fried chicken, and the delicious Wuhu rice. The ham-and-winter-melon soup is so delicate and sweet. If we have to be trapped, I am so glad we are trapped in the best and most entertaining restaurant in town.

After lunch, I return to the computer room, and the Net pops on for a moment and then freezes. Miss Smith and Mr. Chen turn to each other, and she declares in her plain, no-nonsense way, "It's the post office," and he nods resignedly.

The post office, I note, must be the site of the remaining controls of communism, because nowhere else are they particularly evident anymore. I assume the post office has shut off Internet access to all of Wuhu. I wonder what will happen.

While Lu naps, I take stock. The bombing is the end, for a time, anyway, of any help coming from the university. We shall have to go on without an interpreter. I decide that we will watch more TV for language purposes and we will both study, too. And, of course, everything depends on whether the Chinese government wants to continue rousing hostile feelings. Jiang's demand for an explanation from NATO could fuel hostilities for months, because, of course, no explanation could possibly be adequate.

When Lu wakes up, we go out to skate and Lu collects beetles by the lake. She's falling less and getting better, and I'm getting in good shape, too. I am beginning to take in more about the hotel, and the landscaping is really something. Constant breezes blow softly on this little mountain. It is gorgeous here and I feel like one of those ancient Chinese women forced to live in a beautiful compound for all of her life. It's not as bad as I thought.

I am particularly intrigued by a circular metal moon gate that leads to a walled-in area next to the car wash/basketball court, opposite the lake. The gate, once turquoise blue, is rusted now and quite magical in its distress. It is overhung with vines, and I think it opens into a secret garden. Another day, when we are not on skates, we will explore it.

Tuckered out, we leave our skates in the lobby of Building Two and stroll down the street to the bakery to get milk. The babies are out, learning to walk, and Lu stops to help them, every one. The primary school is quiet, as the kids have all been let out. The bakery, however, is filled with impassioned children. A special event is going on.

A young man inside a glass booth is icing a big cake. The primary-school kids have gathered round it to watch him. The man is creating a *Power Rangers* design, with all the Rangers in their various colors. His painting is perfect. He creates the characters with such precision that it's amazing his medium is icing.

I'm taken back to a chef in Taipei who would carve elaborate, intricate vegetable flowers for my father's cocktail parties. I remember, too, the men who carved the ivory balls inside ivory balls, whose workshop was in our neighborhood. I remember wandering in there and standing by their worktables, watching over their shoulders. The intricate nature of the carving was startling. The fact that they never made a mistake was inconceivable to me. I always felt that the people who could do these enchanted things were more than mere human beings.

The elevation of the mundane into art was a feature of my childhood in China: swans carved out of butter so exquisitely that they stirred you to tears; lobsters molded out of wax so perfectly that you expected them to move.

Now, my LuLu watches in wonder as the master cake icer swirls his blue wand, managing to twist the icing brilliantly, as if he were embroidering with silk.

I buy our milk and some sponge cakes, and the woman behind the counter nods at me in a friendly way. She is getting to know us now, and it's good of her to greet us in this time of tension. These little shows of friendship mean a lot under the circumstances. Being a good Joe in a totalitarian country takes bravery.

We wend our way back up Geng Xing, and in front of the university housing entrance, an old woman, in from the country, is selling silkworms on mulberry leaves. She has them in a cardboard box, fat white squiggles on dark green leaves.

When we reach the hotel and our room, LuLu goes with me to get our ironed laundry, and JingJing invites her to stay and play. Back in the room, I glance at the laundry bill and realize it costs a fortune, about twenty American dollars. I should have negotiated about that, too. Funny that laundry would be so expensive in China. I resolve to wash out most of our things myself from now on.

When LuLu comes back, we phone Neke in New York. The phone, at least, is working. Fortunately, he is home and he says he's been worried. On TV, the networks showed rioting in Beijing. I reassure him, and then he talks to LuLu.

When I take the receiver again, I ask him what our news says about how the bombing happened, and he replies that NATO believes they got a wrong address out of an old map. The Chinese embassy had been in that location for only a short time. Whatever they were going to bomb had moved. I can't believe my ears: my whole trip might be in jeopardy because of such a strange event. Can this be true? I ask. He says that's what they are saying.

After we hang up, LuLu bursts into tears. She misses her dad. I hold her close and suggest we look for cartoons, and in a while she is absorbed in a show called *Da Feng Che* (Big Mouth Crocodile), which is featuring a cartoon about an ancient Chinese superhero.

At eight, the news comes on. It is a "national day of mourning" in China. The deceased are a Xinhua news reporter and his new wife, and an older woman clerk. We see their families. President Jiang Zemin bows three times at a ceremony at the Xinhua News Agency, where the slain trio worked. The mother of the young woman who was killed is quoted as saying, "Should a mother have to decorate the mourning hall for a daughter?"

It is dreadful to see. Killing a child is definitely the cruelest thing you can do to a mother and father. There are shots of the father identifying the bodies in Belgrade, and his grief is something

I shall never forget. He weeps uncontrollably and there is such raw pain on his face. CCTV will show this unbearable piece of footage as an ad for the news over and over for weeks, and every time I will feel bad and personally to blame.

The president's demands are unnerving. Jiang is calling for punishment for those responsible. I wonder how far he will go with that, because I know, and I'm sure he knows, that the chances of finding out exactly who caused the error are incredibly slim.

I call Anne and tell her the latest, and she reports that the dean of students came over to reassure her. NATO is synonymous with the Americans, she explains in reply to my query, because the Chinese believe we control the organization.

The emerging picture is quite ironic, I feel.

In the United States, China is presented as a great menace. In China, the United States is considered the only superpower left and China is depicted as our as yet weak but honorable and innocent disciple.

What is so hard to remember is that China and America were allies in World War II. We sent billions of dollars in aid to Chiang Kai-shek to equip and train his armies to fight not only the Japanese but the Communists. But according to Barbara Tuchman's *Stillwell and the American Experience in China 1911–1945,* although Chiang took the money, he seemed incapable of training and equipping his armies with it.

General Stillwell, who was in China to advise, saw what was happening and telegraphed Roosevelt that we were backing the wrong man. Stillwell knew that Mao was going to win, and pleaded with Roosevelt to make deals and give aid while Mao needed us, to make inroads before China became rigidly Communist. Roosevelt refused. One can only wonder what might have happened if for the last fifty years we'd had a democratic influence in China.

May 13
Cloudy

Lu is very excited about skating and is trilling all the way to school. We arrive early, so she plays in the school playground. The only drawback is that there is no grass, so it gets muddy. It would seem that Chinese architects don't think of grass when they landscape—except for the zoos, Yu Dusheng's house, and that little area in the Water Palace, I haven't seen any. Apparently, lawns are not a common Chinese concept.

After I deposit LuLu in class, I walk down to Laodong Road and cross through the round moon gate where, Anne told me, the market lies. Indeed, it is there, a cluster of tables where chickens and housewares lie beak by towel. I purchase some soap powder in a packet.

I return to the computer room at the hotel, and Miss Smith boots me up. This time I do get onto Hotmail and find that I have about twenty worried e-mails from family and friends, wondering if we are all right. Evidently, the Chinese riots were played to the hilt on American TV. I e-mail Neke and Uncle Lew first, for the latest explanations of the bombing and American attitudes about it. Then the Internet freezes up again, and I am forced to log off.

I have spent so long reading e-mail that it is already time to pick up LuLu. When I get to the preschool gate, I see that her class is across the street, coming out of the university housing entrance. They have been to the library, LuLu exclaims. She is, once again, in a great mood.

We go home and eat a delicious lunch of tomato-egg soup, lima beans and peppers, chicken, and rice. Then LuLu repairs outside to the bug area. The kitchen boys come out to watch her. For the first time, I see the man who must be the chef, and I indicate to him how much I appreciate his cooking. His name is Sheh, and he's a tall, lanky, craggily handsome man in his late forties who reminds me of a weathered Gary Cooper. He is taking his smoking break after lunch by the bug area and has a cigarette dangling from the side of his mouth, Belmondo style.

LuLu is conversing with Mr. Wu today, and when he sees me, he asks me about her. I tell him the story (*Wuhuren*, etc.), and he is amazed that she is from here and that we have come all this way to see Wuhu. I feel very comfortable with Mr. Wu, and as I look at him I see why. He reminds me a lot of Ah-To, the cook in our house in Taipei. Same overall shape of face and gentle manner.

I drop Lu off and head for the Xin Bei department store. My objective is to buy knee pads for my child. And I can't stand the feeling that I'm confined to the hotel. I have to break through my anxiety now or we will never go anywhere.

I start out walking, but as I am the only Westerner on the streets, I chicken out and jump in a taxi. It stops near LuLu's bridge, and I climb over the rubble and amble inside. I have noticed that, in China, the entrances to stores are rarely imposing. Often a store looks grungy from the outside, only to reveal quite a wonderful place within. I think the Chinese like an element of mystery to things. The idea that a plain shell will open to reveal something opulent amuses them. Perhaps it is that way with the Wuhu orphanage.

Xin Bei is quite nice inside. The first thing I see is an ice-cream freezer with ice-cream cones for sale—wait until LuLu hears about this. Flavors are green, pink, and brown. No names are pictured; you pick by color. They also have fast food here: barbecued chicken, a leg and thigh on a stick.

The store is very well stocked. On the first floor are cosmetics and groceries. On the second are appliances—washer/dryers, refrigerators, air conditioners, TVs, VCRs, radios, and cameras. On the third is women's wear—mainly blouses, skirts, and some pants—and menswear—suits and shirts. There is no casual wear for adults, only cheaper-quality suits and skirts. On the fourth floor, the children's department contains three tiny amusement park rides and an indoor playground. The upper floors smell faintly of DDT.

So, you can leave your child and go shop, as at Ikea. Adjacent to the indoor playground, two giant toadlike vehicles sit silently. They measure about four feet by four feet and are black and shiny. It turns out that they are huge video-game pods for total immersion.

The furniture they sell here seems faintly 1940-ish, heavy-wood, low-to-the-ground sofas and chairs, also kind of podlike. In bedding, they do not sell box springs. Mattresses sit on wooden platform beds, with tops that lift up for storage. Some of the bedroom sets—bed frame, armoire, and dressing table—are decidedly Deco, crafted in light, delicate woods.

The furniture and home furnishings department is tiny. My impression is that interior decor is not a reality in China yet, just a taste that will someday become a mass craving. They have some window blinds with tiny roses printed all over them, which I like very much.

I ride down the escalator, noting that no one seems to care much that I am here, which relieves me. I cross the street, where an enormous, yawning rubble pit stands between me and the other department store in Wuhu. This one is called Insu. You have to tightrope-walk along a narrow ledge to get to the doorway, and if you lose your balance, you fall in the pit—jagged rocks, garbage, and instant tetanus.

As I'm doing the tightrope act, I notice that the fronts of the buildings across the pit, opposite Insu, have been sliced away. Exposed electrical wiring dangles in the breeze. I don't think I'll come shopping when it rains.

Although Insu is less modern than Xin Bei and doesn't have escalators, it, too, has an indoor playground, and the little-girls' dress department is equally inviting. One item of everything they have is pinned up on the wall for display, just as in Shanghai. The way it works is, you look at the wall first to decide what you want, then look for the size.

When you buy something, you leave the item with the salesgirl, who gives you a little bill for it. You take the bill to a glass booth, usually in the center of the floor, and pay the cashier inside. She gives you a receipt, which you return to the saleslady, who presents you with a wrapped package. It is not that dissimilar from payment procedure at the hospital.

I wander back around Jing Hu Lake, which twinkles in the morning sun. At water's edge, stonemasons are at work, creating borders for future flower beds. On one bank, they are rebuilding an old pagoda-style pavilion. Anne told me that at the start of this year, one side of the lake was entirely shanties and garbage. It has all been razed and rebuilt. It's hard to believe it's the same place, she said.

Halfway home, I come to a beautiful old A-frame structure that looks very Chinese, with pagoda curls. Caroline said it is a tea-house, which means you can drink tea there but you can't buy any. Tea leaves are sold in shops that also sell nuts and seeds, the preferred snack food here. There are different grades to both tea and rice, and the top grades cost as much as a thousand dollars per pound.

I'm beginning to feel more relaxed after my foray. No one scowled at me or hissed or any of the possibilities I feared. People were perfectly friendly. I think everyone is back at work. After all, no one here wants bad relations with the United States or the West in general right now. Prosperity is just ahead, and everyone here can see its tail feathers.

LuLu is already skating when I arrive at school. She holds hands with two other girls, and with a huge smile on her heart-shaped face, she whizzes them at top speed around the court. She is beginning to fit in, and it's thrilling her.

As I watch, I try to absorb that she is from here, that this would have been her world. Given another configuration of planets, she

Tie Shan Hotel, plaza entrance.

The huge pine tree
in the hotel's plaza.

Building Two, where we stayed.

Outskirts of Wuhu, where LuLu's birth parents might live, from the train.

Building One, Reception.

LuLu investigates the bonsai nursery.

Tie Shan lake, with canary house.

Rubble on the hospital street.

A feverish LuLu and
the doctor's assistant.

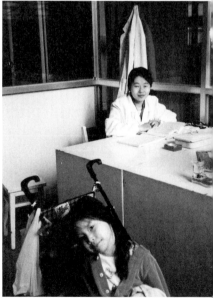

The pharmacist makes
up LuLu's shot.

LuLu greets the security guard at Anhui Normal University Kindergarten.

LuLu in the school playground.

The new building, with feng shui mirror.

LuLu's classroom at naptime.

Skating after school with friends.

LuLu with Yu Jie, the principal.

LuLu playing makeup with JingJing, the attendant.

JiaJia, whom LuLu called her "Chinese mother."

TohToh, whom LuLu called her "Chinese father."

Chatting with Mr. Tchang, Mr. Tong, and the chef.

LuLu and "GuhGuh" ("older brother"), whom I didn't meet until we were leaving.

LuLu and her kitchen pals.

Wuhu's Jing Hu (Mirror) Lake.

Mediterranean side of the lake.

Insu Department Store, Disneyesque architecture, rubble, and Xin Bei (at far left).

Qing Yi Jiang Canal, with houseboats.

Caroline approaches the gate of the Wuhu Children's Institute.

Qing Yi Jiang Canal Police Substation, where LuLu was found.

The police are thrilled to see LuLu.

Surreal grounds of the Hefei Orphanage.

Special needs children under the plaster mushrooms.

The lovely interior court.

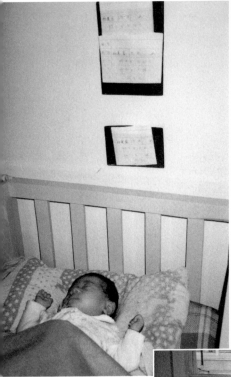

Newborn in nursery, with the date she was born and found written on cards above her crib.

LuLu lined up the babies to pose.

Mom and LuLu pose on humpback bridge at Jing Hu Lake.

would have been going to this school all the time, picked up at lunchtime by her *nai nai* (grandmother).

I look closely at the other children. They are sparkly-eyed, full of energy and impishness, as she is, but she doesn't resemble any of them. None of them look like any of the other Wuhu girls we know, either.

I'm impressed at how much better all the kids are at skating now than they were just a few days ago. Few fall down now, but even when they were falling down, they never cried. They are all still wearing heavy sweaters despite the fact it must be 80 degrees. But suddenly, as the skating heats up, they begin to peel off their layers until they're down to their heavy woolen undershirts.

On the way home, LuLu tells me that during the afternoon, one boy pulled her ear and another pushed her. I hope this is boy stuff and not politics, but how can I know?

On the news this evening, emotions are dying down. The top story, aimed at the American business community, stresses that it is safe to do business again. The only ominous note is sounded by a Chinese scientist, who declares that an outdated map of Belgrade cannot possibly have led to the bombing, that such an "explanation" is pretty lame. Who could disagree?

But I think the Chinese would be surprised at how lame some of these strategic planners actually are. NATO troops were working together for the first time in years. The whole incident could have been the result of ineptitude.

During the commercial, I find myself praying, Please God, let it blow over. Please God. As the tension is easing, I realize how nervous I actually have been. It was pretty scary how quickly the universities erupted into riots after the president told them to— unquestioning, on a dime.

The commercial is for Sleeping Tiger lozenges. Mao was not only right about China being a sleeping tiger, he was also an astounding poet. Modern Chinese have taken his phrases and sayings and turned them right into successful advertising.

May 14
Sunny

It is very hot. LuLu and I begin the day by skating together around the hotel grounds. A truckload of sweepers arrives with big sunhats and funny-shaped raffia brooms. They get off the truck and fan out over the hotel grounds, their job to sweep the fallen leaves from every corner of the seven hectares of land and walkways. Along with their sunhats, they wear aprons and long gloves. Their brooms create a soft, scratchy sound as they sweep away the stray leaves and stems and petals.

There is a lot of activity in the plaza. Carloads of policemen are here. Perhaps a dignitary is coming. Last night on the news, I recognized a German man whom I had seen at breakfast in the hotel. Wuhu, it seems, has its own TV station, and the German is probably affiliated with one of those German factories we saw in the new urban area.

We have a simple lunch of hot-sour soup, which is way too pungent for both of us. Then I put Lu to sleep reading *Stuart Little,* which seems the perfect book for China, perhaps because of its combination of sweetness and formality.

In the afternoon, we skate some more by the lake, and I examine the scholar's rock more closely. It is sitting on a stone table. This LuLu dubs, as she has the huge wooden duplicate in our building lobby, a "Godzilla."

The scholar's rock is placed across from the old moon gate I love so much, and LuLu decides to investigate it. Before I can stop her, she skates down the ramp to it and raises the door latch. I reach her as the gate swings open, and we enter together to find a bonsai nursery.

Of course, there are bonsai trees in the main plaza, but it never occurred to me that they would be nurtured on the premises. The nursery is ancient and rustic, the walls and woodsheds and wooden benches green with moss and ivy. It looks just like an English nursery on a Yorkshire estate, except for the pots and pots of bonsai.

Each of the tiny trees that I see here takes twenty to fifty years to form. Bonsai are not, as many people think, trees bred in miniature. They are actually small bits of trees that are wired up and twisted and made to grow in tree shape. A bonsai is a sort of living poem or trompe l'oeil.

Chained in a corner of the nursery is, amazingly enough, a dog! A German shepherd! LuLu rushes toward him and he growls fiercely. She backs away resignedly. She is aching for an animal squeeze.

As the bonsai gardener is nowhere in sight, we relatch the gate and skate back up the little ramp that led us here, back to the lakeside.

For dinner, we buy potato chips and Oreo cookies at the store by reception. We are both having terrific junk-food cravings. We've eaten no sugar or fat for almost a month. As I'm looking around at the other things they sell, teapots, round antispirit mirrors on pedestals, pens, I see the maps. Jeanine has e-mailed me that Francesca has not received the map of Wuhu that we sent the week we arrived. Suddenly, I realize that I have sent maps of Wuhu back to the United States. If the post office is opening our mail, then sending back maps, what with the bombing, will definitely look suspicious. Funny, how the most innocuous things inevitably become suspect in a totalitarian state.

When I visited South Africa in 1984 to do research on totalitarian states for a novel, I inadvertently did my own laundry in the washing machine at the home where I was staying. It was instantly considered a political statement and caused a crisis with everyone from the maids to the madam. I never really convinced anyone that I just wanted to do my wash.

I am growing to love Chinese television. It is as sophisticated technologically as American TV. The commercials are just as inventive, with as many special effects. The shows are well shot, well edited, and well paced. But ultimately, because they do not rely on sex or violence for viewership, the shows are better plotted and more creative. And the anchors and actors are not, as all American TV people are, afraid to use and wear red.

Here's what was on the six channels one Tuesday as I flipped around from nine A.M. to noon: a cooking show, a TV hospital explaining different ailments and what can be done for them, the news, a movie, stock quotes from Shenzen (one of the free economic areas), an English lesson, MTV-type music videos but without the bikinis, a game of go laid out on the screen with two masters playing, documentaries about China, a children's show called *Do Re Mi,* soaps (one that takes place in ancient China and one that takes place in modern Shanghai), a Chinese opera performance, a game show, the doings of the president of China, a basketball game (the Lakers vs. the Spurs, actually), soccer, ice skating, philosophers philosophizing at the camera, and lessons in Chinese painting.

Channel 8, where I saw the German man staying at our hotel, is Anhui TV and concerns the entire province, not just Wuhu, as I had thought. That was a special on Wuhu.

Channel 6 is the movie channel, and so far we've seen a wealth of films, from World War II action to an Olympic skating movie from the 1950s, featuring Chinese skaters dressed like Sonja Henie. One forgets that up until 1949–50, American and Chinese life was similarly sophisticated, so their movies from that period look identical to ours. It's not all Pearl Buck and Mao jackets in Chinese history.

The children's programming is high quality. There are two shows, *Do Re Mi* and *Da Feng Che* (*Big Mouth Crocodile*). Both contain animated cartoons, game shows, some live people doing things, and some sitcom. LuLu's favorite is *Da Feng Che.* The core

of it is a game show called *Big Mouth Crocodile*. Children must do physical tasks like hopping on one foot fast from one side of the stage to another, while carrying an egg on a spoon. If they drop the egg, they must stand in the mouth of the crocodile, which is made of papier-mâché but closes over their heads.

From bits of the game show, they cut away to episodic cartoons, serials that leave you hanging at the end and eager for the following day's installment. LuLu's favorite of those is *Danny Danyao,* about a dog living in Spain at the time of the Spanish Inquisition. Danny is in love with Julia, another dog. A band of mean dogs in ruffs kidnapped Julia in one episode, and it ended when Danny threw open the door of Julia's room and found her gone. He let out the most heartrending howl of *"Juuuuuuuliaaa,"* and that was the end. LuLu was riveted. She couldn't wait for it to come on again.

There is also a sitcom on the same show that takes place in a fantasy modern Shanghai apartment and features three kids around the age of nine, two boys and a girl. They play together after school. More and more, I think, China today is very much as it was in 1955, as if the country has taken up more or less where it left off when Mao and communism took over.

The commercials are much more elaborately colored, and the Chinese like to pile on the effects, the more the better. For a children's product like long-life milk, the ad will rain multicolored confetti, and three goats will change into butterflies, and a princess will appear in a golden dress all in the same minute.

Aside from food, advertisements appear for tai chi lessons, Chinese-language lessons for Western children, instant fishing rods and reels (which actually feature a Western guy with an 800 number), and a computer factory. This would seem to indicate that at the moment, Westerners are doing the buying off TV, although many Chinese people do have TVs.

Tonight on *Danny Danyao,* Julia escapes the mean dogs and runs for it. Then the sitcom pops on. The two boys are playing in

the apartment, which is lightly furnished with a modern sofa and chairs rather like the ones they have at Xin Bei. The little girl comes home from school, and the boys invite her up to play. The kids are running around, playing what seems to be a war game. One of the boys throws a ball at the little girl, and it hits her in the chest. She slumps to the floor.

"What's going on?" LuLu asks me urgently.

"I don't know. She got hurt," I say. The child is not moving, and the little boys are getting really upset.

"She's not dead, is she?" LuLu asks. Her eyes are as wide as saucers; mine, too. The mother comes in, screams, and runs for the phone. We will have to watch tomorrow to see what has happened.

"Wow," says LuLu. Far from being upset, she is excited by the drama. Mostly, children's TV here is colorful, funny, physical, and festive, but there is stark reality, too, and it takes the two of us—bred on Disney warlike bombast or smiley faces—refreshingly by surprise.

The news comes on and the evil American aspect of the bombing is, thank God, no longer the top story. Top is a report on the postbombing woes of American companies here. No one is eating at Kentucky Gi (Kentucky Fried Chicken) in Shanghai. Production has slowed in factories. Clearly the business community has weighed in.

An American businessman, the head of a company based in Shanghai, is interviewed and talks about the horror of the bombing; in particular, he brings up the father's terrible grief and how awful it was to see. The businessman's face crumples up as he talks about it, and he apologizes for the anguish the deaths have caused. I wonder if America saw that clip of the father crying. It was terribly affecting.

There is also a story about the refugees in Kosovo, with the implication that NATO is bombing them as they flee. And still no mention of ethnic cleansing.

After the news, I settle down for my favorite program, *Around China*. It has helped keep me sane these last weeks. Tonight it is about the one man who, it transpires, makes all the stone lion heads in southern and northern China. And that's a lot of lion heads. All, it says, have the same face, the lion face from the Peking Opera.

May 15
Muggy

I wake wondering what's going on with Leo and whether we will get into the orphanage now that the political tension is easing.

There's a business conference at the hotel. Lots of cars and people are milling about in the courtyard. I notice, for the first time, that two stone lions flank our building doors, and I examine their faces with new interest.

There are plants now in front of our building, too, a line of little ferny trees in porcelain pots. The Chinese use this sort of display often in front of houses or buildings, instead of flower beds. Since we have seen the bonsai nursery, I walk LuLu over to the line of bonsai trees in porcelain pots on the opposite side of the plaza. They are arranged before a huge poem in calligraphic lettering, exhorting the hotel workers to do a good job for guests. Above that is a red map of the hotel grounds and little Tie Shan mountain.

We go up to the Canting and there is a long line of people getting breakfast. I fear it will take ages to eat, but they swoop down on the food, eat at top speed, and vanish. It's startling how fast they eat, faster than Americans.

I always eat the same thing: two duck eggs and weak coffee with sugar. LuLu heaps her plate with dumplings, rice, and vegetables and drinks a warm glass of powdered milk. It amazes me that here she will eat all offered vegetables but at home I cannot get her to eat any. Well, the vegetables here are wonderfully sweet.

In the mornings now, as summer comes, the sun filters in through the side glass doors of the restaurant, and the hotel is filling up and bustling. At breakfast we see the new guests. Once in a while, there's a Western or foreign businessman, but most are groups of Chinese businesspeople with cell phones clapped to their ears and briefcases at their sides.

To breakfast, LuLu often brings the humor book she was given on our first day at the Canting. She carries it about with her like a totem. She also sometimes brings Ellie, her elephant.

As the bombing paranoia has waned, I have been thinking about trying to eat elsewhere occasionally, but I'd have to study my Chinese. In a regular restaurant, I would have to be fluent and comfortable, so as not to make Lu nervous.

Equally important, though, LuLu looks forward to seeing her friends here now, and I don't think she cares about eating anywhere else. For her, I think, the hotel and its employees have come to feel like a huge Chinese family, and she is loving that so much.

I realize, as I watch her disappear into the kitchen with JingJing, that the bombing that has more or less trapped us within the hotel grounds has inadvertently turned our trip here into something more important than a fact-finding mission. It has allowed LuLu to really get to know the young people who work here. And now, in her customary manner, she is taking that exploration to the nth degree.

I knew LuLu would lead me to the place where she needed to go in Wuhu, and she is there, in the kitchen or out with the attendants in the hall, or at a playground, or on the concrete skate court surrounded by lots of laughing fellow citizens.

And where am I right now? Frayed at the edges, to be sure, but at least I'm over my terror and coming down slowly. LuLu is in no danger here at all, I see, which has calmed me greatly. On the contrary, out on the streets of town, LuLu is *my* protection, not the other way around. By virtue of being the mother of someone Chinese, I am allowed to pass almost unnoticed.

And as LuLu becomes more accepted and involved with the young people here, in school and at the hotel, she is, in fact, moving over to them. I see her sometimes look back at me, surreptitiously, over her shoulder, wondering who I really am to her and what it means to have me, the Caucasian foreigner, as her mother.

It is scary, but I'm not pulling her back to me. I am going with my deepest instinct that she and we will benefit so much if I let her go free. So I'm releasing her to have her experiences without my hovering over her. I let her go wherever she wants to: the kitchen, the hall, by herself with her Chinese friends, as little as she is. I consider the private experiences she is having here as memories that were stolen from her memory bank as an infant. She needs new Chinese experiences, I think, to fill the empty places up. I have to trust that when she is full up, she will come back to me.

As for JingJing the waitress; and Wei Wei, JingJing, and Ling-Ling, the attendants; and TohToh and Tao Liang; and the kitchen boys: they all seem to have fallen quite in love with her. Is there perhaps ten thousand years of little-sister love in their genes that has been stifled, too, by the one-child policy? Or are they simply mesmerized by her fearlessness in liking them for who they are? They cannot seem to get enough of her.

And, of course, her obvious fondness for them is all the more meaningful because they know better than she where she came from. Sometimes I can see it in their eyes: they simply can't believe that a child with such power over them came out of the Wuhu orphanage. I can see that sometimes, when she hugs them or makes them laugh; they are as moved by her as I am.

After breakfast, I find LuLu in the bug area and she insists we play a new game called Captain Hook, where I tie her up and restrain her. I suggest instead that I make her walk the plank—the plank being the end of the stone-stair banister. She loves this idea, and we do it again and again, with me playing the part of the evil Hook.

It's clear she is working on the orphanage experience, which, while having scared her in some ways, has also brought her a new calm in discussing the subject of her lost first parents.

When we return to our floor, she runs to LingLing, who is on duty, and they instantly start playing. I leave the door open and hear her telling LingLing her English and Chinese names (LuLu and LuLu Romano Prager).

Later, when she comes in for a rest, she says, "When my parents left me at the institute, we don't know what happened to them. You came and got me, and you are my new mother."

"Yes, that's right," I reply.

She is very happy about this, and I think she has it clearly in her mind now. She is talking about her adoption now with the same sense of triumph she gets when she has really learned and understood something.

At lunch, a funny thing happens. We are eating when one of the waitresses walks across the dining room to a table near us. In her hand she is holding a live bullfrog. Yes, her hand covering its back in a special bullfrog hold, she displays it to the couple at the table. They nod in approval. All the waitresses around us shudder and make "ew" and "ick" sounds, so evidently the frog is not to everyone's taste. But it is considered a delicacy.

LuLu is roaring with laughter. She can't get over it and rushes into the kitchen after the waitress. The frog comes back fricassee, not whole, thank God. I am definitely not into amphibians.

After school, I pick up Lu and we go into the university. Anne has invited us for dinner. In front of the foreign visitors' guest house, we run into Kay and her husband, Max, and their friend Lon, a Chinese graduate student.

Lu immediately starts teasing Lon and getting him to play with her. He tells me, as he picks her up and carries her around, that his sister was the first person ever to adopt a child in Anhui Province. She adopted a baby from Wuhu. She and her husband live now in New Jersey, he says. But it was she who began the entire process that led to so many foreign adoptions. "Tell her thank you," I say, meaning it.

Max tells me he is a sinophile. He and Kay have been in China for eight years now. He has the energy of a good teacher, but he says he does not speak Chinese, which strikes me as peculiar. He also tells me that university students have access to CNN on the Web but have made no effort to look at it during the crisis.

Anne is having Stove Top stuffing and chicken, which seems particularly incongruous here. Her Chinese cook, a middle-aged woman who is very sweet and obliging, makes it and serves it. When she returns to the kitchen, Anne mentions that the cook has assured her of her friendship despite the crisis.

Alexandra, a beautiful Chinese girl of about twenty, with an energetic personality and a great sense of humor, is dining with us. A third-year student of Anne's, she wears her hair in a Dorothy Hamill cut and speaks perfect English, even though she has never traveled out of China. She has, however, been to Beijing as part of a conference of English-speaking students. Anne tells me this, and it is clear that to be invited to Beijing is a huge honor for a student. Alexandra hopes to go to a college in Beijing, which is the equivalent of the Ivy League in America.

Alexandra wants to be a teacher, but I suggest that she become a news anchor on TV because she speaks so well and is so pretty. This she has not contemplated, and her reaction makes it obvious that news anchoring is a job open only to those of exceedingly high place in the society. But also, it has simply never occurred to her. She laughs when I say it, and her smile is so wide that it makes her eyes close.

After dinner, Anne takes us to her classroom. We walk across the campus, which has some nice grassy areas but has a worn look of neglect. This university is not rich.

We follow little paths across the greenery to the main part of the campus, which contains two enormous basketball courts in which about a hundred boys are playing basketball. It is crowded in there.

The building where Anne teaches is concrete and looks unfinished inside. As we walk in, it is twilight and the building is very dimly lit. Then I find to my amazement that there is no lighting in the halls at all. No fixtures, nothing.

In spite of this, there are students in the classrooms, studying and watching TV. In these rooms there is some lighting, but it is incredibly weak.

Some of Anne's students come to the door to greet her. Others rise politely to greet us and make much of LuLu. Anne asks me if I would teach a class in the weeks to come, and I'm flattered and excited at the prospect. Should I teach humor writing or what? I have to think.

Anne takes us back across campus and shows us how to get from her classroom to the gate on our street, and she walks us up to the hotel, since she has never gotten a good look at it before. She stays, she says, mainly on the campus, not needing to venture out much. I think she is also a bit shy.

May 16–17
Rain

On our way out to breakfast, we discover that JingJing has opened a door in the stairwell between the first and second floors; this leads to a secret stairway that takes us almost to the dining hall without getting wet. We must then walk along a covered balcony and up a set of inside stairs to get there.

On the way, we discover an enormous spider's web, about two feet by two feet. Since we are now reading *Charlotte's Web,* and

LuLu is so interested in bugs, this is a major find. We stop and admire the web for a long time, charting how it was woven, and find to our surprise that the spider that crafted it is actually quite small.

The nice father is breakfasting today. We say hello and sit down to our usual fare, after which LuLu goes off to play in the kitchen. While she's away, I think about the bombing and my position here as an American, and how it has allowed me to experience a little of what LuLu must experience a lot—being a person of another race, with whatever baggage that entails.

So far, I have forced myself to be as calm as possible, to try to be an ambassador of peace, so at least people are left with an image of Americans that counteracts the one they are getting on TV.

But the day-to-day self-consciousness is pretty daunting. Not only do I stick out here as a Caucasian, I am also the citizen of a nation that is being vilified daily and publicly in the Chinese media. The only other time I came close to this experience was in South Africa, where my book was banned.

I was journeying there to do research for a book I was writing about Nazism. At that time, South Africa was a totalitarian country with slavery based on race policy, the closest living organism to the Nazi state.

As it happened, my book of short stories had just been published there and been banned. My publishing company decided I should go on the book tour anyway, and eager to see what this bizarre state of affairs would yield, I agreed and was taken around to bookstores.

In Pretoria, the Afrikaner bastion, my escort took me to meet a bookshop owner who was a fan. My book was not on the shelves, of course, but the bookshop owner showed me the *Index of Objectionable Literature,* a huge printed tome in which my book, *A Visit from the Footbinder,* was listed under Section 47A, "Danger to Public Decency and Morals." I took a photo of the page, which I display proudly in my office to this day.

I was then driven to my publishing company there. I stood in the office, saying hello to people who scurried by and never replied. After a while, I realized that no one would look me in the face. Finally, a woman was dragged over. Grumpily, she muttered a short hello and then turned her back. I had been banned, which meant that no one could risk acknowledging me. It was very weird.

We go back to the room the new way, past the giant web. LuLu immediately goes out to work with JingJing and the housekeepers on all the floors. I have given her one rule: she may never enter a room without JingJing or LingLing with her.

Presently, she returns with a little fluffy cat, a toy that JingJing has given her. We watch *Da Feng Che* and find that the little girl did die from being hit in the chest with the ball. I strain to understand the point, but I can't get it. But there she is, with angel wings now, supposedly up in heaven. The parents, hers and the boys', are crying in the boys' living room, leaving LuLu and me amazed.

May 18
Rain

In the morning, LuLu again plays with JingJing and the housekeepers. I tell them to send her home if they need to, but they seem eager to have her.

She comes back later with makeup on, including the red dot in between her eyes, similar to the dot East Indians wear, that here connotes beauty. The Chinese put it on children. LuLu is wearing that red dot on one of her Chinese adoption photos, one that they gave me when I got to China in 1994. I remember when I first saw that photo, I was dumbstruck: she looked exactly like my mother when she was young.

In the evening, there's another wedding, so we walk down to

the bakery and get dinner. Watermelon (*xigua*) sellers are in from the country, and we buy ourselves a big watermelon in front of the entrance to university housing. LuLu also samples one of the pancakes made by the pancake seller. It is very good and sweet, like a Swedish crepe.

As we walk along, a dad pulling a child on a tricycle happens by. LuLu stops to play with the child, and the dad calls her "LuLu." He asks me a bit about her and I tell him the story, even though he has obviously heard it from someone else. We are getting to be known, and it pleases LuLu.

As we reach the vase-shaped entrance to Tie Shan Park, we hear the sounds of Chinese opera and Chinese orchestral instruments. It is so lovely to be looking at this ancient gate and hearing the ancient music wafting out. We must try to see a performance. Alexandra says that the park has a zoo on top of the little mountain.

Back in the room, we eat tons of delicious melon, starved as we are for fruit. After the news, which is still quiet, I find a program that is hosted by Barbara Walters Wong, a roundtable discussion. Tonight it's about the bombing. The panelists are several Chinese scholars versus a man who is from the UN refugee commission.

Basically, the scholars are dubious that the bombing was an accident and give their reasons why. Then Barbara asks the UN man why we would bomb at all, and the man squirms and mutters that it has to do with what people call "ethnic cleansing." He does not explain further, and it is clear from the way he says it that he has been warned not to discuss it in detail and has taken a bit of a risk squeezing it out of himself to begin with. I'm left wondering why the Chinese want to present us as aggressors—and why we want to present them as a people to be feared.

May 19
Rain

Some sort of storm is raging outside, but I'm determined today to find a good view of the Yangtze River. Wuhu is the fourth largest port on the Yangtze, yet you'd never know this is a river town at all. Surely there must be some café or hotel on the river. We are getting in a cab and going to find it.

First, I ask at reception this time for some postcards of our hotel and discover that they don't know what a postcard is. I resolve to take some pictures of the hotel and show them.

Then I dart into the computer room while Lu plays with Toh-Toh. I'm still trying to catch up on my e-mail. The Chinese are growing curious about the amount of time I spend e-mailing, since initially I told them I might need ten minutes once in a while, tops. Because of the bombing, and all the mail I'm getting, I'm spending an hour a day, at least.

Later, LuLu and I pop into a cab, and I tell the driver to take us to the Yangtze River. After driving a ways, he stops before a long, low wall. There is a small opening in it, and I tell him to wait and Lu and I hop out.

A grim industrial scene confronts us—a filthy, iron-and-garbage-littered shred of riverbank with an old crane stuck in the mud-filled water. Overhead, the sky is low and yellow. There's got to be a better view than this.

A clerk at the reception area has told me that the "autoport" (the terminal for the car ferry to Hefei) would be a good place to see the river, so I tell the driver. He drives us a bit farther, then says we have to walk and points. The street to the ferry is one-way, the wrong way for cars, so we get out and start walking through another old high-rise neighborhood. We pass a dry-cleaning establishment that is half out into the street. Everything is outside—the clothes hanging in plastic bags, the man pressing with a mangle—but otherwise the cleaner's is exactly like any of the American counterpart.

We never get to the autoport because LuLu can't make it. It is much farther than it looks. We manage to get a taxi coming the other way and return to the hotel. In the cab, Lu says suddenly, "We should go live at the institute, because that's where I was born."

This takes me by surprise. But I seize the opportunity to ask, "Did you like it there?"

"Yes," she says happily. "Yes."

I wonder at this moment whether I should tell her the truth: that she was brought to the institute from the bridge by the police and not by her parents. Now that we are here, I can no longer in good conscience ameliorate the story. I don't know what to do, so I do nothing, which I will live to regret.

As we drive back and pass an old moon gate in a piece of wall that, for some reason, has been left standing while all around it has been torn down, Lu tells me how much she likes that kind of door. The ancient Chinese beauty really appeals to her.

TohToh's on duty when we get back, and LuLu runs up and hugs him and kisses his hand. I have never seen her so affection-ate with people at home, although she has always been a hand kisser, especially when she is particularly happy with someone for some reason. But here she does it frequently, and it has a tremen-dous effect on these young people. I don't think they are kissed and hugged all that much.

As we leave TohToh, she tells me, "He's my father and Mr. Tong is my uncle. And you are my special mama." And she kisses me on the hand. She seems very, very serene.

While I wash clothes, LuLu goes off to play with LingLing, who is on duty. LuLu phones me from the third floor to say hello and tell me where she is.

While she's out, I watch a documentary on python hunting in the Cameroons. Here's how it's done: the hunter puts his wrapped leg and foot down into a hole that leads to the snake's nest. The snake bites onto his foot and he pulls out his leg and cuts off the snake's head. There's a summer job.

There's a lot about Africa on TV here. I remember when I went to Zambia in 1973, I went on a boat down the Zambezi River with ten Chinese Communist ministers. It was just after Zambian independence, and the ministers and I were the only tourists in the country. We went everywhere together. They drank Coca-Cola and took tons of pictures. We Americans had very little presence in Africa then. The Chinese have always had an interest there. They worked on the trans-African railroad in the 1970s.

At lunch, LuLu is wild. She plays some with the Zimbabwean guy, who tells me he is on the road six months of the year and misses his daughter. Then she rushes off and takes Mr. Tong's keys. He doesn't seem to mind at all and thinks she's funny. It's phenomenal how tolerant everyone is of children in China. They just don't expect them to be adults.

We eat beef with hot green peppers, bean curd, and pork shreds soup and, of course, the superior rice. Wuhu food can be very spicy. After lunch, I come out and there's a big crowd in the bug area. Watching LuLu has become a pastime, and she's enjoying the attention a lot and kisses everyone's hands and hugs them. There is something so profound about her joy that I can't bring myself to limit her affection, even though I can see that the managers with children are wondering about her openness.

Mr. Wu, who speaks a little English, indicates that maybe she's too affectionate. I think he is embarrassed when she kisses people's hands because it looks and feels too supplicating. And I know what he means, but it comes from a pure impulse in her. To her, it means that she likes you a lot, not that she's your servant. And it is perhaps more noticeable in a culture in which overt displays of affection are rare. That the freeze caused by the bombing is background to this extraordinary, spontaneous warmth makes the feelings she elicits all the more complex.

When we return to our room, she asks me to play Captain Hook, and I tie her hands with a scarf and she escapes again and again. She is working hard to put it all together in her little mind.

In the evening, Neke calls. I tell him things are getting back to normal, which I think, thank God, they are. As long as the Chinese government doesn't insist on a cogent explanation of the bombing, everything may turn out all right. LuLu chats with him, and when she hangs up, she cries because she misses him so much.

Around China, this evening, is about the "Ballet Madams of Wuhan." This is a ballet class for women over thirty-five that enables them "to regain the privilege of being a woman," as the report puts it. Middle-aged women abroad, it continues, prefer taking ballet to going to gyms. "At our age," says one woman, a breast cancer doctor, "we are no longer so beautiful. We now want to possess our elegant quality instead of our beauty." Nicely put. I will remember that.

May 20
Rain

I decide we will go to the exercise room, which is located, according to the sign in the main plaza, in Building Six, the luxury building.

We walk over to the lake in our raincoats and take the steep road past the nursery up to the building, where, we discover, Tao Liang is the doorman. He and LuLu are delighted to see one another, and she chats with him while I look for the exercise room.

Building Six is rather fancy. It has a nice, shiny wood reception desk, with clocks telling the time in Hong Kong, New York, Sydney, and Singapore. It has been recently renovated. The exercise room is not open yet. We have to wait for half an hour.

I take Lu and we go down a path from Building Six to the lake to explore. We are on the side opposite the nursery, standing on the red-pillared walkway, near the viewing pavilion. The first thing we find is another giant web about two feet by two feet, strung between two bamboo trees in a giant X. It's astonishing to see webs this big. LuLu examines the new one for a long time.

We discover several new paths and take one that leads us into the pavilion. We sit there for a while, gazing at the lake. The landscaping, Alexandra said, is modeled on that of a famous imperial garden in Beijing.

We pad gingerly around the narrow stone edge of the lake, back over to the other side, where LuLu opens the moon gate to reexamine the bonsai nursery. A lady, perhaps the gardener's wife, is arranging roses in the potting shed. The dog is asleep.

It is interesting how a Chinese garden has so many secret paths, just as a Chinese box has so many drawers to open, with only one that actually leads to the prize. I hadn't realized how much the Chinese like secrets. Perhaps that is one reason they are puzzled by our desire for information about the girls.

The exercise room is open when we return, and I discover that it contains a lightweight kind of Nautilus equipment, most of it broken. There is a small running machine, which the reception clerk helps us with, although she cautions LuLu against using it. "Too fast," she says, which turns out to be the understatement of the year.

Lu and I do some stretching and some free weights together, and then something possesses me and I hop on the running machine. I turn it on, and it's so out of control that my foot is pulled into the mechanism. I fall and somehow at the last possible moment before my entire foot vanishes, I manage to switch it off.

Oh God, I pray as I sink to the floor in agony, don't let my foot be broken. LuLu runs over, concerned. I can barely speak, I am in so much pain. "Sweetie," I manage, "go get the lady. I'm hurt."

LuLu runs out and returns immediately with the reception clerk, and I call, "Ice, ice." As she runs out, I hope I've been understood.

I am cringing in a corner. I have removed my sock and seen that there is a mangled bit around the toes. The top of the foot is black already and swelling.

The clerk returns, God bless her, with ice. As I apply it to my foot, I recall how when LuLu was a baby and would fall, she would always call out, "Ice! Ice!" It was really funny.

Actually, I'm trying not to cry. My luck has been so bad on this trip that I can't believe it.

I sit there, my foot immersed in ice, for about fifteen minutes, during which time I resolve to keep away from any Chinese imitations of Western luxury. What the Chinese do better than anyone are the basic things of life—food, dealing with children, gardening, friendliness, tailoring, and anything to do with humanity and labor. We do well with the labor-saving luxuries.

Three young women show up to accompany me to the hospital, all genuinely interested in me and my condition. I indicate I need only one, and one assists me down to the main plaza, where I decide to visit the Tie Shan doctor on the premises. I can walk okay; it just hurts.

The doctor's office is in the reception building. The doctor is an imposing woman in her late forties who wears a white coat over her dress, and her graying hair in a French twist. She bathes my foot and applies a poultice and a bandage, and cautions me to wear sneakers next time I use the running machine. I advise her that the machine is dangerous, that it runs too fast, and that the hotel should get rid of it before others get hurt. But the party line is already set: it was my fault. I'm about to say, "Listen, I know running machines better than you," but I see I can't win. I accept blame. The doctor tells me to return the next day and get a new bandage. The hotel pays for me.

LuLu and I take a long nap, after which I e-mail Neke about my foot and LuLu plays with TohToh. We go back to the room and eat chips for dinner and watch the news. Topping the broadcast is a report on the Three Gorges Dam, a controversial project that is supposed to prevent excessive flooding of the Yangtze River but will also submerge some of China's most beautiful scenery. They have made progress on the dam and have relocated an entire old village into new concrete high-rises. Echoing Miss Swallow, villagers say they are glad to see the old buildings go. It seems that the original idea for the dam was Sun Yat-sen's.

May 21
Sunny but cold in the morning

On the way to school, Lu breaks away in front of reception. She runs to the lobby to see if her "Daddy" is there. She is referring to TohToh.

"I have found my Chinese father," she tells me as we walk on.

"What's his name?" I ask.

"TohToh," she replies. She takes a beat, then asks, "What were my parents' names?"

"I don't know," I reply.

"TohToh? LuLu?" she says, and laughs.

School is adorable and welcoming. The boys are tumbling over each other like baby tigers. LuLu takes my purse with her for a backpack.

While she's at school, I stroll over to Xin Bei. It's not open yet, so I stand on LuLu's bridge and take a good look at the pagoda, which I now realize is many-tiered and imposing. I look down at the area beneath the bridge and see a market I hadn't noticed before. I'm nervous about going through it alone, however. It looks densely populated, and I'll be the only Westerner. Given the current political climate, I have no idea how I will be treated. But I decide to press on anyway: I climb down the side of the bridge, traverse some rubble, and there I am.

Looking around, I realize this must be the place Mrs. Chang wanted to take me to when we discussed getting rain boots for LuLu. The market extends as far as the eye can see—stall after stall of different items on either side of a narrow path. Overhead are tarpaulins that shield patrons from the rain. This market is clearly the major buying center for Wuhu, yet it is quite hidden beneath the bridge. As with the old *hutong* street near the orphanage, you thread yourself through it as through the eye of a needle. I squeeze past the umbrella stall, the bath towel man, the stationery man selling postcards (at last!), the hair ornament stall, the plastic slipper stall, and the purse stall. Then I turn a corner to find the underpants stall, the knitting wool stall, the kitchen towel stall, the brassiere stall. Another turn and there's the pots and pans stall, lighting and bulbs, rattan furniture, fans, air conditioners. There is also a kitchen stall, where you can buy packs of ten little Kleenex packets—a necessity, since toilet paper is never provided anywhere.

I inch along, fascinated. The hair ornament stall consumes me for a long time. LuLu has very long hair, and she is a prime candidate for the wonderful ponytail ties that they sell, very colorful and very big—a modern version of the big, boxlike hair ornaments worn in ancient times, just as it is with the clothing. I pick out ties in all colors and purchase them. Pressing on, I find the children's shoe store. There I buy bright-blue rain boots for LuLu.

As there is no end in sight, I finally turn around and walk back the way I came. Everyone has been friendly, and I breathe a sigh of relief now that I'm on my way out. The tension is over, I think.

I make a right turn and come out by the button sellers, who have a fantastic array of buttons, absolutely dazzling. I stand for at least half an hour, examining them all. I would stand longer, but there's a huge mound of garbage right opposite the stall and it reeks. This block has rubble on it, and I wonder what will become of the market after all the buildings are completed. I walk on into the knitting wool stall—wonderful bright pinks and greens and Chinese reds. A little boy of two toddles about unsteadily.

Everyone appears to be in a good mood again, including me. I hail a pedicab and am pedaled home, past the bookshops and several outdoor secondhand book stalls that have suddenly appeared.

When I get to school, LuLu is eating lunch. The school provides food for the children, just like Red Apple. Today, they have been served some sort of noodle soup with vegetables. LuLu is glowing with satisfaction.

Just as we are back and settling in for her nap, there is a knock at the door. It's JingJing and Wei Wei, the waitresses. They were worried because LuLu did not come to the Canting for lunch. They wanted to see if she was all right. They stay a while and chat, then leave Lu to her nap.

How sweet they are, these young women. They have opened themselves to LuLu as guilelessly as she has opened herself to them. In our little hotel room we have more things than they probably have in their houses: a laptop, two watches, a Walkman, tons of clothes, several thousand dollars in traveler's checks. It's embarrassing. What they have is genuine pleasure in people and life.

After school, Lu skates with her classmates. She takes the hands of different girls she does not know and they never push her away, as I have seen children do back home. "Don't do that. You're not my friend," they said to her the first day at American camp when she tried to take some girls' hands. But here, there is a different training.

I once read a book on how children are brought up in Communist China. Baby clothes, it said, are deliberately designed with buttons up the back so that when kids go to preschool, the first thing they learn is that they need their neighbor to help them do basic things like take off their coats. And the children here are always open to being joined.

The other side of that communality, I guess, is the kind of groupthink that allowed President Jiang to call the students to riot. He all but snapped his fingers and they obeyed.

At dinner, we have Beijing duck, no longer "Peking" duck. A man stops by our table and introduces himself. He is Chu Dong, from CCTV. He would like to interview me and LuLu. He is interested in our story.

I'm kind of amazed by this, but it makes perfect sense. Our trip to introduce LuLu to China, against the background of the bombing, is a great story for CCTV right now. I tell Mr. Chu about LuLu and he asks if we have visited the Welfare, as he, too, calls the Wuhu orphanage. I tell him no but we would like to. We are trying to get permission. He says he could help us get in. Could he come along and film us?

How ironic, I think, if we end up getting into the orphanage through CCTV. It's definitely a parable for the modern age, in which the media is as powerful as the politicians. I agree immediately. At this point, we need all the help we can get.

When we return to the room, Neke calls, very worried: he thinks the foot problem is LuLu's, not mine. I calm him down.

May 22
Sunny and warm

My foot hurts a lot. After breakfast I go to the doctor, who re-dresses my wounds while LuLu plays with Toh-Toh. She now calls him "Baba," which means "Father" in Chinese, and she calls him that across the plaza when she sees him.

He laughs happily at this, and I wonder what everyone thinks of her doing this. This is the very un-Chinese part of her, her comfort with complexity.

We go back to the room so I can wash out some of our things, and LuLu plays with JingJing in the hall. Our morning outing is to Tie Shan Park. We stroll down the plaza and greet the sweeper lady, who is there in her big sunhat. She gives us a merry hello. Finally, we come to the beautiful vase-shaped entrance beneath the gorgeous pagoda roof.

The doorway and wall on either side are very old. The wood of the pagoda looks like teak and is exquisitely carved. We step through the opening and discover that there are two parks here, not one.

On the right lies the Tie Shan teahouse and an old people's park. On the left are steep stone steps leading up the Tie Shan mountain to the zoo.

A woman sits on a chair just inside the doorway, near a little booth. A ticket taker tries to charge us ten yuan apiece. The woman on the chair demurs and tells the ticket taker who we are. We end up paying four yuan for two.

I feel really good about this. I know it's an honor to be charged Chinese prices.

We enter the Tie Shan teahouse and rock garden. Here is a stunning old teahouse, no longer open, that hangs out over the edge of a miniature pond. It is surrounded by huge, scraggily shaped rocks. There are many paths through and around the rocks and therefore many ways to view the lake and teahouse.

This is where last Sunday's opera performance was given. It must have been delightful to sit in this picturesque place and listen to Chinese music. At the moment, a pair of middle-aged lovers sit on a bench beside the teahouse, resting and holding hands.

Beyond the rocks lies a most bizarre glade of entirely leafless trees with yellowy bark. They cross one another so that they look like big Xs and probably have been trained that way. Through this alien landscape we can see some elderly people frozen in tai chi animal poses and others playing cards on round stone stools set around stone tables.

LuLu runs off to climb the rocks, and I follow her and we come upon two muddy boys, about age nine or ten, who are obviously very poor and are playing hide-and-seek.

"His toenails are dirty," LuLu says of one of them. "Where's his mother and father?"

I explain to her that he probably doesn't have much chance to wash and that his parents are working. Perhaps he's the child of the ticket taker.

She follows the boys and does what they are doing, but it makes me nervous because there are little nooks and crannies that might hide spiders or snakes. So I try to limit her explorations by pulling her away, but she is taken with the boys. And I know she is trying to grasp the concept of poverty. In her life in Manhattan, she does not see children this obviously needy.

We go back past the woman on the chair and try to climb through the left doorway, which leads to the Tie Shan zoo. But the woman on the chair grabs LuLu and wants to play with her and hug her. LuLu is good-natured about it, and when she is finally released we walk up the steep set of stairs into a forest filtered with sunlight.

As we trudge along an old stone path, a man comes up behind us. Lu turns back to look at him, and then turns to me and says, "A man is following," whereupon the man bursts into laughter.

He is a tightly muscled, slender fellow with a ready smile and dancing eyes. He says to me in Chinese, "That caught me off-guard. I expected her to speak Chinese," and he laughs again. It is a curious fact that everything this man says to me—in Chinese—I understand perfectly. I don't know why. He laughs again and chugs past us on his way.

When we reach the very top of the Tie Shan mountain, there is a pavilion from which we can view all of Wuhu. We sit for a while, just looking at this new important place in our lives. Then we choose another path and come down through the forest at a run, only to bump into some boys with a pail of fresh-caught fish, which they allow LuLu to fully investigate. We pass another small building, a museum of sorts, where the man we just met is laying out his mat. It seems he is a fortune-teller. We greet him and he points to LuLu, thumbs up.

Next to him, two women sell soft drinks. I buy a can that has a bilberry-type fruit on it for LuLu and ask directions to the zoo. Everyone points us down another stone path to a plateau and the gate into the Tie Shan zoo.

LuLu bounds inside as I am paying and immediately clambers onto a short stone wall that surrounds a pit of baboons. The ticket taker scolds her and then me, and I apologize profusely. I'm with him: I do not want her to fall in there. It is a deep pit, and contains a fetid little pool and a pueblolike dwelling for the monkeys.

But when I walk through the gate, a wave of gentleness washes over me. It's the soft coo of a thousand doves, and that lulling sound combined with the soft Anhui breeze is an extraordinary sensory experience. As if that weren't enough, before me lies a deep green grassy lawn, like an enormous flokati carpet. The other animal cages are situated on a rise behind it. Doves wander freely on it, but surprisingly, it seems pretty clean.

A huge dovecote borders the grass. We visit some other monkey cages scattered around the edge, but one of the monkeys has a chain around its neck, and LuLu and I cannot bear it.

Past the grass carpet, there is a little stone area beside a canal. People live on the water, and their windows open onto it in a Venetian way. A family of swans glides there.

The water feeds into a stone tank, where a sea lion swims. We look down at him and he casts his eyes upward. A man indicates to us that he sells fish to feed the creature, and when LuLu figures this out, we spend the next half hour nourishing him. Feeding an animal is one of my daughter's greatest pleasures. I will never forget my red-suited baby surrounded by reindeer in Lapland as she scattered their lichen around the corral.

Behind the fish seller, up some more stone stairs, there's a python cage fronted by glass and some rather vocal roosters.

For ages, it seems, we sit on the grassy plateau, lulled by the cooing of the doves. It's like a dowdy Shangri-la. A fellow zoo goer sits down by us and shares her dove food with LuLu, who spends another hour going about her feeding duties.

Bored, I wander back to the baboon pit, and stare at the pueblo monkey house and the troop of about ten baboons and their babies. The babies are cannonballing into their pool, which is quite funny. Then I notice some odd scurrying and see all the rats that live in the pueblos, too. Not so amusing. Still, the monkeys don't seem to care.

Finally I drag LuLu out the gate, promising to return, and we take a stone path down the back side of the Tie Shan and happen on a Buddhist temple complex so vast that it must once have been the center of the city's religious life. I pay four yuan and take LuLu in to see the myriad huge statues of Buddha. There is also, on one side of a big temple, the steepest possible set of steps going down into the narrowest of spaces. I wonder if this has some kind of zen meaning. The complex is elaborate and, from its situation, must have been a stronghold in battles. Little Wuhu must have been a rather important religious place at one time.

We reenter the forest and wend our way downward, past a group of donkeys tethered to a tree, to ground level, where we end up on the street opposite the Bank of China. We take a pedicab back to the hotel and lunch on dumplings, then go off to Xin Bei for ice cream. LuLu has the pink color, which she says is delicious.

On our way home, I show Lu the market I found yesterday. We visit the stationery seller, and when he sees LuLu and me together, he realizes instantly what our situation is and insists upon giving us the postcards we want for free. As thoughtful as this is, it is a bit agonizing. It is clear that he doesn't sell much, and it seems wrong to take something from him. But he isn't finished with his gift: he adds to the packet a little magnet with a picture of the Wuhu girl who's a TV star. She's an actress on the historical soap on TV and a local heroine. Very pretty, she, like LuLu, is a Wuhu girl who left town and made good.

While LuLu goes from his stall to the knitting stall next door and plays with the vendor's little boy, I stand watching and remembering a shoe store I visited in Beijing in 1979.

It was full of patrons, and they all stopped short when I entered, staring at me with awe. Our tour was among the first to visit China in twenty-five years. I was probably one of the first very young Americans some of these people had ever seen.

I approached a glass case and spotted a pair of tiny black velvet slippers no bigger than six inches long, with oddly padded insoles. I pointed to them, and the patrons all giggled. The clerk took them out. When I had them in my hands I understood what they were: orthopedic shoes for women with bound feet who had had their feet unbound when the Communists took power in 1949.

This was a tremendous find, the perfect gift for my collector friend Michael! I indicated to the clerk that I wanted to buy them. He shook his head no. A woman in the crowd took a little book out of her pocket and showed me: cotton coupons, you needed cotton coupons to purchase them.

I was disappointed but resigned and had turned to leave when another woman whipped out her book of coupons, tore off the amount I needed, and thrust them at the clerk. "No," I told her. "No, no." God knew what these coupons meant to her. But she insisted. I tried to pay for some shoes for her in return, but she declined. I walked away with the slippers, mortified but vowing to write something worthy of this gift.

I collect Lu, and we stroll over to her bridge and look down. The walkway along the canal beneath runs all the way to the

s me hardly anything for her time. I love looking at her. She
tately, and I know she must have gotten her medical degree
where around the beginning of the Cultural Revolution.
minds me of Hu, my second Chinese baby-sitter.

en I came home with LuLu, I wanted a Chinese baby-sitter
Lu could continue to hear the language. I made some calls
pread the word, and finally got in touch with a woman who
Chinese baby-sitter. She recommended Yan Li.

spoke perfect English, which she had picked up during her
of study in Germany. She was a doctor of Western medicine
as still studying for the American medical boards. It was Yan
old me originally that girls tended to be second children.
so said that she had never heard of orphanages, that children
generally left at hospitals for adoptions.

en Yan went off to study for her exams full-time, she
ght Hu to work for me. Hu was a medical researcher about
ge. She spoke no English, which was not a problem because
as a highly educated, simpatico person with a brilliant and
ning twelve-year-old daughter. I never worried that she
d have any trouble caring for a one-year-old baby or finding
layground.

was so wonderful with LuLu that my neighbors came up to
nsolicited and gave her the ultimate compliment: "She is so
" they said in awe. "She cares for your baby as if she were her
"

had suffered terribly in the Cultural Revolution, as her par-
were doctors. She was short and square, with a face and head
nd and flat as a ball that had been cut in half. She wore her
pulled back in a tail at the base of her neck and, of course,
used makeup.

ere was something so genuine about her, so poignant, some
of understanding that just drew me to her. And she was so
ated. I intended to reciprocate by teaching her English. Then
usband graduated from Columbia University in computer

Yangtze and the pagoda, but though we try, we can't get down
there. The gates are locked. I wonder how people manage it.

Exhausted, we journey home in a pedicab, which takes a ridiculously long route and emerges through the market moon gate on
Laodong Road opposite the bakery. Maneuvering a pedicab
through that narrow space is almost impossible, and Lu and I are
both embarrassed because the cab is mashing things and people
and being a general menace.

But we get home in one piece, and at dinner there is another
wedding. This time, though, we get to sit in the dining room and
hear a full folk orchestra play, which is divine.

May 23
Cloudy

In the morning, we stroll over to our lake and find a giant
new cage filled with singing yellow canaries. The top of
the cage is a pagoda shape, with little bells at the ends that *ting* in
the wind. LuLu presses her face against the screen and peers inside. Then we notice that a flock of twenty Chinese ducks has
taken up residence in the lake and carpenters have fashioned a
duckhouse beneath the viewing pavilion. New little pegs in the
lake, which I take for water jets, turn out to be duck perches.

I am sad today. I woke up grieving for my mother. How I wish
I could phone her and tell her what it's like here. But I am glad she
didn't have to worry through the bombing, watching all the rioting from bed, where she spent most of the last ten years. She
ended her life a reclining philosopher.

LuLu loved my mother and called her every day from the time
she was two. She figured out the button on the phone that was
linked to my mother's number and would dial her up at dawn

when she awoke. For the first year, she just said, "Hi, Grandma," and then hung up—which my mother found hilarious, in spite of the fact that it was five-thirty A.M. My mother was like that. When she found something funny, no inconvenience really mattered.

When my mother died and LuLu chose to believe in rebirth, she asked me if Grandma would be reborn as a baby. I said, Well, one didn't know. Only God knew about these things. But that's what she decided. And from time to time, she would ask me, Do you think Grandma is grown up yet?

When the gardener appears to feed the canaries, Lu immediately rushes over to this older man. There is a weary wisdom in his face that reminds me of my mother's. The man is in charge of the entire landscaping effort here and has worked with these plants for thirty years. My mother was a magician with her hands, just as he is.

His name is Zheng, and he is in his early sixties. He is another of the Tie Shan team of artists, and his genius is with plants, trees, and bonsai. He immediately enlists LuLu's help in feeding the birds, and sets about teaching her how to remove the little bamboo trough from the cage and fill it with special seeds.

She is hanging on his every word, following his instructions to the letter. This man is a grandfather of her dreams, who knows so much about the earth and growth and patiently passes the knowledge to her. If we lived here, we would get to know this man, who as a horticulturist is as brilliant an artist as the flutist who plays at dinner.

When the feeding is done, Lu and I take a walk to Jing Hu Lake and note that new flowers are being planted in the brick planters they just built. Looks quite nice. Over near the pavilion that is being rebuilt are some giant rocks to climb on, and LuLu runs into two university students who play a lot with her and ask about her.

We have yet to run into a single person who has not played with her upon first meeting. Everyone here seems to love a game with

a child. And she seems to be considered so... she came from Wuhu and yet speaks flawl... dual-language ability is definitely a mark of... ture.

It starts to drizzle and we hurry over to t... at Xin Bei. The store is hopping because it's... ground costs ten yuan, and parents sit outsi... sit for a bit, and another mother converses... like her father," the woman offers, referrin... litely.

I walk around and browse while LuLu pl... partment store I visited in Hefei in 1994 tha... long counter devoted only to animal-head... counter it was! The only thing they still d... spray-on insect repellent. I can't think why.

I get LuLu at lunchtime and, as we leave... place is surrounded by little open-air resta... peared out of nowhere amid the rubble. E... again after lunch.

We struggle over the rubble to find a taxi. W... Insu, which, it appears, is without electricity. S... ing team must have cut the wrong wire. Un... have lighted the store with candles. We drop... department store, and it is wonderful and wh...

We grab a pedicab and ride home under a... sive cloud cover. As we roll along, I take a g... Disneyesque skyscrapers. They are pastel... pinks, and make me think of the Magic Ki... that the bits of old Wuhu that remain among... moon gates and vase-shaped doorways set in... have been left on purpose, as monuments t... spected aesthetic.

When we get back, I go have my foot dress... still hurts. The doctor, though, is happy wi...

science several months later and immediately got a job in Minnesota.

LuLu and I visited her about two years later. I got an assignment for a piece that took me there, and I looked her up. She and her family were living in a high-rise above the only racist in liberal Minnesota. He complained about them constantly to the landlord and generally made their lives hell. I offered to go down and tell him off or talk to the landlord, but of course, that was not her way. I've always regretted it.

So the doctor at the Tie Shan reminds me in some way of Hu. It's the stateliness, I think, and the hidden tragic knowledge.

In the evening, Anne and Alexandra come to the hotel for dinner. There are two weddings on, and we eat in yet another special room, this one rather lovely and newer than the others, with wood paneling and new silk wallpaper.

Because Anne is fluent in Chinese, I get a chance to talk in depth to Mr. Tong, the manager of the Canting. He says it was he who told Chinese TV about us, because he finds it quite moving that I have brought LuLu all this way to see China and Wuhu. In China, he tells me, families would not tell children they are adopted until they are all grown up.

I point out that I didn't really have a choice, but he shrugs. I tell him about our wish to visit the Wuhu orphanage, and he says he will go to the police station for us. He does not foresee a problem. There is no law against it that he knows of.

He also tells us a bit about the hotel. It has four hundred employees and is owned by the Wuhu city government. This last makes me laugh, because I now realize that the government knows everything we are up to.

Four hundred employees makes the hotel a major employer in Wuhu, with vast connections throughout the city. Consequently, I feel better about spending so much time on the premises. It is what it seems to be: the hub around which the life of the city turns.

I ask Alexandra about all the building that's going on in China, and she tells me that "the concrete palaces," as she calls them, have more room for the married son. She laughs when she says this.

At this moment, LuLu, who has been playing outside, returns sobbing. Some little boy has pushed her down and frightened her. Mr. Tong takes her in his arms and comforts her, and then gives her to me while he rushes away to get Mercurochrome. When he returns, he applies it gently to the broken skin on her knee.

I run downstairs and try to buttonhole the boy, but the wedding is over and he squiggles away in the crowd.

The girls come back to the room with us to chat. The rain is beginning to drive us all nuts. Perhaps, I think, this is a good time for our journey to Hefei, to the Anhui Hotel, where I first met LuLu.

May 24
Rain

On the way to breakfast, we examine the giant web. It is still there, but much simplified with all the water pouring down on it. At breakfast LuLu says, "Mom, when my Chinese parents took me to the institute, I think they had another child. Then they had another one."

"That's possible," I reply, and leave it at that. But I determine to tell her, when the moment is right, that she was not taken directly to the institute.

When we come back to the room, she goes off to play with JingJing, and when she comes back she announces, "So, Mom, I have found my Chinese parents. TohToh is my father, and the other room attendant, JiaJia, is my mother."

I have not met or heard of JiaJia before, and I am curious. "Why JiaJia?" I ask.

"Nice and *piaoliang* [pretty]," LuLu replies. "Tao Liang, JingJing, and Mickeyman [a young clerk at reception] are my brothers and sisters."

She is very pleased with her selections for her family group and I am once again impressed at how she is helping herself. She extracts the life-affirming elements from her situation and arranges them around herself like pillows. She is positively snuggling down in the Chinese familial warmth that she has called forth.

As for me, I'm still standing on the outskirts, trusting that she'll come back to me sometime. Right now I don't know how it will come out, I know only that she needs this very much. And as the days go by, the frantic, always-moving quality about her relaxes and calms, and the emptiness she has tried to fill with perpetual motion slowly swells with being. And slowly, slowly, this little girl, the one who was abandoned far away, is no longer that in her own mind. I see her changing before me.

She is now a proud citizen of Wuhu, joined in her heart and head to the people here, to the university preschool, to the Jing Hu Lake, to the doves of the Tie Shan, to the ice-cream cones of Xin Bei. And no one, as long as she lives, no matter where she goes or what she becomes, can ever take that away from her again.

Frankly, I want to fall down on my knees and kiss the hands of every person here who has given their time and love to her. I wonder if they have any idea how important it has been.

As we duck out to dinner at the Canting, LuLu brings JiaJia down from the third floor so I can meet her. She is about twenty, with the kindest face imaginable, and she is the only girl in Wuhu with chunky legs. Since I'm thin and my legs are chunky, this secretly makes me feel pretty good.

At dinner, LuLu hops onto the stage when the flute player arrives and goes into the wings to watch him prepare. Tonight he is accompanied by a rather handsome man who plays trumpet. From this moment on, LuLu will always go into the wings and get flute lessons. As usual, everyone is fine with this. And I finally get it: showing children how to do things beautifully is obviously one of the recognized pleasures of Chinese adulthood.

On the news tonight, there is an ominous call for an explanation of the bombing. The announcer reports that most Chinese think the bombing was deliberate.

"America," the announcer says, "has lost touch with reality now it's the only superpower." There's an antidrug exhibition in Beijing, and on the Wuhu news is the story of a man who stabbed a woman somewhere in the city.

**May 25
Cloudy**

LuLu is in a bad mood. She had diarrhea after eating. But she wants to go to school and insists that I do her hair in pigtails, with numerous colored bands circling each tail from top to bottom, Wuhu style.

At school, something unspoken has happened. All the children are dressed for summer, suddenly. No more sweaters, layers of pants; now all the girls wear white blouses with embroidered scenes on the collars and puffy sleeves, circle skirts with petticoats, white stockings that end midthigh, and sandals. The boys wear light pants and short-sleeve shirts.

One thing I realize after living here for a month: overdressing affords protection. Many layers will protect a child playing on rubble and concrete from scrapes and infection. And the midthigh stockings make a lot of sense. LuLu's legs are covered with scratches from gravel and bug bites. I determine to get her some stockings the next time I see them.

Amazingly, I run into Anne on the street and she takes me to the foreign languages bookstore. Browsing for English-language books, I spy a copy of *Five Children and It* by E. Nesbit, the British children's book author.

When I was small and living in Taiwan, my father brought me British books from Hong Kong, which was then an English colony. *Five Children and It* was one of my favorites. It brings me such delight to give this book to my daughter while we are here in China.

I present it to LuLu back in the room and begin reading it to her. It turns out to be an abridged version for students of the English language, but that's fine. She's a bit too young to be able to follow the original, and the simplification—editing, really—is just right for her. She loves it immediately.

She can't sleep, however, and becomes very snarfy. We fight and she yells, "If I had the money, I would get a new mommy!" In spite of everything I tell myself, this hurts my feelings.

We are both going stir-crazy from the rain. I keep her home in the afternoon because she isn't totally well. I get her to eat just rice at lunch, which helps a lot, and we set out for a walk during a lull in the rain. Then we have to get a taxi back because her stomach cramps.

The strange thing is that after she gets rid of the food she has eaten, she feels perfectly fine again, which makes me think she has a passing bug that will be gone by the morrow. Since she feels okay, we go out to skate and she finds Baba, as we now call Toh-Toh. Later, when he gets off work, he takes the time to play with her again. He is an adorable guy.

At dinner, there are lots of smoking men who spit on the dining room floor. LuLu gets really angry about this and complains loudly. It is disgusting, but I try to explain that in China this is permitted. She is having none of it and complains to Mr. Tong, who looks bewildered.

Despite all this smoking, it said on TV that only one million people in China have cancer, which is not very many, relatively speaking. And people are smoking less now in China than they were in 1994.

As we leave, Mr. Tong tells me that he has gone to the police station, and all we have to do is go ourselves now and we will get our permit. I'm surprised by this, but I thank him for it. I hope it's true.

May 26
Sunny

Finally, the sun's out again. This afternoon I'm taking over Anne's class. I've decided to teach investigative journalism, primarily because I heard on CCTV that one of the big problems in China is that people do not know how to make use of information.

I walk LuLu, who is still in a bad mood, to school. She wants to eat lunch there again, so I set this up with the teacher.

I go back and prepare my lesson, and when I return to get her for her nap, her stomach is acting up again and she hasn't eaten. Plain rice at the hotel, then sleep, during which time I ask Mrs. Chang if she might baby-sit if Lu proves too sick to go back to school. But she wakes in better shape, so I walk her down and then head onto campus.

My class is a bit scary. The students are very quiet, staring at me expressionlessly. These are sophomore students in spoken English. When I tell them that I am a writer and that I have written six books, they gasp in reverence. It takes me aback. I forgot that writing is a very respected profession in China and powerful, too. You can be put in prison for what you write, after all.

I tell them they must write a piece about something they have wondered about and fervently wish to know, and that they must interview people to get a complete picture.

I give as an example the rubble pit in front of Xin Bei and Insu department stores, and how I wonder when it will be gone and why so little has been done to protect citizens' safety while the pit is there. When I suggest that the pit is dangerous in its present state, the students laugh at this sardonically. I suggest that they interview the Wuhu city planning board. They look dubious.

Or, I suggest further, what about the fact that there are no lights in the university hallways? They are very hesitant at this, like rabbits that sense a fox. Interview the university, I suggest. They lower their eyes.

I am struck once again by how much personal hardship the average Chinese person puts up with in a day. It also strikes me that being radical is second nature to Americans, even though we don't think of it that way. We tend to characterize the Left as radical, but conservatives and right-wingers protest as much and as continually as left-wingers.

Anne suggests I tell the class exactly what to do, so I write it on the board: 1) idea; 2) interviews; 3) your thoughts; 4) write article, weaving all into it; 5) make conclusion.

After class, Anne accompanies me to get LuLu. On the way, we discuss an article she has given me about how children are taught in China.

The authors, two American teachers, cite as an example their own child, age two and a half. He insists on opening the hotel door with the key. They give him the key and let him try. He fumbles around with the key, trying to fit it in the lock and failing. The Chinese room attendant can't stand this. She rushes over, puts her hand around his hand, and helps him put the key in the door over and over until he gets it.

At the school, Anne helps me consult the doctor about LuLu. I get some pills for her and instructions, if she's not better, to go again to the hospital.

Anne and I relax at the edge of the concrete court and watch the skating. Lu is having her usual great time in spite of the way she feels. But in the evening, she falls too sick to go to dinner. I order rice up to the room, and Lu sleeps while I watch a documentary about the "Comb Girls," a society of women in the nineteenth century dedicated to remaining virgins and so named because they wore big combs in their long hair. The society was led by a Ms. Chang, a rich lesbian. If any of her girls dared to have sex, they were drowned in a pond. Kind of a feminist story, and yet not.

May 27
Sunny

I am dreading going to the police station. I don't know exactly why, I'm just dreading it. Maybe tomorrow. I hope Leo will call with good news so I don't have to go.

In the morning, we walk up into the forest again to the zoo. It is so lovely along the old stone paths. Birds are chirping. Dragonflies are whizzing about. Wildflowers are blooming. And it's quiet, a respite from the constant hum of city construction.

The breezes are blowing even today, when it's hot, and LuLu sits on the deep green grass for ages, surrounded by cooing white doves, until finally she gets two of them to climb on her knees. Then she picks them up, as she saw a little girl do in a commercial on TV, and I take pictures.

A very fat and bouncy baby boy around ten months old is carried over by his dad. His mother has been sharing dove food with LuLu. The dad wants to take a picture of his boy with her. And they pose together with LuLu propping him up, which is a funny sight.

We walk up to the summit of the zoo to see the lion and pass a new building, which we see from the road when we go to the Bank of China. There is a big hole in the back of it, as if someone kicked it out through the wall. And I suddenly recall from Frances Wood's book that shoddy construction may be a Wuhu failing. In the 1870s, the roof of the British custom commissioner's house cracked in two, revealing that builders had quite forgotten the iron supports in their haste to complete it.

The view of Wuhu up here reminds me of the vista from the one skyscraper that had been built in Minneapolis when I went there in 1978. A small city and, beyond, farmland.

There are other things about Wuhu that remind me of the Midwest twenty years ago: a certain innocence among the people, a friendliness and neighborliness, an industriousness combined with a sense of humor, and a hardiness that comes from enduring harsh winters and hot, hot summers, droughts and floods.

We come back to the hotel and Lu skates before lunch. She skates all the way down to the bakery, with me trotting behind. At Laodong Road, we encounter a filthy, demented boy of about twelve. He is wandering about, and I end up giving him some yuan. I wonder where he is from, because I have seen only one homeless man in Wuhu, lying prone near the bank. Does this child live in the streets?

At lunch, LuLu is helping the waitresses and chatting with people, and a lady at the next table starts talking to me. She is Hua Mei from the Foreign Affairs Bureau. She asks all about LuLu, and I tell her the story and mention that we are off to the police station soon to try to get a permit to visit the orphanage. She immediately offers to call the station and take us over there herself. What a relief! She speaks perfect English. Like Mr. Tong, she doesn't think there will be a problem.

After lunch, we return to the room and find that Mr. Tchang has left a huge bag of sweets for LuLu in honor of International Children's Day, a big holiday here.

LuLu is beside herself. Most of the sweets are from the hotel store and consist of Oreo cookies and chocolate. But there are also the little pots of sweet jelly that she used to get at preschool in

Chinatown. After her nap, she writes a thank-you note to Mr. Tchang, which we will deliver later when she finishes her skating.

I'm not skating myself because of my foot, which the doctor is dressing every other day now. I escort Lu down to the lake, and she sees the gardener there and skates over to help him feed the butter-yellow canaries.

Black-and-silver dragonflies are everywhere. Ocher butterflies are fluttering around. I'm drowning in the voluptuous beauty of the helmet-headed, brown-velvet Chinese ducks perched among the pink-edged lotuses and dripping pines sprawling over the pavilion. I'm afloat in fantasyland when a couple of obvious prostitutes clump down the path from luxury Building Six.

I'm startled to see them. They are wearing the prostitutes' uniform: hot pants, thigh-high platform boots, and very heavy makeup. Both are smoking, and their faces have that angry, hard look.

Regular Chinese girls never smoke, and they don't wear much makeup. They do, however, sometimes wear short shorts and high platforms. But it's the hardness in the faces that gives these two away. I guess there must be a service or two in Wuhu. For a fleeting moment, I wonder if the unadopted girls ever end up like this. Then I push the thought right out of my mind.

We walk to reception so I can e-mail. Everyone we pass greets LuLu and she says to me, rather astutely, "No one says hello because you are not Chinese."

Although she's right about this, it's also true that I have become invisible when I am with her. Perhaps, like the people in our summer community who always think she is one of the other Chinese girls who live there, many people here do not see my face clearly. Perhaps I am a Western blur to them, kind of a nanny figure to one of their own.

As we enter the lobby, Mr. Liu barrels down the stairs carrying an enormous stuffed duck toy (about two feet high), which he presents to the three-and-a-half-foot-tall LuLu. Her mouth literally drops open in amazement. TohToh is standing by happily, as are Mickeyman and the lady who cleans this building, who are fond of her, too. Everyone is beaming at her, and she is overcome with joy and surprise.

She hugs the duck close and names it Tie Shan on the spot. Her smile lights up the entire reception floor. She gives Mr. Liu the note for Mr. Tchang and says thank you in Chinese. She insists on taking Tie Shan up to dinner.

When we enter the Canting, about twenty of the waitresses are standing around, looking like adorable young cats that just munched on canaries. They seat me and then LuLu, with her back to the kitchen. While she is drinking her milk, Mr. Tong sneaks up on her and taps her on the shoulder. She whirls around and there he is, carrying a huge plush mouse also around two feet by two feet.

"I'm calling him Tong," LuLu says when she finally manages to speak, and she clasps the mouse to her passionately. The waitresses are laughing and chattering. Mr. Tong bends down to kiss her cheek, and she hugs him hard. I feel like a kid, too. Like LuLu, I am overwhelmed, because it seems that everyone was in on this.

After dinner, at which the flutist and trumpet players are, wonderfully enough, now a permanent fixture, we carry Tong and Tie Shan back to the room and LuLu shows them off to JingJing.

Around China tonight is about foreign adoptions! It shows Westerners notarizing documents and receiving round dumplings of babies from their nurses. It is interesting that they are broadcasting this story. The spin is very positive, although basically just about the process.

LuLu is quite excited by the program, too. "See those adopted children?" she says. "I was adopted, too. One of those children could be me!"

The program discusses the larger issue of the social welfare program the Chinese are trying to design. Education of the handicapped is debated: should a teacher come to the home, or should handicapped children be sent to school with other children?

When I was here in 1979, you never saw a handicapped person

on the street. They were kept, the guide told us in response to my question, in the house. So what the Chinese are trying to do now, it seems, is what we had to do: reeducate everyone about the handicapped, the mentally challenged, the orphans. It is the first step in laying out a modern social welfare policy. They must take the bad fortune aspect away.

May 29
Cloudy

We are getting ready to go to the police station when Hua Mei calls. The officials are off today, she tells me. We will go Monday.

I breathe a sigh of relief. Perhaps we could just do without visiting Wuhu orphanage. But then I would never know about the files, and just in case there is something—not only for LuLu but for the other girls, too—I have to try.

After lunch, Lu and I go along with Anne and her fellow professor Leslie to a tailor shop to have a Chinese dress made. I also want to order some padded coats for LuLu and for Martha's daughter, Gianna.

We walk up to Sun Yat-sen and then take one of the right-hand spokes to the tailor's street. It hasn't been rebuilt yet, and remains crowded with markets and shops and bicycles and pedicabs. But there are many tailor shops along it, too. You can tell them by the dressmaker's dummies that stand outside as advertisement. Each tailor has about twenty bolts of cloth hanging up, and you choose the one you want for your dress. Pinned on the upper walls inside the shops are different made-up dresses in the cloths available.

The thing that for me most characterizes the run-down Chinese street are broken melons in the gutter. In fact, *The Street of Broken Melons* is a good name for a novel about changing China.

As we walk along, over the crushed and dirty melon rinds, dodging bicycles, stumbling over rubble and uprooted street bricks, I cannot imagine children being left by the road in this atmosphere. Yet they are, and it happens every day, to the tune of one hundred thousand girls a year and more.

Leslie, a native of Wuhu with a daughter age eight, is married to another native who is himself a university professor. She suddenly mentions to me that her husband wants to adopt a girl from Wuhu orphanage but that she is nervous about money—that is, having enough money to bring up a second child. I take the opportunity to ask what happens to the girls who are not adopted. Leslie grimaces.

"Their lives are pathetic," she says.

"Why?" I ask.

"They don't get educated," she replies. "Education costs money in China."

"You mean there's no free education? No public school?" This astounds me. For some reason, I assumed that in Communist China education would be free to all.

"No," she replies.

"So education is not compulsory, either?"

"No," she says. I am amazed.

A lack of education, she assures me, is one of the worst things that can happen to a Chinese person. She adds that there is prejudice against the orphan girls, too. I ask her why. She replies, clearly embarrassed about it, that she doesn't really know why.

I mull this over as we reach the tailor shop. Anne introduces us to the tailor, a man in his late thirties with a buzz cut who is robust and kind of hip-looking. He is, it seems, an expert in traditional clothing, and Leslie helps me explain to him what I want: padded coats for LuLu with matching Red Army–type hats.

Next door to his shop is a fabric store, and we go over there to choose what I want for LuLu's coats. I remember from 1994 how adorable the textile designs for children were in China, and I ask to see the flannel. It is terrific. I choose a cherry-red flannel with a bright-blue pattern and a bright-blue flannel with a red pattern. The colors are bright and pure. I also choose a complementary color printed with teddy bears for the linings.

The design for the coats is traditional. I want them like long Chinese scholars' coats from the 1900s, the kind Sun Yat-sen used to wear in photos I've seen from the period. They will both be mid-calf for the winter weather.

It takes forever to plan this, in spite of its simplicity. We discuss it and rediscuss it, and I realize that this is a ritual. There definitely is a slow, southern feeling to Wuhu; people are rarely in a hurry here.

Because of us, Leslie has delayed picking up her daughter, which is typical of the lengths people will go here to do others a favor. It is a long chain of connection: someone at Leslie's end will do her the favor of watching her daughter until she gets there. For this reason, people are not hysterical about their lives; they are relaxed about offering help.

It will take a week or so for the coats to be ready. We leave the shop and stroll back down the street of broken melons to Sun Yat-sen and then across to the university main gate. When we reach Anne's guest house, Lon is outside. I ask him what happens to unadopted girls, just to make sure I have it right. He tells me that the girls are supported by the state until they are sixteen, then they go into the factories. If they are lucky, he adds, they marry a decent guy.

I fantasize for a moment about all the girls I know being left uneducated, going to work in factories, being unable to marry a decent man. I see that life clearly, standing here in Wuhu. It is the life of a poor person, more or less inevitably the life of a person without connections. I wonder whether LuLu would still be a sunny girl if she lived that life. Somehow I think she would.

We accompany Anne and the other teachers to Mama's, a little restaurant across Laodong Road. It is boiling hot out and the sky is yellow. Anne says the farmers are burning wheat in the fields before they plant again, and the air of the city is thick with the yellow haze of smoke.

After a dismal-tasting meal, which makes me glad that I have eaten so often at the hotel, LuLu and I walk home to the Tie Shan and go sit by our lake. The setting sun is a giant red dot in the sky. We visit the nursery, but no one is there. We follow a mossy path to the greenhouse, and find chickens and enormous pots and heaps of dirt.

On TV, I watch a class in Chinese painting and am struck again by the fact that people here are interested in the process, the *way* things are done, not just the result.

May 30
Sunny

At breakfast today, there is a Chinese family of four from Boston. The dad is very handsome, in his early thirties, from Shanghai. The mom, pretty and perhaps in her late twenties, is from Wuhu. They have two boys, one a toddler and another, five, named Eric. LuLu and Eric take to each other.

I go over to chat with them, and the mom tells me she visits her parents here in an apartment complex, where they live with ten of her aunts and uncles. Unfortunately, she is taking Eric there for the day, so LuLu and I go out to skate.

That afternoon, we go for lunch to a little restaurant across from the main gate of the university. Once we are inside, everyone starts chatting about us, to us, and also making gentle fun of us. I imagine the proximity of the university makes this area more anti-Western. But I am up for it.

I answer all the usual questions about LuLu and they find out that I taught a class at the university. In the end, the very nice lady owner charges us two yuan for lunch (twenty cents), much to the derision of some patrons, who feel we should be charged more. The lunch is noodles with pork shreds and pickles (the Wuhu hamburger) and is good.

I am saddened that the bombing cast such a pall over our visit. I would have loved to explore all the restaurants and neighborhoods in Wuhu. But we will come back and explore more another time. And as far as LuLu is concerned, she has a lovely picture of Wuhu, which is all that counts.

May 31
Cloudy

Today, the police station. We get all dressed up. I get our documents, the letters in Chinese stating who we are and why we want to enter the orphanage, and we go to the lobby to wait for Hua Mei. Baba (TohToh) is in the lobby this morning and is darling with LuLu. She proudly shows everyone the picture of herself as an infant, the one I received from Spence-Chapin.

I can see Baba's heart melt as he is reminded that LuLu is from the orphanage. He is trying to deal with the contradiction he is feeling. LuLu is so proud of it, and here it is not something to be proud of at all. As I look around the lobby at all the young people who work here, whether they are reception clerks, doormen, or maids, I see them having to amend an attitude. It is at once very difficult for them and extremely emotional.

The police station is right next door to the dreaded post office. We go through the gates and a guard passes us in. The building is an old one, similar to city government buildings of the 1950s, when this one was surely built. We wait for about fifteen minutes until we meet with a young woman in a green, ill-fitting Mao outfit with cap. Hua Mei explains what we want, and she tells us we have to wait for the head man. We go back outside and wait some more.

We see no one coming in or out. It is definitely not a busy place. LuLu seems very jumpy, and is running about frantically and not listening, which makes me more nervous. Just as we are about to go nuts, the head man arrives.

He's a guy in his early forties, also in a green Mao suit with cap and a nondescript face. He invites us into his office, and Hua Mei and I sit down while LuLu floats about. His manner is gruff and suspicious as Hua Mei explains our situation.

"What have you done in Wuhu?" he asks, and I tell him that LuLu is getting to know the people and the town.

"How long have you been here? Why do you want to visit the orphanage?" Hua Mei translates.

I hand him the letters, and point out that the orphanage is LuLu's only visible link with her infant past and that she would like to meet her special care nurse.

"Sorry," he says in English. "Closed to foreigners."

The suddenness of this makes me cry, which embarrasses me and them. But I can't help it.

The man softens a little when he sees me crying, and Hua Mei seems to be reasoning with him. Neither she, nor Mr. Tong, nor Mr. Tchang can understand what the big deal is about seeing the institute. People visit there every day.

"The child can go by herself," the man says then.

This surprises me, and I consider it and then decide no. Though Leo has said the institute is okay inside, I would want to be there with her. Hua Mei, a lovely, motherly woman, offers to take LuLu in, but I say no. I am afraid to let her go alone after the incident with the old man guarding the gate there. I just am.

"She is too little," I tell them. But I thank the official for trying to help us. Hua Mei and I leave. LuLu has already rushed outside, bored and very anxious.

In the cab, Hua Mei and I discuss it. I tell her that I want to know if anything is in the files, and couldn't we perhaps meet her nurse outside of the institute? Hua Mei is saddened by the whole thing.

When we return to the Tie Shan, Mr. Tchang is in the lobby and Hua Mei tells him what happened. He immediately calls the higher-ups in the police department, with whom he is friends. I see him nodding. He tells her something, and she turns to me and repeats that "sentiment is not with you right now because of the bombing."

Hua Mei and I now have the second, but not the last, conversation I will have in China about the bombing. She tells me the Chinese really feel we did it on purpose. Did we? She looks so hurt when she asks me.

I reply to Hua Mei's question by talking about Chernobyl, the Russian nuclear plant, and the explosion there in the 1980s. Supposedly, I tell her, the United States had satellites so sensitive, they could see the minutest details from the sky. Yet for weeks no one had any idea what had actually happened there. In the end, we found out when the Russians decided to tell us.

My point is that a nation's real abilities are not always commensurate with its propaganda. Ineptitude is not as impossible as you might think, I tell her. But I know from Chinese TV that ineptitude seems entirely unlikely from a people with as much technology and power as we have.

I then cite Clinton's friendliness toward China, and Hua Mei replies that some think the right wing was responsible, acting secretly in retaliation for Weng Ho Lee's alleged theft of nuclear secrets. Interesting theory.

I don't know, I tell her. I only know it was a grim surprise to everyone. And it definitely has screwed us up royally.

I straggle back to the room and recover myself while LuLu goes off to play with LingLing. After over a month here, I can see that the People's Republic of China and its citizens have recast their image in a way that we are not comprehending.

They have sloughed off the Maoist simple man as an ideal and have embraced the Sun Yat-sen–type scholarly modern theorist, a far more avowedly sophisticated and sensitive individual. They think of themselves now not as peasant revolutionary fighters for equality, but as scholars and entrepreneurs moving toward democracy. Sun Yat-sen, after all, though he saw the point of working with Russia, never thought communism was suitable for China.

So, they were looking up to the West, working closely with us, learning from our expertise, building madly toward a new China. To say that our bombing their embassy was a shock to the Chinese is an understatement. They were thunderstruck by the occurrence and deeply hurt.

After a restful afternoon, we go out to roller-skate and Alexandra visits. She comes up to the Canting with me to plan LuLu's birthday party. On June 8 LuLu will be five, and since the only way I can repay everyone is with a dinner (there is no tipping allowed, for example), I have decided to arrange a birthday banquet.

We consult Mr. Tong, who insists on donating the cake for the party. I tell him I will invite about twenty-five people or so.

I write out the invitation, including a line stating no presents are to be given. No one can afford it, and we already have two huge stuffed animals to take home. My present to LuLu will have to wait. I am getting her a real puppy, which she has wanted desperately since she said her first word: "dogda."

We photocopy the invitations, and Lu gives one each to Mickeyman at reception and LingLing. I try to pay Alexandra for her time translating for me, but she won't take money, period.

As if on cue, in the evening, the news has an account of children with problems recently caused by Chernobyl. We see them on the beach in Cuba, recovering from various treatments. Later LuLu comes back with a hangdog expression. She has gotten into trouble with LingLing for jumping on one of the beds she had made. There's a promo for an upcoming TV special. It is called *The History of American Aggression*. I can hardly wait to see it.

June 1
Rain

Today is the actual Children's Day, and it's the second time I'm teaching my class.

We breakfast with Eric and his parents. As I watch him run around, I can see how American he looks here, even though he is fully Chinese. For one thing, he is very gawky as he runs, his hands and feet too big for his body. He is as floppy as a big puppy. You never see that here. Even the tiniest children are compact and coordinated. Or perhaps growth patterns are slower and more regular here than in America, where boys can suddenly shoot up four inches. Also, both he and LuLu have that confident curiosity just bursting out of them. Neither one of them ever hangs back. They have no fear of consequences.

Eric's mom tells me that the cost of water in Wuhu is exorbitant. (Perhaps that accounts for the price of the laundry.) In the 1970s, she says, Wuhu was very poor and children begged in the streets. I ask her about the Yangtze, and she calls it a "violent river." "The people try to block it out," she adds.

Her name is Louise, and she describes herself as a "China hater." She claims she can't stand anything about it. Her husband is from Shanghai, born and raised there. Eight years ago they left for Boston, where they have lived ever since. On this trip to Shanghai, her husband tells me, he would never have known where he was if it hadn't been for the street signs. So much has been torn down and rebuilt.

When LuLu and I leave the restaurant, we walk past the Chinese magnolia trees. They have put out buds so big, they look like white footballs. We just stare up at them for a while, because they are so huge and lush.

On the way down the hill, we greet the sweeper lady and give her an invitation. Then we go over to the nursery and give one to the gardener and his wife. Then we give one to JingJing, the waitress, via Wei Wei—it's JingJing's day off. And we leave one for Mr. Tchang, Mr. Liu, Mr. Chen, and Mr. Wu.

There's a general one for reception and the kitchen, in case we forgot anyone. And one for Mrs. Chang, Yue Yue, and the reception maid and her son. And one for all the housekeeping staff.

Mrs. Chang has kindly offered to baby-sit for LuLu while I teach my class, so I leave her with Yue Yue in the lobby of our building and go off to the university.

When I get to class, the students hand me their papers. They are very long and remarkably good, considering the students have been studying English for only two years. They also followed my directions to the letter. They seemed to be hardly listening last week, but boy, did they hear every word. Topics they came up with are surprising and solid: "Should Homosexuality Be Legal?" "Why Do Women Read Romance Novels?" "Should College Students Fall in Love?" "What's the Purpose of Education?"

One female student wrote an impassioned outcry against conditions in the dorms. According to her, there is theft and they have rats. Another girl, at my suggestion, wrote a piece about the rubble in front of Xin Bei and Insu, and reported that the work would soon be finished.

As expected, they had trouble interviewing the authorities to complete their stories. The student who wrote about the dorms neglected to interview the university for views on dorm conditions. The student who wrote about the rubble did interview city government officials, then subscribed entirely to their point of view. Nonetheless, she did interview the city government, which took some bravery.

Anne is impressed with everyone's work, and I am amazed at what they accomplished after hearing just one lecture.

At dinner, major dignitaries are visiting, and they are screened off in the dining room. They are living in the special low building near Building Six.

China Business, another program I've discovered, is reporting that very soon consumers will no longer be subsidized by the government. I assume they are talking about price controls. At the moment, most things are inexpensive to me, but probably just affordable for the average Chinese. With the loss of subsidization, everything will change.

June 2
Sunny

Lu wakes at five-thirty with a bad dream. Power Rangers are fighting, and she's fighting with them. A pink robot "destroys her." She is sad. The Power Rangers take her back to their spaceship. Then she tells me that she thought of Grandma on Children's Day.

"Do you think she's still a baby?" she asks.

"I think she still is," I reply, and hug her.

I take her to school and go off to the tailor. When I get to his store, he's not there. His assistant calls him on the phone and wakes him. While I'm waiting, I browse at an underwear stall down the street and buy thigh-high stockings for LuLu and some awfully smart rubber rain shoes for myself. The vendor is very friendly, so I also buy a pair of crocheted lace gloves for myself.

The tailor arrives and we chat about the dresses. While I am talking with him, a mother comes in with a girl of about eight, who looks exactly like LuLu. I don't have my camera and I don't have an interpreter, so I just stand transfixed, staring at the child and then at her mother, who looks like neither her child nor LuLu.

Since our business is done for the moment, I walk to the Bank of China. Inside, I get my money in five minutes by the timer; the teller is getting more efficient. As I come out and walk to Sun Yat-sen, a grubby-looking guy who is dressed like a farmer leers at me and makes a rude money gesture, rubbing his fingers together to indicate I'm a rich foreigner. A bit unsettled, I go to the school to pick up Lu. The headmistress asks if everything's okay, because LuLu is not in a good mood. I ask LuLu, and she says she's too hot and tired. She was feeling all right this morning, thanks to the school doctor's pills, and now she says again that she is not feeling sick.

We stop at the bakery and get milk, and then, as we pass by the primary school, we watch as classes change. It's an orchestrated cacophony that begins and ends on a shut door.

Back in our room, LuLu falls instantly to sleep. I can't get her up for school at two-fifteen, so I let her sleep. When finally she does awaken, we go on an outing to a pleasant place by the Yangtze that Alexandra has recommended. She has written the address on a piece of paper.

We get in the cab and—lo and behold!—the driver takes us to the pagoda beyond Lu's bridge. What we couldn't see from the bridge is the beautiful old teahouse on the canal right by the ancient structure. You get up to it by a stairway from the street.

It's breezy above the little canal, and we buy some soft drinks and sit for a while, watching the houseboats. We stroll to the end of the canal and stand by the pagoda, gazing at the swirling, muddy yellow water. LuLu stares fixedly at the houseboats, little wooden shacks on barges stuffed with families who poke their heads out the doorways to check on their progress through the canal.

"Perhaps your first parents lived on one of these boats," I offer.

She looks quite happy with this thought. One passes by with a small child toddling around on it, and she stares thoughtfully at him.

We climb down from the pagoda into the spice market and have to thread our way past a group of men playing cards. One of them continues this day of rude gestures by asking me, "You want to fuck?"

Strangely, I can't think why he is saying that to me. He could be leering, but he doesn't look that way. I decide it must be some crazy reference to LuLu's father being Chinese.

We go to Xin Bei for ice cream and then to Insu for the indoor playground. The rubble pit is vanishing. Trees have been planted and brick edging has been started. They've done a lot of work since we were here about a week ago. I wonder if the article that Anne's student wrote might have spurred them on. At any rate, it's going to be quite a nice plaza here soon. I feel some sadness that we won't get to see it all done and beautiful. We have both become quite attached to this sweet town and its mighty efforts to move forward.

In the evening, the dignitaries are still here, and Messrs. Wu, Tchang, and Tong are on hand to eat with them. LuLu delivers her invitations to them anyway. I ask the flutist and trumpeter to attend her banquet, and they agree. LuLu scampers away with them for her flute lesson.

After dinner, we walk down to the lobby, where Baba is on duty. LuLu shrieks with joy and plays with him for a bit. Suddenly, for no particular reason, I have a revelation: Shanghai Zoo's "Pets World" was supposed to be a petting zoo! That's what zoo officials intended it to be, only they had misunderstood the term. They thought the "petting" part meant *pets,* so they put pets in cages and called it Pets World. But they had been trying for a petting zoo. This makes me feel better somehow.

I cannot say enough in praise of the Huabao air-conditioning system. Each room has its own unit, so if one breaks, it can easily be replaced. It works wonderfully in this brutal heat.

On *China Business,* the story is about bringing electricity and refrigeration to the farmers and the general problem of modernizing rural China. One scheme they are trying is to ask/insist that successful businesses adopt and subsidize a rural area, thus funneling some of the profits back into the land. Makes sense.

The phone rings and it's Leo. I steel myself for the decision. It has been decided that we can visit any orphanage in Anhui Province *except* Wuhu. I laugh. Is this a Communist joke?

Leo is very apologetic. It seems the Wuhu orphanage is quite old and they don't want me to see it. Very true, I think. And, he continues, a road will be going through it. They intend to tear it down and build a new one. Next time we come to China, we can visit it. Well, that's something, I think.

Is this the real reason? I wonder. Or is it the bombing? Undoubtedly they are uncomfortable with the institute's grimness, given the fury with which everything shabby is being torn down. Can we at least meet LuLu's special care nurse outside the orphanage somewhere? I ask. "Yes," Leo says, "you can."

I decide immediately that we will go tomorrow to Hefei to visit the capital orphanage there. This will allow me to show LuLu the Anhui Hotel, where I first met her, and an orphanage at the same time. And we can take Leo's family to dinner as a thank-you.

We will leave in the morning by hired taxi. When I ask Leo how long the trip is by vehicle, he replies, "Between two and four hours." I'm perplexed by this discrepancy but arrange to call him when we get to Hefei.

June 3
Foggy

It's a grimy, overcast day, so foggy that when the taxi drives onto the car ferry to cross the Yangtze, we can't even see beyond the prow of the boat. The air is yellow. The river is yellow. My fantasy of the Yangtze had a lot more blue in it.

We drove out through the new urban area to the car ferry, past

the bridge they are building over the Yangtze that will revolution-
ize business between Wuhu and Hefei. This bridge is destined to
be finished in the year 2000, like all the buildings.

Cars, taxis, vans, and farmers with bicycle-driven barrows piled
high with wicker crates of chickens and roosters all sit side by side
on the ferry. One farmer is pushing a wheelbarrow full of ducks.
They are crammed in so tight that their heads make a duck-head
bouquet, and they are quacking to one another amiably. It looks
very funny, and I point it out to LuLu.

The ride across the Yangtze takes about twenty minutes or so.
Then we drive onto an unpaved dusty road, past rice paddies
being worked by water buffalo in the way they have been worked
for thousands of years. The villages consist of several old two-
story houses, brown with dust.

Suddenly, the road changes into a superhighway, the Hening
Freeway, which speeds ahead with rice paddies on either side. I'm
beginning to have the feeling that everything in China right now
is metaphorical.

The freeway, like all third-world freeways I've ever been on, is
empty of cars but vast. We motor past water buffalo slowly plowing for farmers who as yet have no electricity.

LuLu and I play count the water buffalo as a travel game. She's
not feeling so well. Her tummy is back to being fragile, or maybe
she's just nervous.

After about two hours (not the dreaded four), we pull into
Hefei. The driver is not sure how to find the Anhui Hotel, so
while he drives around, I find the city completely changed.

The air was heavily polluted when I was here in 1994, so polluted that you could see the grime. I remember thinking as we
drove in from the airport that it was a grim industrial city.

Now it looks a bit like south Florida, with its wide planted
boulevards and pastel-colored, whimsically shaped buildings.
Clearly, it is a lot more prosperous.

The Anhui Hotel is so changed that I hardly know it. Outside, the shanties and market stalls have vanished to reveal wide side-walks planted with trees, hedges, and flowers. The lobby still has the hanging balcony over the reception desk, and vines still dangle down its sides, but whereas it used to give a kind of soviet impression, now it looks Western and luxurious. Perhaps there is more brass and glass.

Upstairs on the mezzanine was an open area with a restaurant, where I subsisted on dumpling soup while I got to know my baby. Looking up, I see that it's gone, all closed in and fronted by a wooden and pseudo–Tiffany glass door.

The gift shop that flanks the elevators sells fine art in addition to painting kits and tchotchkes now, and almost everything costs one hundred U.S. dollars or more.

Our room is very different, too, half the size but brighter, and the windows, then streaked with pollution, are sparkling clean. It was a soviet-style room, big and brown, boring but serviceable. Now it's small and light and festive, if a bit cramped. There is even a minibar. Welcome to modernity. What we would have given for a Coke or a glass of wine in those incredible ten days!

I begin to tell LuLu all about it: How we arrived from Beijing and how excited we all were, awaiting our children. How I went to my room and unpacked her little clothes and laid them on the bed. Here, I show her, here. How there was a little metal crib for her when I arrived, and how I fixed the bedding in it just so. How Xion Yan had told us the babies wouldn't come until two, so I was just waiting nervously, wondering what my baby would be like, when the phone—I pick it up—rang.

"Hello?" I say.

And I answer in Xion Yan's voice, "Would you like to meet your baby?"

"Yes, I would," I reply. And I say that very soon I hear baby noises in the hall and a knock. I walk to the door and fling it open, and it's you, LuLu. And your nurse holds you up, and you give your little bow and break into a smile as big as the Yangtze River, and I fall in love with you on the spot. I am hugging her now, and it's the happiest moment of my life.

Of course, now I'm crying and I show her how I took the infant her in my arms, and Xion Yan asked if we were all right together, and I said yes and forgot to ask about her feeding schedule or anything. How I closed the door behind them, eager to be with her alone, and looked deep into her eyes and kissed her little cheek.

You were so little, I say to her, only eleven pounds, all hands, feet, and a head. And so pretty. And so willing to be loved.

Hi, I think I said to you. Hi. I'm so glad you're here. Hi.

And I suddenly thought you might be hungry. I laid you down in the middle of the bed—I do this now—and I apologized. Would you like milk? I asked. I didn't make it yet. I'm sorry.

I rushed into the bathroom—I do it now—where I was keeping the can of formula. I had to make your milk, I say, by mixing the white powder with boiled water from the thermos, and I hadn't even read the can yet to find out the proportions. I did it, hands shaking, rushing back out to smile at you and check that you hadn't moved to the edge of the bed. You were lying there, looking all around.

You were wearing, I say, the little clothes I've shown you, two Day-Glo-colored sweaters and the padded jacket covered with planets and the three pairs of knitted pants. They had knitted the armholes in your two sweaters so high up that your arms stuck out from your body in a T. You couldn't move that much. They call it swaddling.

I rushed back into the bathroom, and made the formula and dropped things and spilled a lot, and finally returned with the bottle of warm milk. Warm, everything had to be warm, because Chinese babies are never fed cold things.

I took you—I do it—in my arms, as I had done with so many baby dolls in my childhood and placed the bottle in your mouth, and you sucked it in and drank it all. Lu pretends to drink. And when you had finished the last sip, you went to sleep. And I

e afternoon, Lu and I go shopping in a department store.
ave some of the same things Xin Bei and Insu have, but the
oe department is great. LuLu picks out pink Roman san-
t are decorated with rhinestones and fasten up to the ankle
cro.

aleswomen go nuts over LuLu and plague her with the
estions. She gets annoyed, and they give her balloons to
down.

we all meet again to visit John's new apartment. He rides
re on his bike. I can tell from the look on her face as she
that she is somewhere near heaven. She is holding on to
ck demurely, as she has seen girls do for weeks now.
ctly like a coed, she pops off the back of his bike in front
ance to his apartment complex, she announces proudly,
really Chinese!" And I believe it.

to John's building through the complex gardens in
ess. I keep waiting for lights to pop on as they do in
sensors detecting the movement of people walking by.
e no lights, and amazingly enough, when we get to his
ere are no lights in the hall. He lives on the fifth floor
flashlight.

that anomaly, his apartment, when we reach it, is a
e-bedroom in one of the new buildings. There is
icularly Chinese about its detail.

ut for a while and chat, and I invite them to the hotel
hen we get a cab home to the hotel and I can't get
at main street Hefei looks. It's got one of those ele-
ys and clearly was reconstructed to resemble the
ghai.

the orphanage.

thought, It works just as they say: you give them their milk and
they fall asleep.

And that's where I started crying, LuLu, I say, that night, because my heart was so filled up that my body had to let some over-
flow. And it has continued to this day.

She listens happily to the story, playing her part, making fun of
me because I cry, and I marvel at the fact that it has been four years
since those incredible ten days that changed my soul forever. To
say that I am a different person is beyond understatement. I am a
mother now, her mother, LuLu's mother. She taught me how,
with her particular quirks and talents. And she's a daughter now,
my daughter—not just a name on a bed, but a deeply loved member of a family, a hope for the future for whom great things are
prophesied, someone I would not now want to live without. Part
of a legacy; her name appears on wills.

But before she became my daughter, she was someone else's.
She had another mother, who, most likely because her baby came
out female, was forced to give her up or make the family suffer.
And because I'm who I am, I can't forget that mother. She's my
silent partner here and guides the Eastern aspect of the training.

Lu and I walk downstairs now to see the room where she was
officially adopted. The process began late on the afternoon we got
the babies, I say. We all went down to meet the notaries in this
large, brownish room. It was the first time we saw each other's babies, our first public moment as parents.

And we all looked at each other, and we laughed and laughed
because we'd never felt so open in our lives. Nine couples, three
single women, twelve babies between the ages of seven and fifteen
months: your friends LiLi, Sasha, Emily, Emma, Maya, and Gianna among them. The very air was throbbing.

The notary, in a Mao suit, said to me somberly when I sat opposite him, "Do you like LuLu?"

And I replied, "I love LuLu," because I already did. And he notarized the first paperwork of the adoption.

I'm facing a door that didn't used to be there. I try it and it's locked. A little plaque on the wall reads "Rose Room." Tears sprint down my face as I look through the glass panel into the once brown room, now opulent and appointed in brocades. It was here that I adopted you, I manage.

LuLu stands on tiptoe to see. Ohhh, she says. The room looks so fancy now that I have to laugh through my tears.

I take her round to what was once a second dining room, next door. Here, I tell her, the older babies like Sasha ate every morning. It's just a conference room now.

And here—we run down the front carpeted stairs to what is now a bakery but was once an area with couches—I gave you orange juice. A big bottle, because I didn't know. You're supposed to water it down, at least, but I gave it to you full-strength, and you gobbled it down and got the worst stomachache. It was all my fault. You were healthy as a horse.

LuLu loves this.

It was also here that Bernice and I ran into the most beautiful young woman I have ever seen. Sitting here with you and little Emily, trying to be mothers, and along she wafted, like something out of an ancient scroll. She picked up each baby in her graceful arms and lulled you both to sleep. Then she floated away.

And it was here—I don't tell LuLu but I think it—that on the third day I had you, late at night as you slept, out of my psyche popped a memory so long suppressed, its emergence was akin to enlightenment.

I suddenly recalled being in Hong Kong at the Royden House School on the day we were visiting an orphanage in the New Territories. Our embroidery class was going there to deliver the bibs we had made for the children. I was nine years old and all dressed up in a silk shirtwaist dress with a bow at the neck. I can still remember the papery feel of the silk on my skin. I remember getting a window seat in the car, squeezed against the headmistress. I remember staring out the window as we drove and drove through miles of rice paddies.

The car parked on gravel and I can sti[ll] shoes on the polished floors as we ente[r] looked like a big English manor house that. We were led through several room then into one where there were some

One crib near me contained a bab who was sitting, propped up against into this baby's eyes, and she locked tensified her gaze into a glare of suc to burn with shame. I felt what it w crib and to see me, a privileged litt dering by, as if at a zoo. I bowed from the room. But her pain was a me for half a lifetime.

Leo arrives at this moment, a doors and into a taxi. He is takir lives in a small three-room apar small New York apartment, with shower, although there is no ro sits in the living room, along books. He and Mrs. Leo broug

Leo explains the situation v ered an eyesore at the momer that LuLu didn't care about mattered. But the higher-u help.

Actually, having now bee see a show orphanage, one ters are right: if the origina torn down, what's the di matter.

After a lovely lunch of by Mrs. Leo, I return to who is twenty-two, ride time, I vow, we will get

In t
They h
kids' sl
dals tha
with Ve
The
usual qu
calm her
Later,
LuLu the
rides off
John's ba
When, ex
of the ent
"Now, I a
We wal
pitch dark
Europe, by
But there a
building, th
and carries
Aside fro
spacious on
nothing part
We hang o
for dinner.
over how gr
vated walkw
Bund in Shar
Tomorrow

June 4
Grim, foggy, overcast

We both awaken, nervous. I have explained to LuLu what we are going to do, that we are going to her orphanage. I don't know if she quite understands the difference between the Wuhu Children's Institute and this orphanage or if it matters to her. She and I both are approaching this as if this is the one she came from.

We go down to the old Chinese restaurant, now the new, redesigned restaurant. It features a central stage, with a mock scholar's study complete with pens and desk. This room, too, is a far cry from the smoky, oily, clamorous place I couldn't eat in because I was too tired to cope with chaos. It is genteel now and expensive.

The breakfast buffet has strong coffee and French toast with syrup, and Lu and I both rush the table. It's funny how exciting it is to see American breakfast foods after not seeing them for a long time. They are absolutely adorable-looking laid out on a table: French toast, cornflakes, orange juice, eggs. We do have the cutest breakfast food in the world. But somehow, in a foreign land, they never seem to taste as good as they look.

Leo calls and I go to the reception desk to get the phone. He says that a Miss Ping is coming to take us to the orphanage. He must go to a meeting.

I'm a little disconcerted by this, but I cope. After breakfast, Lu and I go to the lobby to wait. While LuLu careens around like a dervish, I mull over the last few days.

It's odd the mistaken attitudes we all seem to have about one another. Leo, for example, asked me whether this is the first time I ever did my own wash. Of course it wasn't, but I don't think he fully believed me.

For our part, we are taught to think of the Chinese as formal and rigidly disciplined, but from what I've seen, they are among the most relaxed, fun-loving, and tolerant people I have visited.

Miss Ping suddenly arrives, and I corral LuLu and we drive to the outskirts of the city. We get out before a gated compound and wait as the guard telephones. Then we are allowed in.

I am holding LuLu's hand and she is very tense. "Are you all right?" I bend down and whisper.

"I'm scared," she answers.

"Do you still want to go?" I ask. We could turn back.

Suddenly she bolts ahead.

We are in front of a four-story white high-rise building. She runs around the corner of it, and I follow. What greets us is a terrific surprise.

How can I describe it? We seem to have walked into an elfland. White stone paths traverse a huge, plush, gorgeously kept dark-green lawn that is landscaped with flowers and bushes and topiary pine trees shaved into ball shapes. A group of three-year-olds is playing or sitting on white plaster benches underneath three giant white plaster mushrooms. The Anhui breezes blow gently. A wispy white fog is swirling round visibly. And the effect is a stunning gentleness. I'm completely taken aback but immensely relieved. I'm so glad we came here.

LuLu runs full-throttle up to the children. Their nurses are young women in their twenties, all wearing light cotton pajamas. Mr. Zhao, the director, appears, and Miss Ping and I walk over to him. He is a friend of Leo's. He has a craggy, worn face that is both gruff and kind. He wears a worn Mao suit.

He escorts us over to the mushrooms, which really are fantastic-looking, and I introduce him to LuLu, who refuses to acknowledge him. To cover the awkwardness, I compliment him on how pretty it is here, and I can see he is pleased that I think so. Then I inquire about the children I'm looking at.

"They are all unhealthy," he tells me. "They have heart conditions, skin pigmentation, eye problems, retardation, leg deformity." He looks weary as he says this.

I will myself not to cry. Most of the children look normal, except for one lively little girl who has bandy legs. They do not stop her, however, from running about full-tilt.

Mr. Zhao motions us to come inside the orphanage with him, and I notice several other four-story buildings dotted about the compound, all white with antiglare blue glass windows. One houses the elderly. One is the hospital. The others are administrative. We follow Mr. Zhao inside the orphanage and climb a wide stone staircase to the second floor, where the babies live.

The building, like Lu's school in Wuhu, is built around a lovely central courtyard, with covered balconies on every floor. Painted blue and white, they are hung with colorful little mobiles. Concrete staircases are set at all four corners of the building. This must be a standard Chinese design.

LuLu is so nervous that she is levitating. We move a ways along the balcony and come upon the one-year-olds. There are about twelve of them in wheeled walkers, being fed by two nurses. While two babies eat, the others wait their turn silently.

LuLu bounds forward and indicates to a nurse that she wants to help. The nurse hands her a bottle and she sits down to feed a baby. I can tell from her demeanor that doing this is calming her a little. The look on her face is utterly serious.

The atmosphere in the place is jolly. The nurses laugh and chat together. The babies are washed and sparkling and adorable. They are, of course, all girls. Mr. Zhao tells us that all will be adopted within two weeks. They will all be gone, he says, smiling. I tell this to LuLu.

When she has fed some babies, we walk farther along into the room next to the newborn nursery. Here, ten babies ranging from eight months to one year sit in wheeled walkers near their cribs. From there I walk by myself into the newborn nursery and will myself not to cry.

In here, ten pretty little blue cribs are pushed close together. In each crib is a tiny newborn girl, sleeping. On or above each crib is a handwritten paper telling the day each was found and the estimated date of birth. Each one of the newborns is flawless.

After five years of dedicated observation, I have become convinced that it is not that the Chinese send the prettiest girls to America, as some critics have claimed, but that Chinese babies are universally attractive. Not all Chinese adults are, but there is something totally perfect about the combination of Chinese features and babyhood.

I bend down over one particularly lovely baby. The smell of the tiny one brings me back to a maternity hospital in Taiwan. The cook's wife, Ah-Mei, has had another baby. I am going with her husband, Ah-To, to visit her.

The maternity ward is neat and friendly, with little wooden beds placed very close together. We bend over Ah-Mei and see the infant. I remember the oily, warm smell on the child's head—this baby has it, too. How I loved Ah-To. He was tall and smiling, with wavy black hair. He guarded me with grace.

Was this like the place LuLu was carried into? Probably not. They slept five or six to a bed then. Maybe in winter here they still do. My sister watched a documentary on TV that showed women in a Chinese orphanage washing the newborns very roughly just after they arrived. Did that happen to LuLu?

I remember the first time I bathed her in the Anhui Hotel, at the end of that first day. I started to remove her many clothes, and she froze and moved one tiny hand protectively to cover her vagina. When she was nude, I picked her up and carried her into the bathroom but immediately realized she was too little to bathe that way. I put her back on the bed and disrobed myself, then ran the bath and, holding her, got in with her. She was utterly rigid with fear.

Mr. Zhao tells me there is one nurse per eight newborns. One of the nurses is carrying around a newborn, pressed to her breast, as we speak. She will do this with each of the newborns throughout the day. With the older children, he says, there are about three nurses for ten.

The babies are in their own worlds. You can see them spacing out, their tiny minds wandering. It's a happy, peaceful world, filled with laughter and pleasant to look at, but there is not much one-to-one attention. And this may be the real peril of even the best of early institutional life.

Martha has told me that researchers have found that when the mother stares rapt into her baby's eyes during the first year of life, it helps the baby focus its five senses and bring them into line. And it's clear that some of the sensory integration problems experienced by some of the kids began right here.

LuLu comes into the room and lines up the children in their walkers, two by two, until they are in a long vertical line. Then she stands behind them.

"Take a picture," she says to me.

I look to Mr. Zhao and he says, "Go ahead. Take pictures."

So I whip out the camera and take the two shots that LuLu has posed. She stares at the camera seriously.

We continue down the hall to the playroom, which contains some old stuffed animals and a few toys, but not enough. I make a note to send some next Christmas. Some Lego sets, toys to help the children focus.

When LuLu see this room, she rushes into it and starts playing with the toys. She particularly likes a stuffed cat. She plays with it for a while, trying to inhabit the life here. Then she looks up and says, "I like the institute," meaning this orphanage.

When we move on, Mr. Zhao insists on giving her the cat, which upsets us both a little. I'm upset because there are so few toys and she has so many, and she's upset because she is not sure she wants to take a piece of the orphanage with her.

The nuances are lost on Mr. Zhao, who is trying to be kind, so LuLu takes the toy reluctantly. We walk back down the hall and see some more babies. Lu, who is feeling more comfortable now, sits down and cuddles some of them. While she is sitting there, a little girl with no arms runs upstairs. Lu is stunned; she stares fixedly at her.

Mr. Zhao tells us with genuine happiness and pride that this child is going to America in two weeks to someplace in Pennsylvania. She has already been adopted. I quickly inform Lu of this, and she smiles about it and nods affirmatively to herself. God bless those Americans, I think.

Mr. Zhao escorts us down to his office, where he shows us some pictures and letters that adoptive families have sent him. Things are different, he tells us, now that Chinese couples can adopt, and more and more Chinese are doing so. After filling out paperwork for the adoption process, they simply come to the orphanage and pick out a child—which must be a wrenching experience in and of itself.

He also admits when I ask him that although every orphanage contains files on each child, it is policy to give out no information. I seize on this. Perhaps, then, there is more in the files than the documents we were given at the time of the adoption: where they were found and estimation of birth date.

He walks us out past a little classroom where, he says, they have some daily schooling for the older children.

Outside again, LuLu is running amok and doing nothing I ask her to do. Mr. Zhao says, "All adopted children I have seen are naughty."

"It's not my fault," I shoot back, smiling. "She came that way. It's your fault." And he laughs out loud at my gibe.

Ahead of us, a woman suddenly comes out of the hospital building, carrying a newborn baby wrapped in padded quilts. She crosses in front of us and goes into another building.

"A new one has just arrived." Mr. Zhao points at the retreating figure. Chills run down my spine.

"Unfortunately, the hospital is off-limits," he says, anticipating my desire to see where the babies arrive.

He walks us over to an outdoor playground reminiscent in its beauty and incipient rustiness of the one at Lu's school. There are three boys there between six and eight years old. Two clearly suffer from Down's syndrome. One looks normal, but Mr. Zhao says he is severely retarded. He will live here for the rest of his life, as will others like him, in a complex of old buildings on the far side of the playground.

If I had more money, I think, I would adopt lots more children.

I remember that one of the things that surprised me most about our adoption group was that they were all, save two, like me: over forty and childless. I expected them to be young and infertile. What was it about our generation that it took us so long to understand what children could bring us?

I stare at the boys with Down's syndrome, and instantly I'm driving in the car with my dad in Taiwan. We are going to visit the French ambassador so I can play with his two daughters, who are around my age.

The ambassador had a beautiful big mansion on the beach. I recall being led out to the sand to meet the girls. I remember to this day exactly what they looked like: they were redheads and, I thought, twins, because they looked so alike. But there was something odd I couldn't put my finger on, something that in the late 1950s was never discussed, never mentioned.

I spent the day with them and they never spoke much, which I assumed was because they didn't speak English. I forgot about it until, one day when I was in my twenties, the memory rose up and I suddenly understood: they suffered from Down's syndrome. That was why I couldn't quite figure them out.

We go back to Mr. Zhao's office and thank him, and I get the address of the place so Eshel and Elizabeth can send toys if they want at Christmas. Mr. Zhao has asked for pictures for his bulletin board.

As we leave through the gate, LuLu doesn't say much.

"Was it okay? I thought it seemed nice and very pretty," I add.

"I like the institute," she says again, and directs her attention out the window.

I ask Miss Ping to ask the driver to take us to a store with a good toy department after he drops her off at work.

She does this and I sit back, drained, against the seat. I will never forget rounding that corner and seeing those white mushrooms on the deep green grass, softened with swirling fog. I wonder if it had a similar effect on LuLu.

Well, I think, it's done. She has seen the type of place where she spent the first seven months of her life. Now, if we can meet the special care nurse, she will have a grasp of her beginnings to take back home.

She and I snuggle up against each other until after Miss Ping leaves us and the driver stops before a big store, in front of which stand two stone elephants. A live band is playing.

In we rush and walk around and up the stairs, until we find the toy department. LuLu chooses two toys, a framed magnetic surface with little colored magnets to create pictures, and a set of Chinese blocks with pictographs on them, obviously for learning Chinese characters.

After lunch at Kentucky Gi down the block, which is expensive and spicy, we return to the hotel. Lu lies down and instantly falls asleep.

When she wakes, we go out to the nearby park, which is quite elaborate. There they have two great slides. One is in the shape of an elephant, and you slide down his trunk. The other is a complex of stairways and slides at different levels, way up in the trees. It's the kind of thing kids adore and adults shudder at. Lu is up it like a shot and running from level to level with some little boys.

When she tires of that, we walk around and find an area where she can rent a little car painted like a panda and drive it all by herself. She does this over and over.

We walk on and come to two rides. One is called the Challenger: you get inside, and it lifts up and rolls over and makes a giant noise. It looks so wild that she and I both watch it and then wait to see what people look like when they come out. Frazzled, is the answer, but sparkly.

The other ride is called the Dragon Boat, and it's the pendulum ride we saw at the Shanghai Zoo. Lu and I get on it, and immediately I know I have made a big mistake. The boat we are sitting in is swinging way up and then down and way up again, and I am just cowed with terror. For one thing, I am afraid of heights; for another, I hate rides like roller coasters. I am holding on to the side of the Dragon Boat with a white-knuckled grip, whimpering. Finally, I start to laugh because I am so scared, and LuLu laughs, too. Thank God it finally stops.

We go over to the swings and a little boy joins us. I like him immediately. He is the same height as LuLu, with similar jet-black eyes that shine with intelligence and humor. He is wearing a three-piece tweed suit and seems very jaunty, even though the suit is a tad dirty and he is clearly poor and not in school.

He wants to play with LuLu. She likes him and teaches him to pump the swing, which he is happy to learn to do. I chat with him a bit and find out that he is eight; I decide he must be undernourished, because he is pretty small.

His name is Jimmy (Zemin), and he is a darling child. His father and rather thuggish brother emerge from the background as Lu is trying to teach him to pump. They yell at him because he is not learning fast enough, but he seems used to it and, ignoring them, continues to play with us.

Jimmy indicates that he would like to go with LuLu on the airplane ride, which is in another section nearby. We walk over there to investigate. The airplane is a ride that lifts off the ground until it's about fifteen feet up. Lu wants to go, but I check and find the seat belts are broken, and I have to tell him no. I give him two tickets, though, and he soars into the air with a look of bliss on his face.

Watching him, I curse myself for not being able to speak good

Chinese, because then and there I would have offered his father a deal: that I would take him to America and educate him. Since I can't do that, when he alights from the ride, I indicate to his father that this child is a gem. Jimmy beams with pride.

In the evening, Leo and his wife and younger son come to dinner at the hotel restaurant, which I've dubbed the Sun Yat-sen, and they invite us to go with them on the morrow to the Hefei Wild Animal Park on the outskirts of the city.

June 5
Sunny

The Hefei Wild Animal Park is kind of a foot safari park—an open pine forest that you walk through, encountering animals along the way.

Leo is wearing a stylish Panama hat. Mrs. Leo is carrying a sun umbrella and a picnic basket, and I feel as if we are in a wonderful movie. The style of the park is 1940s Adirondack.

We walk and John rides LuLu through the huge stone gate straight into the peacock area. The peacocks are calling to one another, a mournful, shrieky yowl that sounds almost like monkey calls. Lu chases after them until we come to a bridge on which stands a rather insistent deer. LuLu rushes up to him and hugs him around the neck, which he seems to like. He lets us touch his horns, which feel strangely soft and almost furry. Then he pulls away and tries to yank the lunch bag from Mrs. Leo's hand. Quickly I buy deer-food packets from a nearby stand, and Lu urges her furry friend to gorge himself at my expense. He then proceeds to follows us around for the next half hour, begging. When he finally gives up, he returns to the bridge to strong-arm others.

We stroll along the wide pathways through the pine forest and presently come to the baboon enclosure, which—oh no!—we can go into. A brutal-looking man with a club is standing guard inside. When Lu sees that people can actually go in, of course, she insists we do, too. We stand nervously watching the monkeys unwrapping pieces of candy and discarding the wrappers.

LuLu is awed at being so close to the baboons themselves. All I can think of is what Neke would say if he knew we were doing this. Baboons are enormous when you are close to them, and powerful. I wouldn't like to witness a fight between one of them and the guy with the club.

I finally manage to pull LuLu out, and we move on to the next, rather lackluster enclosure, which is full of emus. After this, we come to a pen of overly friendly camels. One approaches from behind and, much to Lu's delight, tries to eat her ponytail.

The style of the Hefei Wild Animal Park has surprised me. I had forgotten the Chinese Adirondack twig-and-pine, log-cabin style of architecture, but I have seen it before, in Taiwan. My father would take us up to Sun Moon Lake on vacations once in a while, and we stayed in a hotel there that was made of logs. I remember they had very deep bathtubs with sloping backs that all the children would get in at once and slide down, screaming.

We return to Leo's for lunch, and Mrs. Leo cooks noodles and greens, which are delicious. But afterward, LuLu is sick again. When we get back to Wuhu, I decide, she's going right to the hospital.

Leo shows us to the bus station for our return. We board a small van that is packed with friendly people. Leo provides us with a note that reads, "My daughter must go to the bathroom, please stop the bus." We bid him good-bye and thank him profusely. What a nice man he is. God knows what expense and effort he has gone to on our behalf. There are so many things that we take for granted that are costly and difficult to do here. I feel embarrassed at having asked his help in the first place, but we would not have seen the workings of an orphanage without it.

LuLu sleeps the entire trip, which this time takes about two and a half hours back through the dusty villages across the Yangtze to the place we both now feel is home: Wuhu.

The van takes us right into the main plaza of the Tie Shan Hotel. Baba is on duty, and his face lights up when he sees us. He runs right over and insists on carrying our little bag all the way up to our room.

JingJing stands right up and runs to open our door for us with her keys. "Where were you?" she asks.

"Hefei," I tell her.

She is clearly also delighted to see us. Mrs. Chang appears and welcomes us, too. And though Hefei seemed like Paris in contrast, Wuhu is so much sweeter.

June 6
Sunny

After breakfast, Mickeyman at reception writes down the address of the hospital so we can take a taxi. I assume it's the same workers' hospital, but it is not. This one is on the other side of Jing Hu Lake, a block or two from the Children's Palace, and it's fancy.

This hospital is clearly middle-class. It has wood paneling and is clean and bright. It operates the same way as the workers' hospital, however, so I go and pay my money, and they hand me a booklet with a picture of the hospital on the cover and blank lined paper inside. I proceed to the doctor's room, and the ten parents and children who are already in there move aside for us. I'm wondering how I will manage when, as always seems to happen, a nice woman turns up who speaks a bit of English.

She helps me explain LuLu's problems to the doctor, who reaches for the booklet I have been given and writes in it while she translates. He tells her and she tells me that LuLu probably has a parasite, but they have to grow a culture to find out which kind. To tide her over, he will give her some pills that may work. She must, however, give a feces sample to the chemist so that if the pills don't work, they can represcribe the proper medicine.

He writes all this down in the booklet and gives it back to me. The crowd around us in the room nods in agreement. I am used to the group medical experience now and want to stay to see what's wrong with the other children. But the woman helping me needs to go, so I rush out with her and Lu.

I go over to the cashier and pay her again, this time for the pills. I see she is computerizing all our information, too. This is such a good system: having your own record of your child's visit to the doctor to take home with you, including what medicine has been prescribed and when to take it.

We go back to the pharmacist and hand her the receipt, whereupon she makes our pills. LuLu loves this part and stands with her nose pressed against the glass, watching them mash ingredients with a mortar and pestle.

After the pharmacist, we are directed to the bathroom, where Lu gives a feces sample. Then we take the little cup to the chemist, who sits behind a wire-screened window in a full laboratory with beakers and Bunsen burners. He reaches out for the cup, writes something on it, and prepares the petri dish right in front of us. We are told to return in a few days.

LuLu is mesmerized by this. And to me, this is what is so great about China for children: they get to see everything that happens right from scratch. There are no shortcuts, no secrets—it is all out there from beginning to end.

We taxi back to the hotel and play around our lake. I go in to check my e-mail while LuLu plays with Mr. Ni, who owns the antiques store. He has caught a dragonfly for her, and she wears it on her dress like a pin.

I'm trying to decide whether to go to Tongling, which is where Emily and Gianna, Bernice's and Martha's daughters, are from. I had said I would, but something has always come up to prevent it, and I can't find out how far away it is. I ask at reception, How far by car to Tongling? The answer is two or four hours. Big difference with a four-and-a-half-year-old, but they just don't know. If LuLu gets better, maybe.

My e-mail is terrible. Sara writes that our friend Alice is dying. In my bag, I am carrying her daughter's papers. Her daughter is from Wuhu, too, and I am checking the files for her as well.

Oh God, what a tragedy. Alice adopted and, three years later, was diagnosed with inoperable cancer. Now she is dying. It is what all of us fear so much, being older mothers. She had asked me to find out what I could about her daughter, and now I am even more determined to see those files at the Wuhu orphanage.

I go back to the room and reread Alice's letter to me. It is a lovely good-bye from her. I feel unutterably sad for her, her husband, and her daughter. I want to write to them, but honest to God, I don't know how.

June 7
Fog; hot, steamy rain; yellow smoke

As we make our way up the hidden staircase to the dining room, the air around us is yellow and tropical. The huge spiderweb is gone. They must be harvesting wheat again.

After breakfast, while LuLu plays with Baba in the lobby, I phone Hua Mei about a reading of the files and meeting Lu's special care nurse. She says she will phone the orphanage and see about setting this up.

I pick up LuLu and we take a cab to the indoor playground at

Insu. As we round Jing Hu Lake, LuLu turns to me and says, "I'll remember where I was adopted."

"I will, too," I say. "I really love it."

We are both looking out at the little pagoda on the tiny island, beyond which tower the skyscrapers. I remember again what Anne told me: that several months ago there was a midden around the lake, mounds of garbage and shanties. Now, through sheer will and effort, Wuhu has turned this area into something beautiful, something worthy of the new China that the Chinese are so clearly building, the new China that reveres Sun Yat-sen, not Mao.

When we return to the room, LuLu plays with the magnetic picture from Hefei. She sets up a vertical line of numerals and says, "These are the floors we were on in the institute." She is beginning her work.

I sleep and dream of Alice. It's a long dream I can't remember, but we were having a good time. I am sending her a message that I will do my best to find out everything I can, when the phone rings. It is Hua Mei. LuLu's nurse is long gone, she says, and we cannot see the files.

June 8
Torrential rain

It is LuLu's birthday. Or is it? The documents say her birthday was an estimation. The note from her mother says it was June 8 at eleven-thirty P.M. Leo said to trust the note from the mother, so I am.

I owe Penny from our group for LuLu's mother's note. While we were getting notarized in Hefei, I got Xion Yan's husband, who spoke English, to ask if there was a note, and there was. Her

nurse handed it to me. Can I have it? I asked. The orphanage director said no. Penny, sitting nearby with her new daughter,
Emma, also from Wuhu, called out, "Take a picture of the note!"
This I immediately did, and that is why I have a copy of it today.

So I think it is Lu's birthday. I read somewhere that if a child is
born near midnight, the Chinese will give the birth date as the
next day, so she could have been born June 7. But the date we celebrate is June 8. And today at lunchtime is her birthday banquet.

I try to make the wake-up as rousing as possible. I give her
some presents I bought at Insu, some stationery accessories,
which she likes, the Sailor Moon backpack. But weight and space
are considerations, and I have promised the puppy.

I think so much like a mother now that it's unbelievable. My
mind is totally changed. I remember once having coffee with
Alice just after we both became mothers. We met at a coffee place
and had to wiggle by a woman with a stroller to get in. I remember Alice looked at her and said, "I used to complain all the time
about mothers with strollers blocking the doorways of stores.
What was I thinking?!"

I knew exactly what she meant. If you have a baby in a stroller,
it's hard not to block every doorway, even if you don't want to. It's
a design flaw of strollers. The things I complained about as a
childless person make me blush today. I thought I knew everything. I didn't know anything. What, as Alice put it so well, was I
thinking? Oh God, Alice.

I take LuLu up to the dining room, and as we are eating, a lady
from the Xinhua News Agency approaches us. She's young,
seems nice, and speaks excellent English. Her name is Pray.

It seems that she and her photographer were supposed to do a
photo essay on a fossil dig that is going on somewhere near here,
but they have been rained out. So Mr. Tong has told them our
story and they have decided to interview us instead.

I invite them to our birthday banquet, and they agree to come.
On the way down the stairs from the dining hall, my purse

opens and my camera falls on the stones and breaks. It hardly fazes me: I seem to be resigned to disaster at this point, or maybe I'm becoming more Chinese. At any rate, I think immediately, at least a photographer is coming to her party.

Then I realize this is madness. I have got to have a camera. So I bundle LuLu into a taxi and head for Xin Bei, where the only camera with a zoom lens that I can afford is 998 yuan, a huge price for Wuhu, about a hundred dollars. I buy it grumpily. I have left LuLu upstairs in the indoor playground. Today, the lady there charges me only five yuan instead of the usual ten. It turns out that her daughter is in Lu's class at school.

I get film on the way home at the film store on Laodong Road. I've noticed it but have never gone in. Now I've decided to have my film developed and see how it goes. I hope it turns out well.

We go back to the Tie Shan and change for the party. As we come out, LingLing is waiting with a little music box, which immediately puts LuLu in the spirit of the day.

Up in the dining room, the guests begin to arrive. Tao Liang appears with a huge bouquet of flowers for LuLu, who is struck speechless. Baba comes with an enormous stuffed dog, bigger than LuLu. Mr. Wu also brings a huge stuffed animal. JingJing arrives with her baby nephew, for whom she sits on her days off. Mr. Ni from the antiques store comes. Leo's friend who helped get us the room is there. Even Mr. Tchang drops by. The Xinhua people are there, snapping pictures. The reception staff comes, and the waitresses. The only people who don't show up are the gardener and his wife and the sweeper lady, and I hope it's not because they are lower on the totem pole than these more urban types. I will never know.

The banquet is terrific: endless courses of fish, chicken, duck, soup, and our favorite vegetable, *xiao cingsai,* which LuLu and I have taken to eating all by itself for dinner. The flutist and trumpeter play, and I invite them to join us. They will not take money for playing, which just astounds me.

Mr. Tong comes out with the cake, and we all sing "Happy Birthday," and I toast our friends and thank them for their kindness to us.

Total cost: one hundred dollars. What a treat.

By the time we get back to the room, LuLu is raw with fatigue. She falls asleep clutching her new dog, which she names Baba.

In the evening, Neke calls to say happy birthday, after which we go to the lobby for our interview with Pray.

I am explaining to her how I adopted LuLu when Lu interrupts to say to me, "I chose you. I knew you were the right mom for me. I love you." And she hugs me on the spot.

Like all the other journalists, Pray is intrigued by us. She and the photographer are going to follow us around for a few days. She tells me that the way China is moving ahead now, couples don't even want to have children—too much of a burden.

June 9
Torrential rain

LuLu's finger has gotten infected. She got a tiny paper cut in Hefei and we forgot to spray with Medi-Quick, and within three days: a big infection. We go down to the Tie Shan doctor, who didn't come to the banquet and apologizes when we walk in. I stare at her perfect French twist as she makes a poultice paste, smears it on the infection, and wraps a bandage around Lu's finger. My foot is still healing, but I no longer come for bandaging. My middle toe is still tender.

We were going to have pictures at breakfast, but the photographer (who is obviously the boss here) decides against it. The Xinhua crew will accompany us to the tailor, where Lu will try on her coats. Before we go I check my e-mail, and there are lots of birthday greetings for LuLu from her uncles and grandfathers.

First thing, we drive to the bank. The end of our street is two feet deep in water. There's a veritable flood on Laodong Road, raging through the moon gate and into the market. Taxis are stalling. The photographer barrels through, and we drive over to Sun Yat-sen and take a left spoke.

At the bank, a lady takes my raincoat and I'm done in four minutes, the fastest yet. The lady helps me back into my coat, and I dart back into the car.

On the way back to Sun Yat-sen, I ask Pray if people don't miss having big families. For centuries it was such a protection for them.

She replies that young people now feel there is "more in life than responsibility," and I think, Uh-oh, here come the sixties.

The tailor is not there when we arrive. We hang out in the store for about twenty minutes until he finally shows up, which is kind of agonizing because of the rain. But LuLu's coats are wonderful, exactly as I envisioned them. My dresses, however, are way too big, and I don't want shoulder pads in them. I fiddle around for a while, getting them just right, while the photographer takes pictures. He is irked, Pray tells me, that we are doing nothing traditional. I don't go into the Children's Palace fiasco. I think he's just irked that I am an American. After all, the three people killed in the bombing were from Xinhua. Frankly, I doubt the photo essay will ever see the light of day.

But I like Pray and she likes us, and it's restful to talk to someone in English.

We go back to the hotel for lunch, and after Lu is finished, she goes off to play in the kitchen—her preferred place to be now. The kitchen boys are very young and full of fun, and she enjoys their games. They throw bread and joke and generally laugh a lot.

That's one thing about Wuhu: people laugh a lot here. I'm forever rounding a corner and seeing someone having a joke. The room attendants and floor maids laugh. The sweepers smile and laugh. The car-washing boys laugh and joke. The reception crew laughs and chats. The managers stand in the bug area, and smoke and laugh with the cook. The taxi drivers are laughing and playing cards while they wait for fares. The salesgirls laugh and giggle at Xin Bei and Insu. There's laughter in the market. The depiction of China as one long horror show of anguish and pain has not been our experience at all. Quite the opposite; it's unusually jolly.

After lunch, I wait around for LuLu by the bug area but can't find her and decide she may have gone down to the room. Her independence is growing day by day, and she knows the place so well now that she just might have zoomed down to see JingJing.

Several minutes after I get to our building and to our room and realize she isn't there, one of the waitresses appears with a sobbing LuLu. I hold her close, and explain what happened and why I left the dining room without her. But it is clear that she is terrified that she might be left, that her mother might vanish.

"No matter what happens, I will never leave you," I say to her. "I will always be here for you. I will always be your mother."

I like to think of myself as an honest person, so when I say this to her (and I have said it before, when I think she needs to hear it), I always feel dishonest. Because if I died, I would be leaving her, and I'm not young. This makes me think of Alice, and I silently utter a little prayer for her and her daughter. But I long ago decided not to include death for the moment in our picture. This four-parent, two-country business is hard enough for a small child to grasp without adding the possibility of my death.

But, of course, Lu will hear about Alice, and she will know right then that Western mommies may not leave but they can die. Is there no end to the shoals ahead?

Back in the room, I switch on TV to dull my thoughts, and there is a film about Tibet, with Tibetans gathering firewood in the grasslands in summer. Strangely, it's about the lyric qualities of Tibetan life, and shows Tibetans singing and dancing around the campfire.

June 11
Cloudy

I am thinking that we might move on to Guanzhou. There are several reasons. First, as inexpensive as it is here, it has been more expensive than I thought, what with foreigner's prices, and I still have the most expensive part of the trip ahead: the White Swan Hotel in Guanzhou. Guanzhou (the old Canton) is the city where Americans must go to get immigration visas for their adopted children. Everyone who adopts in China ends up at the White Swan Hotel. Then we are stopping over in Hong Kong on the way to Hawaii, where we are meeting Cheryl, LuLu's godmother, and seeing her new house on the Big Island.

It is also getting much hotter, and there is nowhere to swim in Wuhu. The hotel pool doesn't open until mid-July. We can't spend the next month in the indoor playgrounds. The Chinese, in spite of their Olympic diving prowess, don't seem to go in for water sports. And they don't like to expose their bodies to the sun. I've noticed, since it got hotter, bicyclists wearing little sun shawls to cover their shoulders and necks. The women are all wearing hats with wide brims or carrying umbrellas, or both.

Since we are not getting to meet Lu's nurse or read her file, our literal business here is finished. And LuLu misses her dad and her cats and her friends and her American home, and it's just getting time to go.

LuLu finds Baba on the door and plays with him for a while before we set off to find a large suitcase to contain all the stuff we have acquired. I tell LuLu that unfortunately, we cannot take all the giant stuffed animals home with us. She must choose two.

She has bonded to Tong and Tie Shan, whom she often brings

up to dinner, so she chooses them. Baba's dog and the other creature will have to stay behind.

We walk up Laodong Road to Sun Yat-sen, where I had seen a luggage store on one of our travels. Inside is a kitten with a rope tied around its neck, tethering it to the store. I find this odd; don't they know cats will stay around a home? Or is it theft they fear?

LuLu plays with the kitten while I learn that there are no big suitcases here. It takes a long time to pry her away again, but finally I do, and we walk around the lake to the mall opposite Insu. Jing Hu Lake looks lovely now, all planted with flowers, and the little pavilion where LuLu played with the students is restored and very pretty.

We go into the mall and pass by the store where I got the Sailor Moon backpack, and the owner comes running out. LuLu forgot her bracelet there a month ago and he's saved it all this time for us. I try to buy a suitcase from him but, alas, they are all too small.

We have ice cream at Xin Bei and then go down into the market to stock up on hair things as presents for our Chinese girl-friends.

As we pass the knitting store, the wool seller calls out, "Hi, LuLu!" Lu goes right in and plays a while with her little son. Next door is the kind man who gave us postcards. Today I buy more from him, along with another kitchen magnet with the picture of the girl from Wuhu who made good.

We return to the hotel for lunch. We can't stay out too long at one clip now because of the heat. When we are finished eating, LuLu takes me into the kitchen to meet her friends. It's a rabbit warren of industrial-looking rooms back there, an enormous place. Her friends the kitchen boys, who look mighty mischievous, are making duck. The chef, my friend, is frying up something in another room. I take a look at the cooking oil he uses and vow to find some. I must be at least fifteen pounds lighter than when I arrived, and I've eaten more healthfully than ever in my life. How I will miss this diet, such lovely fresh vegetables.

After a nap, during which the news reports that Henry Kissinger is visiting, too, we set off for the tailor. Interesting about Kissinger; he must be doing backtrack work in Beijing, apologizing, placating, promising things in return for forgiveness.

The tailor is having his hair cut across the street when we arrive. He hops out of the barber chair and rushes across the street to see us. The winter dresses are fine now, but the summer ones are still too big.

We walk back and visit the hotel antiques shop. I want to buy some presents here to take with us. I tell this to the owner, and when he hears we will be leaving, he gives LuLu an antique porcelain box with pictures of children playing on it.

It's going to be wrenching to depart, really sad. But we'll come back, I promise myself.

After dinner, at which the flutist plays more beautifully than ever, LuLu goes off with JingJing and Alexandra calls with information about the train to Tongling. I'm still trying to get there before we go. It's two hours away, she says. A friend of hers took the train there recently. I couldn't get much of an answer when I asked how far it was by car.

"Two hours. Four hours," Mickeyman said. I asked if there might be a map so I could check the distance, and he looked at me oddly. No map.

I finally realize that no one travels here except businesspeople, and rarely by car. So they only need overnight bags, and no one knows how far anything is.

After dinner we pick up the photos, which turned out very well. They did a good job developing them, too, and it is quite cheap. I determine to develop all my pictures of the last few months here, in China, instead of waiting till I get home. The Chinese camera produces a photo with a velvety feel to it. It seems to be an excellent device.

On TV this evening, *China Business* is about the making of law in China. They don't have law as we know it, which fascinates me. They saw that they had to make law when they started building buildings and one fell down because it was shoddily constructed and killed a lot of people. Several American lawyers working in Beijing are interviewed. They say diplomatically that practicing law in China is unique, because you can be in the process of suing a firm and it just disappears off the face of the earth.

June 12
Cloudy

At breakfast, LuLu is allowed to help put the fresh eels into the bank of fish tanks by the entrance. For her, this is a real mark of belonging. Then we go down to reception and Lu plays with Baba while I ask about train tickets to Guanzhou. The woman at reception, whom I don't know all that well, doesn't really understand me; she orders the tickets, and it's done. Suddenly, we are leaving Wuhu in three days.

The knowledge that we are going slowly dawns on everyone in the lobby. They are all upset, but Baba looks stricken. I immediately take down his name and address as everyone starts playing with LuLu as if to get just a little more time. I feel awful.

We walk down to Laodong Road to the photo store and pick up the rest of our pictures. In the shop, there is a panoramic shot of Wuhu; I inquire about it and the owner, a young man into technology, gives it to me. I thank him profusely. This will be one of the prized things I take home, to remind me of our time here.

We continue on to the bank, but for some reason it is closed. We take a taxi back and Mickeyman, or "Older Brother," as Lu now calls him, tells me we have spent seventy-five hundred yuan out of twelve thousand, which is great news. I will need the rest for the remainder of our journey.

We go up to the Canting and eat according to our simple drill, a four-year-old's drill, whose very consistency has made us part of the landscape here, and the landscape part of us.

When I leave, LuLu is out in the bug area with Mr. Tchang, Mr. Tong, and Mr. Wu. I take their pictures with her.

"When will you come back?" Mr. Wu asks. It's amazing how much more English everyone speaks now than when we arrived.

"I don't know," I tell him. "If I had my way, I'd come every summer, but it's expensive. We will come back, though." And we will.

As Lu and I walk down to our room, I think that Wuhu will be much different when we do come back. The bridge across the river to the Hening Freeway will change life here. Hefei will be only an hour away. Wuhu has always been cut off from the capital, but now it will be within easy reach. People could even live in Wuhu and work in Hefei. But when I mention this, most people cannot even imagine such a thing.

Sometimes it seems that modern life is all nostalgia. You come to love something, and soon after, it vanishes. You don't get a lifetime to enjoy it anymore.

On the way down the road from the Canting, through the trees, bushy with leaves and bending in protectively toward us on either side, LuLu inhales the warm, oilcloth smell in the air.

"I don't want to leave China," she says sadly. "I wish my life was here."

"Me too," I say. "I feel the same way."

For a while, I fantasize how I would make money in today's China if we lived here. Journalist, yes. But what they really need here are coin-operated Laundromats for busy working folks and college kids. Perhaps they would use less water and be a lot cheaper.

When we get back to the room, I try to make a decision about

Tongling. We are not going. If only Lu were well and I actually knew how far away it was . . .

Around two, Alexandra comes to help with a few things. First the tailor. Most of the things are great. The two summer dresses are a bit dowdy, but I'll live with that. While we chat with the tailor and get his name and address, LuLu eats watermelon seeds and plays with a boy who works there.

Then we three get into a taxi and head for the hospital to see about Lu's culture.

When we get there, I go to the cashier and pay. It is much less expensive than last time. We walk through the building and up a ramp to the chemist's lab, where the chemist heats his pipette, does something with the culture, and then looks at it under the microscope.

She does have a parasite, he tells Alexandra, and he writes down the prescription in the booklet, which I have brought with me so we can take it to the pharmacist. I am upset but relieved that finally LuLu will get the right medicine. I wonder where and how she got the bug.

We walk back around the Mediterranean side of the lake to the university entrance and stroll across campus. The feeling is happy and lively, and everyone is out on the basketball courts, playing.

When we get to the plaza, Baba is on duty. Alexandra helps me talk to him. I thank him profusely for his kindness to LuLu, and he replies that he loves her. I ask him whether he will continue in hotel work, and he says probably not. He is interested in becoming either an auto mechanic or an interior decorator, two professions that are about to take off here.

I drop by the lobby and quickly get my e-mail. There's a message from Martha about our not being able to visit Wuhu orphanage. "Take the director to lunch," she writes.

That pretty much underscores the misconceptions we have been laboring under, which I understand far better having been here.

We go back to the room, and while LuLu plays with JingJing, I watch a soap opera that takes place in ancient China. A maiden has been put in a wooden prison with a bevy of loutish women.

I turn to the soap that is set in modern Shanghai and discover that the new wife, Huler, has been beaten by her new husband. Her grandmother does not want her to go back to him, but she has to. The entire family is there, crying.

In the evening the special finally comes on. *The History of American Aggression* begins with the invasion of Grenada and continues through the Gulf War and up through the bombing of Belgrade. It almost could have been made by a left-wing liberal. I hope it won't rile people up against us just as we are leaving Wuhu.

June 13
Sunny

We breakfast and then spend some time in the bug area chatting. Mr. Ni, from the antiques store, gives LuLu a gardenia and she asks for another, which she gives to me.

Then she runs off into the kitchen and plays throwing-food games with the boys. It is one of those days that she has a plan, and as we walk down the hill, she tells me she wants now to go play with JingJing, as she is learning some Chinese songs. She sings me one: it's a pop song called "Doshe Nida Tong," which means "Give Me Your Heart."

I drop LuLu off with JingJing, and go to the room and call Leo again to say good-bye, but I don't get him. There's a knock and it's Baba with a paper I must fill out. It is a declaration of moneys spent in Wuhu. It also asks my age and how I felt about such things in the city as the public bathrooms.

Alexandra has told us of another park we might visit. It is called

Tien Tong Park, and she has written down the name and address to give the taxi driver.

The park lies on the Buddhist temple side of the little Tie Shan and turns out to be very pretty. The first thing we see is a lake and a man fishing by the side of it. He is wearing a suit, and this combination of formality and rusticity is such a metaphor for the new China.

We walk on and find an old Duesenberg from the 1930s in which, for a fee, you can sit and have your picture taken. I can't help but wonder who in Wuhu used to drive it.

On the way home, we stop off at the bakery because the man who ices the cakes is performing. The primary-school children are cheering him on.

We meander up the street to the Tie Shan, cross the plaza, and enter our building. There, grouped on the stairs, are all the attendants, floor maids, and employees of our building, with Mrs. Chang. They start applauding as we enter.

I am so moved by this, I can't speak, and LuLu is delighted. She rushes to them and hugs them all and dances about. I, of course, as usual, am trying not to cry.

Instead, I whip out photos to show everyone. I have duplicates if people want copies. Mrs. Chang is especially interested in photos of the Hefei orphanage.

"They look very nice," she says, referring to the babies, and a look of puzzlement comes over her face. I can see that she expected them to look gnarled and ugly somehow, to confirm that the prejudice against them is justified.

She had made, perhaps, an exception in LuLu's case; now, as she sees so many perfectly adorable babies, she is realizing that she may have thought wrongly about the children. And all this clearly crosses her open, kindly face as she looks through the photos.

I go down to reception and find that they have gotten a bid of a hundred and fifty yuan to drive us to Nanjing, where we will

rhaps she will end up being as great a cook as he is
xperiences here.

I wrest her from her buddies and we go down to the
ournalist is an hour late. The Xinhua people were also
. As a sometime journalist myself, I wouldn't dare be
, but then journalism is new to China.

rter, who calls himself Stephen, is in his mid-twenties,
onable, and very enthusiastic. A young Chinese
d Beth, who teaches in the English Department at the
as brought him over. Both speak very good English.
exactly like young journalists in America. He has the
ess and drive, and his thinking is just as sophisticated.
about us because, of course, we are a great story.
a lot about us already. Either he's really done his
work or it's such a small town that everyone knows
yone else. He knows we hang out at Xin Bei and get
r example, which isn't common knowledge. Or

estion is whether we came here to find Lu's Chinese
I answer, we came here to find Wuhu, her home-
she could see China and meet the people. This, I tell
st; she needs to love and respect it.

in why I would bring her all this way, and I decide
nd reply that if there is a chance that LuLu is a one-
aby, then I feel I owe it to the woman who was not
ep her to make sure she knows and loves China.
t I can do in return for having this wonderful child.
ve China myself and that I spent part of my child-
n.

e have been to the Welfare, and I tell him part of the
saying that I would prefer he didn't even mention
ause I don't want to offend the Wuhu city govern-
why do it now? We went to the Hefei orphanage
ne, so better not to mention it.

catch the train to Guanzhou. It would cost two hundred yuan to
go to Tongling, but I don't think I have the strength for that.

This evening, there's an extraordinary program on TV. It's the
Barbara Walters Wong discussion hour and the topic is "Should
the Handicapped Be Allowed to Live? Should the Fetus Have
Rights? Yes? No?"

There's a bioethicist, an ethicist, and a geneticist, all discussing
sex discrimination and how to improve the quality of human beings, and whether we should.

Barbara says, "If we were allowed to abort unwanted children at
will, there would be only males in this country and no future gen-
erations."

And all the professors at the table nod sagely. And there it is,
right on the table. In LuLu's Wuhu school class, twenty-three
boys and ten girls. In one immigrant class at Red Apple, twelve
boys and two girls. But it is amazing to hear the TV moderator say
it out loud like that.

My mother used to say that the one-child policy was the one
hope China had of teaching men to value women. The fewer
there were of them, the more valuable they'd be, she would say.

The curious thing about being here is that the young women
we have met, from Caroline to JingJing to Alexandra to Wei Wei,
all have lots of strength and confidence. One does not sense a pall
over China's women; quite the contrary.

The ethicist declares that parents should abort only for medical
reasons. Then the bioethicist adds that the more children people
have, the less intelligent the children are.

The professor from Beijing says he does not believe in inborn
intelligence. It's a matter of parental input and education.

Should we make the Chinese smarter if the technology is available to do so? asks Barbara.

The geneticist says no, we can't make the Chinese smarter. It's
impossible. Geneticists are not able to make people smarter.

The professor from Beijing says that we should make people

smarter if we can. He is pro-technology. He gives as an example how new techniques for delivery of premature babies have lessened the incidence of cerebral palsy. The quality of obstetric service directly influences these things, he says.

It continues to be a wild night on TV. There's some sort of *Ripley's Believe It or Not* game show on. The host is a Pal Joey type in a tux. He is flanked by two girls in cocktail dresses, one in yellow, one in red. One side of the stage is yellow, the other side is red.

The contestants are two men. One is doing situps, one is standing on his head and bumping forward.

That ends, and we are treated to a woman whose hair must be ten feet long. She is standing on a pedestal, and her hair comes all the way down and winds along the front of the stage.

Then comes a mathematician who writes a lengthy and complex problem on the blackboard. A little kid appears and figures it out.

Then there's a guy who makes air sculptures with bubbles he blows. He makes bubbles so big he can stand inside them. Then he blows cigar smoke and decorates the bubbles he blows with it. He closes by covering both hostesses with giant bubbles.

Watching this show, I am reminded of Marco Polo's description of the fairgrounds in twelfth-century China. He, too, was probably entertained by a man who blew giant bubbles and sculpted them.

June 14
Sunny

I take LuLu to school. For the first time in a while, she is feeling pretty well. The pills seem to be working, thank God and that guy with the pipette.

"But you already went to the Welfare," he says, and looks puzzled. It really startles me that he knows of our visits there, and I lie, telling him yes, we dropped by, not knowing we couldn't just visit. I tell him about our interview with the police and being denied a permit.

"Look," I say, "we don't need to visit now. I just wanted to see her file in case there's anything in it she could know. Little details will be so important to her later. And she would like to have met the woman who took care of her for that last month. But we have resigned ourselves. They won't let us. So," I finished, "please, leave it alone."

"I can go for you," he says. "I'll go tomorrow to the orphanage and look through the files for you."

Just like that.

"You w-will?" I stutter. "You can?"

"Sure," he says. "I'll set it up tomorrow."

It takes me a minute to recover. I ask him to wait, and I rush away to the room to pick up all the documents I have for Francesca, Maya, Mary, and LuLu. I also sit for a moment and write a list of questions for the orphanage director.

When I return, I ask Stephen if he will look for the other girls' files as well. Then I ask about where LuLu was found, just to make sure I saw the right place, and show him the address.

"I'll take you there tomorrow," he says. "And we'll do some photos."

And with that, we arrange to meet again in the morning.

They leave and I sit there, dumbfounded. This is China in a nutshell: like a Chinese box or Chinese garden or Chinese building, with so many secret drawers and paths and entrances and exits, and finally one leads to the chamber of the emperor. Patience is the catalyst, patience and good faith.

As LuLu and I walk back to the room in the hot, starry night fragrant with jasmine and powdery DDT, I feel the goodwill of all our friends in Wuhu behind this. Stephen is their gift to us for sticking it out, and to their little countrywoman, LuLu, for loving them so wholeheartedly.

Just when you think China has abandoned you, she turns around and picks you up again.

June 15
Sunny

Stephen gives the taxi driver directions to the place where the original adoption documents say LuLu was found.

When we get there, it is a different bridge from the one to which Caroline and Miss Swallow drove us. It is on the same canal, though, the Qing Yi Jiang Canal, which extends all the way to Xin Bei; but this bridge is about a mile down from the other one. Aside from location, it is quite similar, a modern bridge but less well traveled.

Right across from it is the police station, the actual police station into which LuLu was taken when she was found. When I surveyed the bridge at Xin Bei, I was so overwhelmed that it never occurred to me that there was no police station there. I stare at the police station for a moment, my heart in my mouth.

This area, Stephen tells me, was until recently all shanties and rather poor. Now it has been cleared out and is a new but nondescript business neighborhood with office buildings and truck lots.

I try to envision LuLu lying anywhere here, and I can't.

Stephen is carrying LuLu and I can see that she is following the discussion closely.

"Would you like to go into the police station," he asks, "to see if they remember LuLu or have records of her?"

I'm shocked. I hadn't even thought that the police would have records, but of course, they would, too.

"Yes," I say. And in we go.

Stephen tells the police who we are, and they are really enthusiastic. They spontaneously hoist LuLu up in the air in triumph. It has given them obvious pleasure to know that one of the girls they find so often has lucked out with a good, warm life.

But, Stephen tells me, they have said they are not the same police who actually found her. Every two years they change stations. He must apply to see the records, which he says he will do for us.

I take pictures of Lu with the police and the bridge, and the surrounding area. Then we get into a taxi and go to Xin Bei for the photo session. The photographer takes LuLu on the Rooster ride in the children's department, sharing it with another child who's there.

While she's getting her picture taken, I tell Stephen that whatever he does, he must not upset the adoption ministry. We are not here to upset anyone, just for LuLu to see where she came from. Then I tell him to phone Leo and interview him, too. I want Leo to be in on this right from the beginning, so there are no problems.

Before Stephen leaves us to go off to the orphanage, he says, "Perhaps her parents will read about it in the newspaper and contact me. Can I give them your address?"

I am filled with both ecstasy and terror at the thought. "Of course," I answer.

"Would you like her to meet them?" he asks.

"Yes," I respond.

In truth, the possibility that this might happen makes me confront this as a reality for the first time. What if LuLu no longer wanted me? whips through my soul. Can I share my most prized love? How cosmopolitan am I, really? I shake off these thoughts with the knowledge that for LuLu to meet and know her original parents would mean so much. It would change her destiny. She is capable of rock-solid happiness, and that would make it possible for her. From terror, I segue into fantasy, and now Lu is spending summers in Wuhu with my in-laws (her birth parents) and I'm learning from them to cook and garden.

I drag myself back to the present, and Stephen, Lu, and I leave the store. While he heads for the orphanage, we decide to lunch at a beautiful teahouse moored on the lake that we have passed all this time but never entered.

The teahouse boat has a yellow pagoda roof and is made of wood, with windows all around it. We get on via a little wooden bridge carpeted in red. Inside, it is adorable, with wooden furniture and lace curtains. The only problem is that it does not have air-conditioning and it is unbelievably hot.

The proprietress appears, a woman with a 1940s rolled hairdo and a shoulder-padded print dress. She insists we move to the one air-conditioned room, which is in the back of the boat. We order dumplings and tea, and then she shuts the door.

Unfortunately, neither Lu nor I can feel this air-conditioning, and we are melting. We open the doors and move out into the stream of a fan in the main cabin, which doesn't help much. We are speechless with heat. It's a pity, because the teahouse boat is lovely.

We eat quickly and stagger outside, where a woman on a bike asks LuLu to take a picture with her when she hears how well Lu speaks English.

LuLu's cheeks are bright red. I am so hot, I can't think. They call this province the Oven of China, and now I know why. The air is so hot that we can't breathe it in.

The oppressive heat makes me feel a bit better about leaving. Beth has told me that it gets so hot here in summer, they have a rule: if the temperature hits a certain mark, people can stay home from work.

When we get home, we take a cold shower and spend the rest of the day inside in the air-conditioning. While LuLu plays with JingJing and the other floor attendants, I try not to get too anxious about what will be in the files.

Finally, blessed evening comes and it cools off a bit, and after dinner we go down to the lobby to meet Stephen and Beth. I sit opposite them and prepare myself. LuLu goes off to play with Baba, who is fortuitously on duty.

Stephen leans forward. "There are no files," he says, disappointment in his voice. "They are gone. Not for any of the girls. Everything was in a jumble. I did find one page from Lao Li's [Francesca's] file, but that was a duplicate of the page you had given me."

Just like that. Over. I don't know whether I am sad or happy to hear this.

He goes on. "I did find other files from the same period and notes—all had to do with the family planning act. So probably LuLu was abandoned as a result of that."

I nod my head. One-child policy.

"They remember LuLu and Lao Li because they were among the first girls sent to the U.S.A., but not because they remember them as people. In fact," he adds, "during the time they were left, they did not expect any girls would be sent out of the country, so they didn't bother to keep their records in order. These are not important people. . . ." He lowers his eyes. He does not want to offend me, but he is trying to tell me the truth. "I told them they must take more care. Perhaps when they move, they will put the records in order and find something."

"But you looked very carefully?" I ask.

"Yes. I did," he says, and smiles ruefully.

I feel a door closing in my mind. An anxiety has left me.

I had asked a number of questions, which he now answers.

1. How did they get their names?

"No particular reason except place. Lao Li was found on the Laodong Road, hence Lao. Li is a common girl's name."

2. Who chooses the babies for us?

"Both the Welfare and Beijing assign the babies to the adoptive parents, but in both cases it is entirely random."

3. What about meeting LuLu's special care nurse?

"LuLu did not have a special care nurse. All the nurses took care of the babies."

I wonder if this is true. It could be.

He goes on to say that the Welfare hopes I am not seeking LuLu's parents, because "Chinese law stipulates that these parents will be punished. It is a crime."

"No," I reassure him. "No."

Now it is my turn to interview Stephen. I ask him if he is disappointed, and he says he is and that he bawled out the director and told him to keep better records and to staple any notes to the files.

I ask him if he got a sense of where LuLu might be from or anything else when he went through the files.

"LuLu," he replies, "probably came from one of three outlying counties of Wuhu City: Nanling, Fanchon, or Wuhu Tsien. The reason she was left was, as I've said, the family plan. Her parents would be around thirty years old, because the average age of parents here is twenty-five, and she would probably be their second child. The parents most likely work in factories. They are probably not farmers, because a lot of people have come off the farms now and work in factories."

I sit quiet for a moment and then thank him for doing this for me. I tell him he seems like a very good reporter, and that as a journalist myself, I do think we are a good story and am looking forward to his piece about us.

He suddenly grimaces and stammers out, "Y-yes, we do more here in China than taking away people's human rights."

It is a strange moment. I think he wants to talk about the bombing with me but won't for some reason. We have become quite friendly, and he knows I am a journalist, too. This remark is as close as it gets.

Since he has done this important thing for me, I take this opportunity to tell him how I really feel.

"I'll tell you what I think: the real human rights story in this country, right now, is the dangerous living conditions of the average person."

I am referring to the pits of rubble, exposed live wiring, no lighting, and so on.

Beth and Stephen look shocked for a second, but they smile at me and nod imperceptibly.

I then give Stephen my address to send a copy of his piece when it comes out, and I get his address. We shake hands. Lu comes over and hugs him, and he and Beth leave. She promises to return on the day we depart to help us.

No files. Gone. I sit for a while in the lobby, digesting the news. No information. Nothing of Maya, Mary, Francesca, or LuLu.

I feel a sense of closure about this now and go over it again. Her first parents are factory workers, around thirty, from the outlying suburbs. Next trip, that's where we will go to have a look. We couldn't go this time because of the bombing.

I take LuLu back to the room, and after I put her to bed, I watch her sleeping and pray that when she gets older, it will be okay with her that she was adopted.

June 16
Torrential rain

We are off to Insu to buy presents for JingJing and Ling-Ling since I can't tip them. We walk down to get a taxi, but curiously, there aren't any. We walk farther and discover a huge flood at the bottom of the street, blocking the entrance. Our choice is to wade through dirty water three feet deep to get to Laodong Road or follow the path others are taking through the university grounds. We take the path and come out through the building next to Radio Shack by the lake.

At Insu, I buy two lavish makeup kits, one a bit more lavish than the other—for JingJing, who has been so great to LuLu. My roller skates are going to Baba. Some hardly worn dresses of LuLu's that she has grown out of will go to Yue Yue, Mrs. Chang's daughter. And everyone got copies of photos.

We come back several hours later via Laodong Road and discover the water is still there. There is no drainage, evidently, and a fire truck is sitting in front of the moon gate to the market, attempting to suction up the flood. We end up removing our rubber boots and, much to Lu's delight and my horror, wading through the water onto our street.

In the afternoon, Anne comes and I make use of her translation abilities to thank everyone and say good-bye properly.

We talk to JingJing, the waitress, and she tells us that all the waitresses come from the tourist school and are doing a work program at the Tie Shan. Then she will go back to school to become a teacher. They make about four hundred yuan a month: fifty-six dollars.

At dinner, LuLu dances to the trumpet, and we tell the trumpet player and the flutist that we are going. The two men are visibly upset.

Anne helps me tell them how much I have enjoyed their musicianship and how beautifully I think they play. I thank them, too, for their kindness to LuLu, who has spent a bit of every evening in the green room, learning from them.

After dinner, we bid good-bye to Anne and I put Lu to bed.

"Tell me about when I was borned," she murmurs, a request she has not made since we arrived.

So I start the story, using everything we have learned here.

"On the outskirts of Wuhu, a Chinese couple, your Chinese parents, gave birth to you. They couldn't keep you, though they wanted to very much—I don't know why, exactly, but probably because the government wouldn't let them have another child. So they took you to the bridge near the police station—"

"And they left me there *alone*?" LuLu suddenly shouts. It is a cry of outrage coming from a place deep inside her, and for the first time ever, tears flood down her cheeks because of something to do with her adoption.

"I'm crying," she says, feeling her wet cheek with her little fingers, astonished at her own lack of control. Then she just lets go.

"I don't want them to leave me alone. Why did they leave me alone?" she cries out through deep, grief-stricken sobs.

What can I possibly say? My baby's heart has broken open and grief is gushing out. I curse myself that I ever held back any information from her. Yet I realize that being left *alone* is just a metaphor for being left.

"My darling," I say, "listen. They left you there because they knew those policemen would find you right away and take you to the institute. It was a safe, known place. I know this because your mother left a note, so she knew they would find you very soon. Lu, you're such a joyful person, I don't think it was a very bad experience. And you know what I bet happened?"

She looks at me. "What?"

"You know how you like to run around and look at everything by yourself?" She nods.

"Well, you were probably looking all around and curious, and then the policeman found you and took you right inside, and you thought, Rats! I'm enjoying this."

She smiles. Then she says mournfully, "I miss my Chinese parents. I'll never know who they are. I love my Chinese parents," she sobs. "I love my Western parents."

"I love your Chinese parents, too," I say truthfully. "Because you have their eyes, their strength, their good humor."

"I'll never know what my Chinese parents looked like," she says sadly.

"Perhaps your father looked like the men you've met. Like Baba."

"He's not my real Chinese father. He's like a brother," she says. "I miss my Chinese father and my Chinese uncles and cousins and my *nai nai* [grandmother]." She weeps for it all and I weep, too.

I hold her close and we weep together. Then I say, "I'm so sorry that you lost your parents, Lu. Sometimes things happen in strange ways. But your mother left me a note so I would find you. And I love you more than anything in the whole world, and Neke loves you more than anything in the whole world. And we are so honored to have you as our daughter."

She throws her arms around my neck and says, "You are the best, best, best, best mama in the whole world."

And we stay like that for a few minutes, then she picks up the TV remote and says calmly, "I want to watch kung fu."

For now, we are finished with our talk. She has never grieved like this before, and while the adoption book said it is important for her to do it, seeing her pain is unbearable.

I go into the bathroom and get into a hot bath. She comes in after a while and says again, "I'll never know what they looked like."

"Look in the mirror," I say, and she does. Her funny little heart-shaped face, with the one dimple just to the right of her full lips, stares back at her. Her jet-black hair falls to her waist. Behind her, I'm in the mirror, too, with my pale skin and blue eyes. "Look. You look like your mama and your dad and your grandmother." I take her hand in mine. "I bet your mama had these beautiful hands."

She wanders away back to the TV, and when I am ready for bed, we read *Five Children and It* together. At the end of it, there are questions, one of which asks the child to make some wishes.

She closes her eyes tight and whispers, "I wish I knew my Chinese parents. I wish I knew my uncles and cousins."

June 17
Sunny

In the morning, LuLu is very cheerful and visibly calm. She is excited about our going now. She is desperate to see Neke and jubilant at the thought of our train ride to Guanzhou.

It is hard to believe we are leaving. We walk up to the Canting for breakfast and notice that the magnolia buds, as big as footballs, are opening into giant blossoms. The dragonflies are everywhere, whizzing about like tiny jet planes. Butterflies are flapping about daintily. And the trees that line the path are twittering, packed with birds invisible to the eye. The sun glints off the pools of water that remain on the concrete from the rains, and steam rises faintly from dew that is burning off the leaves. Every one of these things we will miss like dear friends.

At home we live in a world where we are constantly taking in many things. Here we have focused on a few. How restful it has been, and how human. It is not just LuLu who is wondering who she is.

After breakfast, I pop into the kitchen and take pictures of the kitchen boys, and tell them we are leaving. They all look sad.

At ten, Beth comes to help us with our good-byes. First we go to the bank. In exactly five minutes, we cash our traveler's checks, thank everyone, and say good-bye.

We return on foot, stopping at the photo store to pick up some blowups I had made. There we encounter Kay, whom we thank for her friendship and bid good-bye. She'll be going home for a month in August with the other American teachers, she says. She will think of us.

The flood has evaporated or been sucked away, so it is easy to zip around the corner and into the preschool. We visit Yu Jie, who has moved into her new office in the new building. It is quite different from the old one, white and sparkling. Beth helps me thank her and the school doctor for being so kind to us. I try to indicate without saying it outright that I know it wasn't easy for them, what with the unpleasantness, and that their rock-solid friendliness did not go unnoticed.

Yu Jie takes us upstairs to see LuLu's class, and I thank the teacher. She tells me how much they enjoyed having LuLu in the class, that the teachers were impressed by her bravery and fearlessness. They comment on how friendly she is and how willing to try things. They wish, they say, that Chinese kids were more like that. LuLu says good-bye to her friends, who are taking their naps, as is the way here, on the tables.

Yu Jie invites us to come the next day before we go, as it is class picture day. She apologizes a bit for the school. She wishes, she says, they had more equipment for the children, and, of course, it's not finished. Clearly, her vision of the American preschool is way overdeveloped. I tell her truthfully that her school is wonderful. LuLu had a great time here, which she did.

We walk back to the antiques store in the hotel and I buy some teapots from Mr. Ni for the Wuhu girls back home. Then we go up to the room and I invite Lu's beloved JingJing, the attendant, to sit down with us.

JingJing tells us that she lives at home. She has worked at the Tie Shan for three years and is about to take an exam in tourism, after which she hopes to make more money. She tells me she is shocked that we are leaving so soon, and she looks it. She is not prepared for it, she says, and she is very sad.

I thank her for her incredible kindness to LuLu and say that Lu will never forget her. I tell her how important it is to LuLu's identity to have received such warmth in China and that no present is good enough for that. LuLu, she replies, made their jobs a lot more fun.

"I am moved," JingJing then says, "that you would buy me such an expensive present. Never have guests treated me with such friendliness and democracy."

"It was our pleasure," I say, meaning it.

After a time, we go to dinner. We are sitting at the table when the flutist and trumpeter arrive. They come over to us and give LuLu two presents: from the trumpeter, a music box with a girl sitting on it; from the flutist, a Chinese flute.

Even at five, LuLu knows immediately that these are extraordinary gifts that have deep meaning. She flings her arms around the flutist and thanks him, and then around the trumpeter. Then, all together, they go up on stage, and while they play "Red River Valley," LuLu sways and dances to the tune.

When we go back to the room, I pack while LuLu plays with JingJing. At one point, she pulls me out into the hall to meet a young man in his early twenties who is here to collect four-year-olds who are going to the boarding school where he teaches. It is a private school for prodigy artists and costs around eight thousand dollars a year, a whopping sum for China. The young man is a painting teacher, and he looks exactly like a student at Andover or Exeter or Yale. He is clearly a very privileged kid, one of the new Chinese wealthy, I guess, or maybe not so new. He is adorable and full of fun.

June 18
Sunny

We are leaving today. I've packed all the bags, and except for the clothes we will wear, we are set to go. The train leaves at eight. We decide to head out at four-thirty because no one can tell us how long it will take to get to the station. We go up to breakfast and I pretend we aren't leaving so as to maintain my sanity.

We go off to the preschool, where the class is having end-of-year pictures. All the children are wearing heavy makeup. Many have the red dots in the middle of their foreheads.

Yu Jie invites us into her office. She gives LuLu chocolate soy milk and presents her with four books of Chinese classics for children. *Dream of the Red Chamber* is among them.

I can't believe this. The books are beautiful. These people have been so good to us that I'm just overwhelmed. And again, LuLu, only five, seems to grasp that the books are very special. She insists on carrying them under her arm as we leave and tells me firmly that someday she will read them.

We walk back up the street for the last time, past the primary school, which at this moment breaks into a glorious cacophony of children's voices, past the man selling roast ducks, past the entrance to the university housing and the *xigua* sellers from the country, past the other preschool with its moon gate, past the taxi queue and the pagoda entrances to the Tie Shan teahouse and zoo.

I bid good-bye to the doctor who fixed my foot and Lu's finger. Then I go into the lobby and get the bill. All is correct, except for a phone bill of a whopping three hundred U.S. dollars. Upon inquiring, I learn that this part comes from the dreaded post office. The post office is claiming that I spoke for an hour and fifty-three minutes to the United States and four hours and fifty minutes to Hefei. Because I timed Neke's two calls to us, I know that all my U.S. calls together took no longer than about fifteen minutes. And I called Leo in Hefei about three or four times for a total of about an hour.

I protest, but this part of the bill is up to the post office. It seems that perhaps we didn't hang up properly and break the connection, so we were still open to charges.

The woman behind the desk is someone I don't know well, but she puts up with my protest and calls Mr. Tchang. She takes our address and tells me that Mr. Tchang will look into it. Then she returns in cash the money that we did not spend.

We go up to the restaurant and say good-bye to Mr. Tong. I thank him for everything and order a take-out lunch for the train. He makes a lovely dinner for us, a fish soup and duck with fennel. Lu is not with us; she is down playing for the last time with Baba.

I go back to the room, stopping to collect LuLu. There is so much luggage, I don't know how we will get it on the train. But I'm not worried; I know a bit about China now, and I'm certain that someone will turn up to help us.

I have crammed Tong and Tie Shan, the stuffed animals, into the bags. The giant dog, LuLu is carrying. She hasn't bonded with it but would like to keep it. We make a pact: if we see a poor child, she will give it away. If not, she will keep it. She is fine with this.

She runs off to the plaza as Beth, JingJing, and I struggle with the bags. When we get down to the lobby, Tao Liang is there to see us off. He and Baba pack up the car. We say good-bye to Beth and thank her. LuLu kisses Baba and I direct the driver to go up to the Canting so Lu can say good-bye to Mr. Tong.

We pull over by the Canting stairs and LuLu dashes up them. Mr. Tong is out, but LuLu rushes into the kitchen. She returns with a very handsome young man about twenty, whom I've never seen before but who looks exactly like her. "Good-bye, my brother," she says, and hugs him close. Tears well up in his eyes. Then he releases her and stands mournfully, as we pull out, waving.

Silently, she and I sit side by side, hands clasped, mother and daughter. Despite our sadness at going, there is a calm in both of us, a new intimacy between us that has grown and clarified in these two months of searching. We are back together again, and we stare out the window as one as Wuhu streams by.

When we come to the outskirts of the city with its rich green rice fields and its farming commune factories, I point them out to her. "There are some factories," I say, and she nods and looks.

In the distance, a woman walks out of a doorway and LuLu tugs on my hand. "If I was her daughter," she says, "I wouldn't be able to go home with you."

Then she snuggles up against me and goes to sleep. I look down at her beloved Chinese face, and it is glowing with reddish light, a little red sun that rose in the East but is setting in the western sky.

Epilogue

Tongling turned out to be an hour away by car. We could have gone for the afternoon any time.

We did meet a man begging on the train platform, with a boy about LuLu's age asleep in his lap. Lu gave him the giant stuffed animal, much to the amazement of passengers and, we hoped, to the little boy when he awoke.

The White Swan Hotel in Guanzhou was filled with Americans pushing newly adopted babies in strollers, so LuLu was able to see the final step of the adoption process. It really excited her. She spent a lot of time running up to new parents, asking them about their babies, and then calling back to me, "Look, Mom, she just got her."

We even made friends with a new family, whom we now see in our playground. Darcy is the baby's name, and though neither one of them can recall their introduction in China, she and LuLu are both drawn to each other when they meet.

Stephen's article never appeared. Although at the time he seemed to be exactly what he claimed to be—a young reporter— in retrospect I wonder if he really was. Did he perhaps work for the Wuhu city government, which finally took pity on us? Or both?

And, of course, because I never saw the document room myself, I still wonder about the files. Were they gone, as Stephen told me? I did believe him at the time, although it is just as possible that his editor at the paper decided that since we were leaving Wuhu, the story was over. I've had stories killed in newspapers for such reasons.

As for LuLu, well, I think my friend Stephanie, herself the mother of a Chinese adopted daughter, said it best when she came over to me in the playground just after we got back from Wuhu. "What did you do to LuLu?" she asked. "She's like a different person."

I wouldn't have gone that far, but I knew just what she meant. It was as if a big black ball of confusion had been pushed out of LuLu's head. She came back from China—how shall I put it?—unencumbered by old doubts or anxieties, having reclaimed, I think, some essential part of her self. The frantic behavior vanished. I never saw her that way again.

She speaks often and fondly of TohToh and JingJing. Her flute hangs in her room, one of her most prized possessions. Next to it is the set of Chinese classics, which she looks at and plays with a lot, carrying the books around in backpacks and shopping bags and pretending to read them.

She is now thriving at a Western primary school, where she is able to study Chinese, which she wanted to do, she told me, so "when we go back to Wuhu I can talk to my friends."

One night last month, when I couldn't help her with her Chinese homework because I didn't know the meaning of some words, she had a momentary resurfacing of longing for her Chinese mother, the first in two years, and we wept together again. But there is a location for this grief now, and it no longer sweeps over her being, an incomprehensible maelstrom that threatens her very identity and her attachments.

As I was putting together this book and looking through my adoption packet, I came upon the letter I wrote to LuLu's birth mother during the adoption process. I had all but forgotten it.

Spence-Chapin asked each adoptive parent to do this purely as a therapeutic exercise, since the letters cannot and never will be sent.

In the letter, you are meant to try to say to this woman, whose child you will receive, what you think is most important for you to say. At different times over the last six years, whether with my baby-sitters, or going back and forth to Chinese school, or in Wuhu during and after the bombing in Belgrade, I have asked myself in utter exasperation: "Why are you doing this? Is this really necessary? Couldn't you just raise her as a total American, play-down the birth parents, and have done with it?"

I reprint my letter to her birth mother because, to my surprise, it shows that seven months before I met LuLu, saw her photo, or knew her name, I already knew the answers to those questions.

May 16, 1994

Dear Madam,

The adoption agency has asked me to write to you, but I don't know how. I don't know what to say to a woman whose greatest tragedy is my good fortune. That you should have your daughter forced from your arms by a government who I then must pay to envelop her in mine is the stuff of which I have fought against my entire career. That I should end up tacitly supporting this policy is my shame and, yet, my fate.

What can I promise you? That your daughter will be loved and adored? Most assuredly. That she will want for nothing? You have my word. That she will be wonderfully educated and prepared for her adulthood? To the best of my ability.

If I had my way, she would actually know you. But, they tell me, she will not have a record of who you are. But I assure you she will know of your courage and love in leaving her alive so I might raise her. Of the adversity and animosity you faced in doing so. I shall help her to feel in her heart as I do the gratitude and respect for the risks you faced in giving birth in a place where birth is not a free act.

But I will also instill in her, as I'm sure you would want me to, a love of China, and an identity with the Chinese people. Don't worry. She will know where she came from, that she was born of a great and ancient tradition. Perhaps someday, she would wish to go back. The history of China is, as you know, wide and long.

As your daughter becomes my daughter, I will want for her what I have always wanted for myself, really: to be confident, secure, and jolly. To be at one with life. To find people and work she loves, to take pleasure in nature and art, to find nourishment in the spiritual, and to be eternally curious.

Forgive me, Madam, for my part in ripping off the Women of China and in particular, of course, you. If I did not feel that your daughter would be better off with me than in an orphanage, believe me I would not be doing this.

As your daughter becomes my daughter, your ancestors become my ancestors, and mine become yours. It is an interesting thing and very modern. Please understand that I respect this sacred trust, and should we meet in the afterlife, we would embrace as one family, for that's what we will soon be. I shall think of you as the years unfold as I'm sure you will think of me. My heart is with you.

Acknowledgments

This memoir could not have been written without the generosity and support of the following people: Leo, who worked so hard on our behalf and is a tireless orphans' advocate in China; Hua Mei, the entire staff and management of the Tie Shan Hotel, and the English department at Anhui University in Wuhu, all of whom showed such friendship to us; the government officials of Anhui Province, People's Republic of China, who in a time of tense relations with America, generously allowed us to visit the Hefei Children's Institute. I thank them all.

ABOUT THE AUTHOR

EMILY PRAGER is the author of three novels, *Clea and Zeus Divorce, Eve's Tattoo,* and *Roger Fishbite,* as well as the acclaimed book of short stories *A Visit from the Footbinder* and a compendium of her humorous writings, *In the Missionary Position.* She has been a satirical columnist for *The Village Voice, The New York Observer, Interview,* and *The New York Times,* as well as London's *Daily Telegraph* and *The Guardian.* She is a Literary Lion of the New York Public Library, and in 2000 she won the first Online Journalism Award for Commentary given by the Columbia University Graduate School of Journalism. Her books have been published in England, France, Germany, and Sweden, and next spring will appear in Lithuania and Israel.

She teaches humor writing at New York University, and lives in Greenwich Village with her family.

ABOUT THE TYPE

This book was set in Bembo, a typeface based
on an old-style Roman face that was used for
Cardinal Bembo's tract *De Aetna* in 1495. Bembo
was cut by Francisco Griffo in the early sixteenth
century. The Lanston Monotype Machine
Company of Philadelphia brought the well-
proportioned letter forms of Bembo to the
United States in the 1930s.